내신평정
평가문제집

High School
English

NE 능률

High School English 내신평정 평가문제집

지은이	김성곤, 윤진호, 구은영, 전형주, 서정환, 이후고, 김윤자, 강용구, 김성애, 최인철, 김지연, 신유승
연구원	우지희, 김경호, 이윤주, 이다연
영문교열	MyAn Le, August Niederhaus
표지 • 내지 디자인	디자인샐러드
맥편집	㈜이츠북스
마케팅	정영소, 박혜선, 오하야
영업	한기영, 주성탁, 박인규, 정철교, 장순용
제작	한성일, 김동훈, 심현보

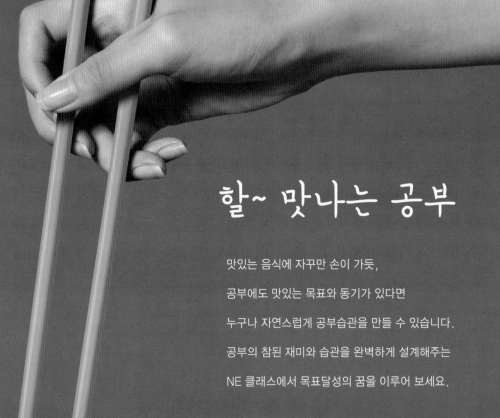

A habit is like a cable.

We weave a thread of it every day,

and at last we cannot break it.

So we must form good, positive, and productive habits.

- Horace Mann

습관은 동아줄과도 같다.

한 올 한 올 날마다 엮다 보면

결국 끊지 못하게 된다.

따라서 우리는 훌륭하고 긍정적이며 생산적인 습관을 형성해야 한다.

여러분은 어떤 습관을 가지고 있나요?
여러분의 습관이 여러분의 꿈을 실현하는 데
중요한 원동력이 된다는 사실을 기억하세요.

Introduction

교과서 파트별
핵심 내용 정리

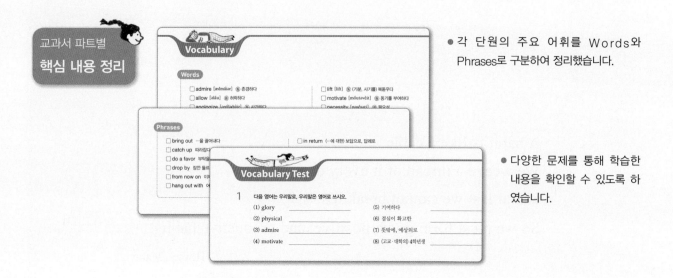

● 각 단원의 주요 어휘를 Words와 Phrases로 구분하여 정리했습니다.

● 다양한 문제를 통해 학습한 내용을 확인할 수 있도록 하였습니다.

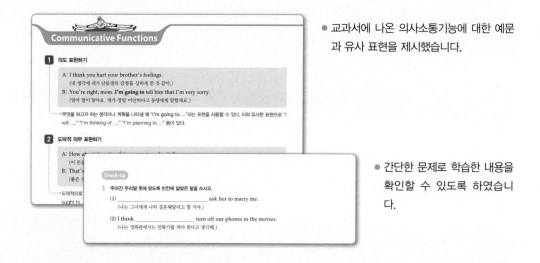

● 교과서에 나온 의사소통기능에 대한 예문과 유사 표현을 제시했습니다.

● 간단한 문제로 학습한 내용을 확인할 수 있도록 하였습니다.

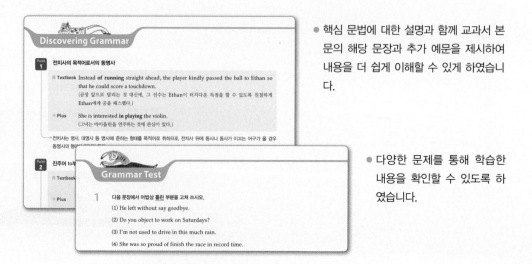

● 핵심 문법에 대한 설명과 함께 교과서 본문의 해당 문장과 추가 예문을 제시하여 내용을 더 쉽게 이해할 수 있게 하였습니다.

● 다양한 문제를 통해 학습한 내용을 확인할 수 있도록 하였습니다.

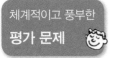

체계적이고 풍부한
평가 문제

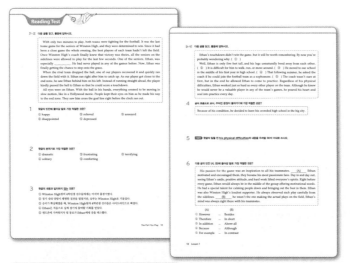

● 읽기 본문에 대한 이해도를 높일 수 있는 확인 문제를 제공했습니다.

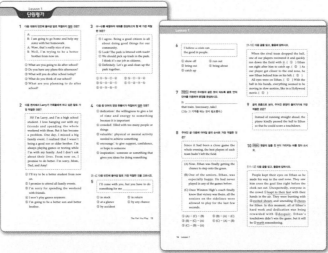

● 풍부하고 다양한 문제를 통해 각 단원의 전체 내용을 철저히 파악할 수 있도록 하였습니다.

시험 대비
실전 문제

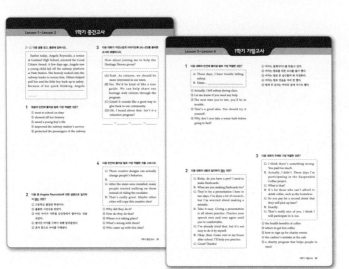

● 실제 중간고사, 기말고사와 유사한 유형의 문제로 구성하여 학교 시험에 대비할 수 있게 하였습니다.

Contents

The Part You Play

Functions

- 의도 표현하기
  I'm going to call and tell my friends that I can't make it today.

- 도덕적 의무 표현하기
  We should be more interested in our town.

Structures

- Instead **of running** straight ahead, the player kindly passed the ball to Ethan so that he could score a touchdown.

- **It is** difficult **for him to walk**, **run**, or **move** around.

Vocabulary

Words

- [ ] admire [ædmáiər] 동 존경하다
- [ ] allow [əláu] 동 허락하다
- [ ] apologize [əpálədʒàiz] 동 사과하다
- [ ] appointment [əpɔ́intmənt] 명 약속
- [ ] attitude [ǽtitjùːd] 명 태도
- [ ] behavior [bihéivjər] 명 행동, 행실
- [ ] bend [bend] 동 구부러지다
- [ ] burst [bəːrst] 동 (강한 감정의 표현으로) 터뜨리다
- [ ] commitment [kəmítmənt] 명 헌신, 전념
- [ ] condition [kəndíʃən] 명 상태
- [ ] contribute [kəntríbjuːt] 동 기여하다
- [ ] crowded [kráudid] 형 붐비는
- [ ] dedication [dèdikéiʃən] 명 헌신
- [ ] defeat [difíːt] 동 이기다, 패배시키다
- [ ] determined [ditə́ːrmind] 형 결심이 확고한
- [ ] disappointed [dìsəpɔ́intid] 형 실망한, 낙담한
- [ ] effort [éfərt] 명 노력
- [ ] encourage [inkə́ːridʒ] 동 격려하다
- [ ] especially [ispéʃəli] 부 특히
- [ ] excel [iksél] 동 뛰어나다, 탁월하다
- [ ] excuse [ikskjúːs] 명 변명, 핑계
- [ ] glory [glɔ́ːri] 명 영광
- [ ] inspiration [ìnspəréiʃən] 명 영감[자극]을 주는 것[사람]
- [ ] intelligence [intélədʒəns] 명 지성, 지능
- [ ] leap [liːp] 동 서둘러 …하다
- [ ] lift [lift] 동 (기분, 사기를) 북돋우다
- [ ] motivate [móutəvèit] 동 동기를 부여하다
- [ ] necessity [nəsésəti] 명 필요성
- [ ] observe [əbzə́ːrv] 동 관찰하다
- [ ] offer [ɔ́ːfər] 동 제공하다
- [ ] passion [pǽʃən] 명 열정
- [ ] physical [fízikəl] 형 육체의, 신체의
- [ ] positive [pázətiv] 형 긍정적인
- [ ] pour [pɔːr] 동 (많은 돈, 시간, 힘 등을) 쏟아붓다
- [ ] practice [prǽktis] 명 연습
- [ ] recover [rikʌ́vər] 동 되찾다
- [ ] remind [rimáind] 동 상기시키다
- [ ] rescue [réskjuː] 동 구조하다
- [ ] reward [riwɔ́ːrd] 동 보상하다
- [ ] score [skɔːr] 동 득점하다
- [ ] senior [síːnjər] 명 (고교 · 대학의) 4학년생
- [ ] shine [ʃain] 동 빛나다
- [ ] sideline [sáidlàin] 명 (경기장 등에서의) 사이드라인
- [ ] sophomore [sáfəmɔ̀ːr] 명 (고교 · 대학의) 2학년생
- [ ] unexpectedly [ʌ̀nikspéktidli] 부 뜻밖에, 예상외로
- [ ] unnaturally [ʌ̀nnǽtʃərəli] 부 부자연스럽게
- [ ] valuable [vǽljuəbl] 형 귀중한
- [ ] victory [víktəri] 명 승리
- [ ] wonder [wʌ́ndər] 동 궁금해하다
- [ ] worth [wəːrθ] 형 …할 가치가 있는

Phrases

- [ ] bring out …을 끌어내다
- [ ] catch up 따라잡다
- [ ] do a favor 부탁을 들어주다
- [ ] drop by 잠깐 들르다
- [ ] from now on 이제부터, 향후
- [ ] hang out with 어울리다, 놀다
- [ ] in return (…에 대한) 보답으로, 답례로
- [ ] instead of … 대신에
- [ ] make one's way …로 나아가다
- [ ] regardless of …에 상관없이
- [ ] run out (시간 등이) 끝나다, 다 되다
- [ ] show off 자랑하다

1 다음 영어는 우리말로, 우리말은 영어로 쓰시오.

(1) glory _____

(2) physical _____

(3) admire _____

(4) motivate _____

(5) 기여하다 _____

(6) 결심이 확고한 _____

(7) 뜻밖에, 예상외로 _____

(8) (고교 · 대학의) 4학년생 _____

2 다음 빈칸에 들어갈 알맞은 단어를 보기에서 골라 쓰시오.

보기	apologize	crowded	passion	worth

(1) The bus was _____ with people on their way to work.

(2) This magazine definitely is _____ reading. It's full of awesome information.

(3) I was impressed by her _____ for art.

(4) We _____ for not replying to you earlier.

3 주어진 우리말과 같은 뜻이 되도록 빈칸에 알맞은 말을 쓰시오.

(1) You must _____ _____ and see us sometime.
(언제 잠깐 들러서 우리를 보고 가야 한다.)

(2) When I'm stressed out, I _____ _____ _____ my friends to feel better.
(난 스트레스를 받을 때, 기분 전환을 위해 친구들과 어울린다.)

(3) She decided to walk to school _____ _____ taking the bus.
(그녀는 버스를 타는 대신 학교까지 걸어가기로 했다.)

(4) He likes to _____ _____ his muscles and strength.
(그는 그의 근육과 힘을 자랑하는 걸 좋아한다.)

4 다음 영영풀이에 해당하는 단어를 보기에서 골라 쓰시오.

보기	defeat	excel	observe	intelligence

(1) _____ : to be extremely good at something

(2) _____ : to win against someone in a fight, war, or competition

(3) _____ : the ability to learn, understand, and make judgments or have opinions based on reason

(4) _____ : to watch carefully the way something happens or the way someone does something

Communicative Functions

1 **의도 표현하기**

> A: I think you hurt your brother's feelings.
> (내 생각에 네가 남동생의 감정을 상하게 한 것 같아.)
> B: You're right, mom. **I'm going to** tell him that I'm very sorry.
> (엄마 말이 맞아요. 제가 정말 미안하다고 동생에게 말할게요.)

• 무엇을 하고자 하는 생각이나 계획을 나타낼 때 "I'm going to …"라는 표현을 사용할 수 있다. 이와 유사한 표현으로 "I will …," "I'm thinking of …," "I'm planning to …" 등이 있다.

2 **도덕적 의무 표현하기**

> A: How about donating this money to a charity?
> (이 돈을 자선 단체에 기부하는 게 어때?)
> B: That's a good idea. I think **we should** help the poor.
> (좋은 생각이야. 난 우리가 가난한 사람들을 도와주어야 한다고 생각해.)

• 도덕적으로 마땅히 해야 할 일을 나타낼 때 "We should …"라는 표현을 사용할 수 있다. 이와 유사한 표현으로 "We ought to …," "It's right/wrong to …," "We must …," "You have to/have got to …," "We're supposed to …" 등이 있다.

Check-up

1 주어진 우리말 뜻에 맞도록 빈칸에 알맞은 말을 쓰시오.

(1) _____ _____ _____ ask her to marry me.
(나는 그녀에게 나와 결혼해달라고 할 거야.)

(2) I think _____ _____ turn off our phones in the movies.
(나는 영화관에서는 전화기를 꺼야 한다고 생각해.)

2 다음 대화의 빈칸에 적절한 말을 보기 에서 고르시오.

A: So did you pack everything?
B: Yes. _____
A: Don't worry. I've checked already. Let's just take out the trash.
B: Oh, wait. _____

> 보기
> ⓐ We're supposed to book a room in advance.
> ⓑ Now I'm going to check to see if we've left anything behind.
> ⓒ We should sort the trash before throwing it out.

Discovering Grammar

전치사의 목적어로서의 동명사

> ▌**Textbook** Instead **of running** straight ahead, the player kindly passed the ball to Ethan so that he could score a touchdown.
> (곧장 앞으로 달리는 것 대신에, 그 선수는 Ethan이 터치다운 득점을 할 수 있도록 친절하게 Ethan에게 공을 패스했다.)
>
> ＋**Plus** She is interested **in playing** the violin.
> (그녀는 바이올린을 연주하는 것에 관심이 있다.)

• 전치사는 명사, 대명사 등 명사에 준하는 형태를 목적어로 취하므로, 전치사 뒤에 동사나 동사가 이끄는 어구가 올 경우 동명사의 형태가 되어야 한다.

진주어 to부정사와 의미상의 주어

> ▌**Textbook** **It is** difficult **for him to walk**, **run**, or **move** around.
> (그는 걷고, 뛰고, 움직이는 게 어렵다.)
>
> ＋**Plus** **It was** hard **for me to understand** the lecture.
> (나는 그 강의를 이해하기가 어려웠다.)

• 문장에서 주어 역할을 하는 to부정사구가 긴 경우, 주어 자리에 가주어 it을 쓰고, 진주어인 to부정사구를 뒤로 보낼 수 있다. to부정사구가 나타내는 동작의 주체가 문장 전체의 주어와 일치하지 않을 때, 「for+목적격」으로 의미상의 주어를 나타낸다.

Check-up

1 다음 괄호 안에서 어법상 올바른 것을 고르시오.

(1) Thank you for (to stand / standing) by my side.
(2) I prefer eating home-cooked meals to (eat / eating) out at a restaurant.
(3) She was responsible for (protecting / to protect) the patients from harm.

2 다음 괄호 안의 단어를 바르게 배열하여 문장을 완성하시오.

(1) It is _____.
(for / Chinese characters / to / him / hard / read)

(2) It is _____.
(it / for / impossible / finish / me / by tomorrow / to)

1 다음 문장에서 어법상 **틀린** 부분을 고쳐 쓰시오.

(1) He left without say goodbye.

(2) Do you object to work on Saturdays?

(3) I'm not used to drive in this much rain.

(4) She was so proud of finish the race in record time.

2 다음 문장의 괄호 안에서 알맞은 것을 고르시오.

(1) I'm sorry for (be / being) late.

(2) I've never thought of (to fail / failing) the exam.

(3) He is good at (listening / to listen) to others.

(4) In addition to (close / closing) the window, be sure to turn off the light.

3 다음 문장을 밑줄 친 부분에 유의하여 우리말로 해석하시오.

(1) It is necessary for you to attend the meeting.

(2) It is important for her to get enough sleep.

(3) It was difficult for him to refuse her offer.

4 주어진 우리말과 같은 뜻이 되도록 괄호 안의 말을 알맞게 배열하여 문장을 완성하시오.

(1) 아이들이 그 산을 오르는 것은 위험하다.

(children / climb / for / dangerous / to / that mountain)

→ It is _____.

(2) 날씨가 그렇게 추운 건 드문 일이다.

(the weather / so cold / to / unusual / be / for)

→ It is _____.

(3) 우리가 서로를 알게 되는 것이 매우 중요하다.

(each other / to / us / know / very important / for / get to)

→ It is _____.

(4) 그가 그렇게 늦도록 외출해 있는 것이 이상했다.

(him / strange / so late / for / be out / to)

→ It was _____.

[1~3] 다음 글을 읽고, 물음에 답하시오.

　　With only two minutes to play, both teams were fighting for the football. It was the last home game for the seniors of Winston High, and they were determined to win. Since it had been a close game the whole evening, the best players of each team hadn't left the field. Once Winston High's coach finally knew that victory was theirs, all the seniors on the sidelines were allowed to play for the last few seconds. One of the seniors, Ethan, was especially _____. He had never played in any of the games before. Now, Ethan was finally getting the chance to step onto the grass.

　　When the rival team dropped the ball, one of our players recovered it and quickly ran down the field with it. Ethan ran right after him to catch up. As our player got closer to the end zone, he saw Ethan behind him on his left. Instead of running straight ahead, the player kindly passed the ball to Ethan so that he could score a touchdown.

　　All eyes were on Ethan. With the ball in his hands, everything seemed to be moving in slow motion, like in a Hollywood movie. People kept their eyes on him as he made his way to the end zone. They saw him cross the goal line right before the clock ran out.

1　윗글의 빈칸에 들어갈 말로 가장 적절한 것은?

① happy　　　　　　② relieved　　　　　　③ annoyed
④ disappointed　　　⑤ depressed

2　윗글의 분위기로 가장 적절한 것은?

① dramatic　　　　　② frustrating　　　　　③ terrifying
④ solitary　　　　　　⑤ comforting

3　윗글의 내용과 일치하지 <u>않는</u> 것은?

① Winston High팀의 4학년생 선수들에게는 마지막 홈경기였다.
② 경기 내내 양팀이 팽팽한 접전을 벌였지만, 승부는 Winston High로 기울었다.
③ 승리가 확실해졌을 때, Winston High팀의 4학년생 선수들은 사이드라인으로 빠졌다.
④ Ethan은 처음으로 실제 경기에 참여할 기회를 얻었다.
⑤ 엔드존에 가까워지자 팀 동료가 Ethan에게 공을 패스했다.

Ethan's touchdown didn't win the game, but it will be worth remembering. By now you're probably wondering why. (①)

Well, Ethan is only five feet tall, and his legs unnaturally bend away from each other. (②) It is difficult for him to walk, run, or move around. (③) He moved to our school in the middle of his first year in high school. (④) That following summer, he asked the coach if he could join the football team as a sophomore. (⑤) The coach wasn't sure at first, but in the end he allowed Ethan to come to practice. Regardless of his physical difficulties, Ethan worked just as hard as every other player on the team. Although he knew he would never be a valuable player in any of the team's games, he poured his heart and soul into practice every day.

4 글의 흐름으로 보아, 주어진 문장이 들어가기에 가장 적절한 곳은?

Because of his condition, he decided to leave his crowded high school in the big city.

5 서술형 ▶ 윗글의 밑줄 친 **his physical difficulties**의 내용을 우리말 30자 이내로 쓰시오.

6 다음 글의 빈칸 (A), (B)에 들어갈 말로 가장 적절한 것은?

His passion for the game was an inspiration to all his teammates. ___(A)___ Ethan motivated and encouraged them, they became his most passionate fans. Day in and day out, seeing Ethan's smile, positive attitude, and hard work lifted everyone's spirits. Right before every game, Ethan would always be in the middle of the group offering motivational words. He had a special talent for calming people down and bringing out the best in them. Ethan was also Winston High's loudest supporter. He always observed each play carefully from the sidelines. ___(B)___ he wasn't the one making the actual plays on the field, Ethan's mind was always right there with his teammates.

	(A)		(B)
①	However	...	Besides
②	Therefore	...	In short
③	In addition	...	Above all
④	Because	...	Although
⑤	For example	...	In contrast

1 다음 대화의 빈칸에 들어갈 말로 적절하지 <u>않은</u> 것은?

> A: _____
> B: I am going to go home and help my sister with her homework.
> A: Wow, that's really nice of you.
> B: Well, I'm trying to be a better brother from now on.

① What are you going to do after school?
② Do you have any plans this afternoon?
③ What will you do after school today?
④ What do you think of our school?
⑤ What are you planning to do after school?

2 다음 편지에서 Larry가 가족들에게 하고 싶은 말로 가장 적절한 것은?

> Hi! I'm Larry, and I'm a high school student. I love hanging out with my friends and spending the whole weekend with them. But it has become a problem. One day, I missed a big family event. I realized that I wasn't being a good son or older brother. I'm always playing games or texting while I'm with my family. And I don't ask about their lives. From now on, I promise to do better. I'm sorry, Mom, Dad, and Amy!

① I'll try to be a better student from now on.
② I promise to attend all family events.
③ I'm sorry for spending the weekend with friends.
④ I won't play games anymore.
⑤ I'm going to be a better son and better brother.

3 ⓐ~ⓓ를 배열하여 대화를 완성하고자 할 때 가장 적절한 것은?

> ⓐ I agree. Being a good citizen is all about doing good things for our community.
> ⓑ Look! The park is littered with trash!
> ⓒ We should pick up trash in the park. I think it's our job as citizens.
> ⓓ Definitely. Let's go and clean up the park together.

① ⓐ – ⓑ – ⓒ – ⓓ
② ⓑ – ⓒ – ⓐ – ⓓ
③ ⓑ – ⓐ – ⓓ – ⓒ
④ ⓒ – ⓓ – ⓐ – ⓑ
⑤ ⓓ – ⓐ – ⓑ – ⓒ

4 다음 중 단어의 영영 뜻풀이가 적절하지 <u>않은</u> 것은?

① dedication: the willingness to give a lot of time and energy to something because it is important
② crowded: filled with too many people or things
③ valuable: physical or mental activity needed to achieve something
④ encourage: to give support, confidence, or hope to someone
⑤ inspiration: someone or something that gives you ideas for doing something

[5~6] 다음 빈칸에 들어갈 말로 가장 적절한 것을 고르시오.

5

> I'll come with you, but you have to do something for me _____.

① in stock
② in return
③ at a glance
④ by any chance
⑤ by accident

6

> I believe a crisis can _____ the good in people.

① show off
② run out
③ bring out
④ bring about
⑤ catch up

7 [주관식] 주어진 우리말과 같은 뜻이 되도록 괄호 안의 단어를 이용하여 문장을 완성하시오.

> It _____
> that train. (necessary, take)
> (그는 그 기차를 타는 것이 필요했다.)

8 주어진 글 다음에 이어질 글의 순서로 가장 적절한 것은?

> Since it had been a close game the whole evening, the best players of each team hadn't left the field.

> (A) Now, Ethan was finally getting the chance to step onto the grass.

> (B) One of the seniors, Ethan, was especially happy. He had never played in any of the games before.

> (C) Once Winston High's coach finally knew that victory was theirs, all the seniors on the sidelines were allowed to play for the last few seconds.

① (A) – (C) – (B)
② (B) – (A) – (C)
③ (B) – (C) – (A)
④ (C) – (A) – (B)
⑤ (C) – (B) – (A)

[9~10] 다음 글을 읽고, 물음에 답하시오.

> When the rival team dropped the ball, one of our players recovered it and quickly ran down the field with it. (①) Ethan ran right after him to catch up. (②) As our player got closer to the end zone, he saw Ethan behind him on his left. (③)
> All eyes were on Ethan. (④) With the ball in his hands, everything seemed to be moving in slow motion, like in a Hollywood movie. (⑤)

9 글의 흐름으로 보아, 주어진 문장이 들어가기에 가장 적절한 곳은?

> Instead of running straight ahead, the player kindly passed the ball to Ethan so that he could score a touchdown.

10 [주관식] 윗글의 밑줄 친 it이 가리키는 바를 찾아 쓰시오.

[11~12] 다음 글을 읽고, 물음에 답하시오.

> People kept their eyes on Ethan as he made his way to the end zone. They saw him cross the goal line right before the clock ran out. Unexpectedly, everyone in the crowd ①leapt to their feet with their hands in the air. They were bursting with ②excited shouts and unending ③cheers for Ethan. In this moment, all of Ethan's hard work and dedication was being rewarded with ④despair. Ethan's touchdown didn't win the game, but it will be ⑤worth remembering.

11 밑줄 친 ①~⑤ 중 문맥상 쓰임이 적절하지 <u>않은</u> 것은?

12 [주관식] 다음 영영 뜻풀이에 해당하는 단어를 윗글에서 찾아 쓰시오.

> to give something to someone because they have done something good or helpful or have worked for it

13 (A), (B), (C)의 각 네모 안에서 어법에 맞는 표현으로 가장 적절한 것은?

	(A)		(B)		(C)
①	for	…	to come	…	Although
②	for	…	coming	…	Although
③	for	…	to come	…	Despite
④	of	…	coming	…	Despite
⑤	of	…	to come	…	Although

14 밑줄 친 ①~⑤ 중에서 가리키는 대상이 나머지 넷과 <u>다른</u> 것은?

15 윗글의 빈칸에 들어갈 말로 가장 적절한 것은?

① Contrary to　　② Thanks to
③ Except for　　④ In addition to
⑤ Regardless of

[13~15] 다음 글을 읽고, 물음에 답하시오.

> Ethan is only five feet tall, and his legs unnaturally bend away from each other. It is difficult (A) for / of him to walk, run, or move around. Because of his condition, ①he decided to leave his crowded high school in the big city. ②He moved to our school in the middle of his first year in high school. That following summer, ③he asked the coach if he could join the football team as a sophomore. The coach wasn't sure at first, but in the end ④he allowed Ethan (B) coming / to come to practice. _____ his physical difficulties, Ethan worked just as hard as every other player on the team. (C) Although / Despite he knew he would never be a valuable player in any of the team's games, ⑤he poured his heart and soul into practice every day.

[16~18] 다음 글을 읽고, 물음에 답하시오.

> Over time, however, Ethan became valuable to the team in <u>different ways</u>. His passion for the game was an inspiration to all his teammates. Because Ethan motivated and encouraged them, they became his most passionate fans. Day in and day out, ①seeing Ethan's smile, positive attitude, and hard work lifted everyone's spirits. Right before every game, Ethan ②<u>would</u> always be in the middle of the group offering motivational words. He had a

special talent for calming people down and ③ to bring out the best in them. Ethan was also Winston High's ④ loudest supporter. He always observed each play carefully from the sidelines. Although he wasn't the one ⑤ making the actual plays on the field, Ethan's mind was always right there with his teammates. Everyone could sense his love for football, and the coaches _____ his commitment.

16 밑줄 친 **different ways**의 구체적인 내용으로 윗글에서 언급되지 않은 것은?

① 선수들에게 동기 부여하고 격려하기
② 긍정적 태도와 노력으로 모두의 기운 북돋우기
③ 사람들을 침착하게 하기
④ 출전 못한 선수들 위로하기
⑤ 매 경기 유심히 관찰하기

17 밑줄 친 ①~⑤ 중, 어법상 틀린 것은?

18 윗글의 빈칸에 들어갈 말로 가장 적절한 것은?

① admired   ② decided
③ requested   ④ expressed
⑤ ignored

[19~20] 다음 글을 읽고, 물음에 답하시오.

For the past three years, Ethan has been schooling us all in the game of life. He always reminds us that everyone is important to a team's success, though their role on the team may be small. Instead of 팀의 최고 선수가 되기 위해 모든 노력을 쏟아 붓는 것, he has done everything he can to make the team better. As Ethan has shown us, _____ is also of great worth. When we help others shine, their light will shine on us in return. Yes, sometimes there is something better than being the best.

19 주관식 윗글의 밑줄 친 우리말과 같은 뜻이 되도록 다음 괄호 안의 단어를 알맞게 배열하시오.

(to / putting / best player / all his efforts / the team's / into / trying / be)

20 윗글의 빈칸에 들어갈 말로 가장 적절한 것은?

① trusting each other
② lifting up those around us
③ having sympathy for others
④ paying attention to details
⑤ being happy with small roles

Lesson 2

The Power of Creativity

Vocabulary

Words

- abandon [əbǽndən] 동 버리다, 유기하다
- amount [əmáunt] 명 양
- appear [əpíər] 동 …처럼 보이다
- approach [əpróutʃ] 명 접근, 접근법
- blend [blend] 동 (보기 좋게) 조합되다[조합하다]
- brilliant [bríljənt] 형 훌륭한, 멋진
- conserve [kənsə́:rv] 동 절약하다, 아끼다
- contemporary [kəntémpərèri] 형 현대의
- convert [kənvə́:rt] 동 전환시키다, 개조하다
- decompose [dì:kəmpóuz] 동 분해되다, 부패하다
- destroy [distrɔ́i] 동 파괴하다
- disposable [dispóuzəbl] 형 일회용의, 사용 후 버리는
- effect [ifékt] 명 영향, 효과
- endless [éndlis] 형 끝없는
- equipment [ikwípmənt] 명 장비
- exhibit [igzíbit] 명 전시물
- facility [fəsíləti] 명 설비, 시설
- flexible [fléksəbl] 형 잘 구부러지는, 유연한
- gorgeous [gɔ́:rdʒəs] 형 아주 멋진, 아름다운
- heritage [héritidʒ] 명 유산; 전승, 전통
- imagination [imæ̀dʒənéiʃən] 명 상상력
- individually [ìndəvídʒuəli] 부 개별적으로
- influence [ínfluəns] 명 영향
- inspiring [inspáiəriŋ] 형 (…하도록) 고무하는
- install [instɔ́:l] 동 설치하다

- junk [dʒʌŋk] 명 쓰레기
- landscape [lǽndskèip] 명 경관, 풍경
- lessen [lésn] 동 줄이다
- magnificent [mægnífisənt] 형 장엄한, 장대한
- manage [mǽnidʒ] 동 관리하다
- marvelous [má:rvələs] 형 놀라운
- material [mətíəriəl] 명 재료, 물질
- mess [mes] 명 지저분한 것
- object [ábdʒikt] 명 물체, 물건
- obviously [ábviəsli] 부 명백히, 분명히
- option [ápʃən] 명 선택(할 수 있는 것)
- original [ərídʒənl] 형 원래의
- perhaps [pərhǽps] 부 아마도
- pleasing [plí:ziŋ] 형 즐거운, 만족스러운
- preserve [prizə́:rv] 동 보존하다
- provoke [prəvóuk] 동 유발하다
- purify [pjúərəfài] 동 정화하다
- reduce [ridjú:s] 동 줄이다
- repurpose [ripə́:rpəs] 동 용도를 변경하다
- resident [rézidənt] 명 주민
- resource [rí:sɔ:rs] 명 자원
- sculpture [skʌ́lptʃər] 명 조각품, 조각
- seemingly [sí:miŋli] 부 겉보기에는
- storage [stɔ́:ridʒ] 명 저장, 보관
- transform [trænsfɔ́:rm] 동 변형시키다

Phrases

- a series of 일련의
- along with …와 더불어
- come up with (생각을) 떠올리다, 생각해내다
- cut down on …을 줄이다
- in place of … 대신에

- one of a kind 독특한 사람[것]
- take place 일어나다, 개최되다
- tear down 허물다
- throw away 버리다, 없애다
- turn ... into …를 (~로) 바꾸다

1 다음 영어는 우리말로, 우리말은 영어로 쓰시오.

(1) blend _____   (5) 설비, 시설 _____

(2) exhibit _____   (6) 저장, 보관 _____

(3) equipment _____   (7) 조각품, 조각 _____

(4) contemporary _____   (8) 분해되다, 부패하다 _____

2 다음 빈칸에 들어갈 알맞은 단어를 보기 에서 골라 쓰시오.

보기	abandon	heritage	flexible	disposable

(1) Don't use _____ products such as paper cups and napkins.

(2) This ancient building is an important part of our cultural _____.

(3) We had to _____ our car in the snow.

(4) This plastic is as _____ as rubber.

3 주어진 우리말과 같은 뜻이 되도록 빈칸에 알맞은 말을 쓰시오.

(1) The film festival _____ _____ in late July.
(그 영화제는 7월 말에 개최된다.)

(2) He _____ _____ _____ a brilliant way to use all the leftover food.
(그는 모든 남은 음식을 활용할 멋진 방법을 떠올렸다.)

(3) You can use maple syrup _____ _____ _____ sugar in most cakes.
(대부분의 케이크에 설탕 대신 메이플 시럽을 사용할 수 있다.)

(4) We're going to _____ _____ that building tomorrow.
(우리는 저 건물을 내일 허물 예정이다.)

4 다음 영영풀이에 해당하는 단어를 보기 에서 골라 쓰시오.

보기	install	provoke	magnificent	repurpose

(1) _____ : to cause a reaction, especially a negative one

(2) _____ : to find a new use for an idea, product, or building

(3) _____ : to put furniture, a machine, or a piece of equipment into position and make it ready to use

(4) _____ : extremely good, beautiful, impressive, or deserving to be admired

Communicative Functions

1 가능성 정도 표현하기

> A: I think we are lost. Let's ask this man for directions.
> (내 생각엔 우리가 길을 잃은 것 같아. 이분께 방향을 물어보자.)
> B: Okay. **Maybe he'll** know how to get there.
> (좋아. 어쩌면 그가 그곳에 어떻게 도착하는지 알지도 몰라.)

• 어떤 일에 대한 가능성을 추측하거나 이야기할 때 "Maybe/Perhaps/Probably it will ..."이라는 표현을 사용할 수 있다. 이와 유사한 표현으로 "Chances are (that ...)," "It is likely that ..." 등이 있다.

2 의견 표현하기

> A: **It seems to me that** they spend too much time watching TV.
> (내 생각에는 그들이 TV시청에 너무 많은 시간을 보내는 것 같아.)
> B: I totally agree with you!
> (네 의견에 전적으로 동의해!)

• 의견을 말할 때 "It seems to me that ..."이라는 표현을 사용할 수 있다. 이와 유사한 표현으로 "In my view/opinion ...," "I think/feel/believe ..." 등이 있다.

Check-up

1 주어진 우리말 뜻에 맞도록 빈칸에 알맞은 말을 쓰시오.

(1) _____ _____ _____ get better grades next year.
(그는 아마 내년에는 더 좋은 점수를 받을 거야.)

(2) _____ _____ _____ _____ that family is the greatest source of happiness.
(내 생각에 가족은 행복의 가장 큰 원천인 것 같아.)

2 다음 대화가 자연스럽게 이어지도록 순서대로 배열하시오.

> (A) Then why don't we go shopping now?
> (B) Okay. I'll call my brother. Maybe he will give us a ride.
> (C) Is everything ready for our party?
> (D) No. It seems to me that we should buy more snacks.

_____ → _____ → _____ → _____

Discovering Grammar

Point 1 명사를 수식하는 과거분사(구)

> ▌**Textbook** The giant pictures **made** from trash by environmental artist Tom Deininger are one of a kind.
> (환경 예술가 Tom Deininger에 의해 쓰레기로 만들어진 거대한 그림들은 매우 독특하다.)
>
> **+ Plus** The movie **based** on true events is attracting a large audience.
> (실제 사건에 바탕을 둔 그 영화가 많은 관객을 끌어 모으고 있다.)

• 분사가 단독으로 쓰이지 않고 뒤에 목적어, 보어, 부사구 등 수식어구를 동반하고 있을 때는 보통 명사를 뒤에서 수식하게 된다. 이때 분사가 명사와 수동의 관계이거나 완료의 의미를 갖고 있으면 과거분사를, 분사가 명사와 능동의 관계이거나 진행의 의미를 갖고 있으면 현재분사를 쓴다.

Point 2 주격 관계대명사

> ▌**Textbook** The German government showed us an excellent example of this with a former steel plant **that** closed in 1985.
> (독일 정부는 1985년도에 문을 닫은 철강 공장으로 우리에게 이것의 훌륭한 예를 보여주었다.)
>
> **+ Plus** I have a friend **who[that]** has been to Africa.
> (나는 아프리카에 다녀온 친구를 알고 있다.)

• 관계대명사는 「접속사+대명사」의 역할을 하며, 선행사를 수식하는 형용사절을 이끈다. 이 중 주격 관계대명사는 관계대명사가 절 내에서 주어 역할을 하는 경우를 말한다. 선행사가 사람인 경우 who[that], 사물인 경우 which[that]를 쓴다.

Check-up

1 다음 괄호 안에서 어법상 올바른 것을 고르시오.

(1) I'd like to meet someone (who / which) is trustworthy and responsible.

(2) They were rebuilding their old houses (who / which) had been destroyed during the war.

(3) A dictionary is a book (who / that) explains the meaning of words.

2 주어진 우리말과 같은 뜻이 되도록 괄호 안의 말을 이용하여 문장을 완성하시오.

(1) 당신은 이 미술관에서 유명한 화가들이 그린 그림들을 볼 수 있다. (pictures, draw)

→ In this gallery you can find _____ _____ by famous artists.

(2) 이 프로젝트에 큰 열정을 보이는 지원자들이 많이 있다. (applicants, show)

→ There are many _____ _____ great passion for this project.

1 다음 문장의 괄호 안에서 알맞은 것을 고르시오.

(1) Who is the man (talking / talked) to my mother?

(2) I took pictures of the mountain (was covered / covered) in snow.

(3) Look at the man over there (holds / holding) a big black umbrella!

(4) Most of the people (inviting / invited) to the party were old friends.

2 다음 괄호 안의 동사를 어법에 맞게 바꿔 쓰시오.

(1) Do you know the people _____ next door? (live)

(2) They questioned the people _____ in the accident. (involve)

(3) He is painting a child _____ a sandcastle. (build)

(4) She has taken care of many _____ soldiers. (injure)

3 다음 두 문장을 관계대명사를 이용하여 한 문장으로 만드시오.

(1) My grandfather passed away last week. He had been suffering from cancer.

→ _____

(2) The people can get tickets for free. They have membership cards.

→ _____

(3) That is the road. It leads to the airport.

→ _____

(4) I bought an oven. It is suitable for baking and cooking.

→ _____

4 다음 우리말과 같은 뜻이 되도록 주어진 단어를 배열하여 문장을 완성하시오.

(1) 책상에 앉아있는 여자는 그의 비서이다.

(who / is / at the desk / the woman / is sitting)

→ _____ his secretary.

(2) 그녀는 바닥에 놓여있는 인형 하나를 집어 들었다.

(lay / a doll / picked up / which / on the ground)

→ She _____.

(3) 너는 공원에서 놀고 있는 그 소년을 보았니?

(playing / that / in the park / the boy / was)

→ Did you see _____?

[1~2] 다음 글을 읽고, 물음에 답하시오.

Obviously, recycling is good for many reasons. We can ①increase the amount of trash thrown away, use less energy than we would to make new products, and ②conserve natural resources by recycling. However, recycling is not a perfect way to manage waste. It still requires large amounts of energy to ③purify used resources and ④convert them into new products. So, what about trying to creatively reuse, or "upcycle," them ⑤instead? This new approach is becoming more popular since it is even more environmentally friendly than recycling. _____, it can also be fun! Here are some inspiring examples of how people have creatively upcycled old, used things.

1 밑줄 친 ①~⑤ 중, 문맥상 낱말의 쓰임이 적절하지 <u>않은</u> 것은?

2 윗글의 빈칸에 들 로 가장 적절한 것은?

① As a result   ② For example
③ In other words   ④ What's more
⑤ On the other hand

[3~4] 다음 글을 읽고, 물음에 답하시오.

Along with small everyday items, much bigger things can also be upcycled—even old buildings that cannot be used for their original purpose anymore. The German government showed us an excellent example of <u>this</u> with a former steel plant that closed in 1985. (①) Rather than destroy the plant's buildings or abandon the entire facility, they decided to give it new meaning as a series of useful public structures. (②) Many of the buildings kept their original shapes, but received extra equipment and new designs in their surrounding areas. (③) Concrete walls of iron storage towers were turned into ideal training fields for rock climbers. (④) Can you believe a building for melting metal is now a viewing platform with a gorgeous 360-degree view? The final result is the Landscape Park Duisburg Nord. (⑤)

3 글의 흐름으로 보아, 주어진 문장이 들어가기에 가장 적절한 곳은?

For instance, old gas tanks became pools for divers.

4 서술형 윗글의 밑줄 this가 가리키는 바를 우리말로 쓰시오.

[5~6] 다음 글을 읽고, 물음에 답하시오.

> When artists _____, things that most people consider junk are reborn as beautiful works of art. The giant pictures made from trash by environmental artist Tom Deininger are one of a kind. Up close, these brightly colored creations look like a mixed-up mess of broken plastic, unwanted toys, and bent wire—all things that cannot be recycled. From farther away, however, they appear to blend together into marvelous landscapes or other paintings. There is also an artist who shows that even disposable cups can be reused as artistic material. For years, Gwyneth Leech has turned used coffee cups into brilliant art exhibits. After a cup is used by someone, she paints a unique design on it and hangs it with many other painted cups in front of a window or pretty background. These works from Leech and Deininger are not only pleasing to the eye, but they also naturally provoke an interest in environmental conservation in people.

5 윗글의 빈칸에 들어갈 말로 가장 적절한 것은?

① take on the role of a curator
② have conflicts with galleries
③ get inspiration from nature
④ work with environmentalists
⑤ add their own creative touches

6 서술형 윗글에서 Tom Deininger와 Gwyneth Leech가 만드는 작품의 역할 두 가지를 우리말로 쓰시오.

(1) _____

(2) _____

[1~2] 다음 대화를 읽고, 물음에 답하시오.

> B: Hey, Michelle. What are you looking at?
> G: It's an advertisement for a handy new product: a flexible power strip. (①)
> B: I've never heard of that kind of thing. (②)
> G: Well, it is divided into sections so that it can be bent into different shapes. (③)
> B: Oh, I see. Maybe that will make it easier to fit it in small places. (④)
> G: That's right. Isn't it amazing how one small change can improve a product so much? (⑤)
> B: Definitely. It is a clever invention.

1 대화의 흐름으로 보아, 주어진 문장이 들어가기에 가장 적절한 곳은?

> How can a power strip be flexible?

2 두 사람의 심경으로 가장 적절한 것은?

① annoyed   ② envious
③ impressed   ④ indifferent
⑤ frightened

3 다음 대화의 빈칸에 들어갈 말로 가장 적절한 것은?

> G: This used to be a lifeless village. But recently, artists decided to paint lots of pictures to raise the residents' spirits.
> B: The residents must have been very

> pleased.
> G: You can say that again. Thanks to these murals, this village has become a wonderful place to live and a popular tourist attraction.
> B: _____

① It's not right for street artist to paint pictures on walls and houses.
② I think it's great for residents to work together with artists for their community.
③ I believe murals are a great tool to hide the cracks on walls.
④ I don't feel it right to turn this neighborhood into a tourist spot.
⑤ It seems to me that the artists breathed new life into this area.

4 다음 중 단어의 영영 뜻풀이로 적절하지 않은 것은?

① purify: to remove bad substances from something to make it pure
② convert: to change in form or character
③ contemporary: modern and relate to the present time
④ abandon: to keep something as it is
⑤ decompose: change chemically and begin to decay

5 주관식 다음 빈칸에 들어갈 알맞은 말을 쓰시오.

> The movie became as popular as the _____ novel.
> (그 영화는 원작 소설만큼 인기를 끌었다.)

6 밑줄 친 부분의 뜻풀이로 적절하지 <u>않은</u> 것은?

① I'm sure your sculpture is going to be <u>one of a kind</u>. (평범한 것)

② She suffered <u>a series of</u> hardships before her success. (일련의)

③ He <u>came up with</u> a great idea to promote the new product. (생각해내다)

④ You need to <u>cut down on</u> salty food. (줄이다)

⑤ He refused to follow the unjust order <u>along with</u> his colleagues. (…와 더불어)

[7~8] 주관식 다음 문장에서 어법상 <u>틀린</u> 부분을 찾아 바르게 고치시오.

7 I've seen the famous library designing like a seashell.

8 Do you know a good restaurant what serves sushi?

[9~10] 다음 글을 읽고, 물음에 답하시오.

Every day during lunch, Jamie enjoys a soft drink and has a decision to make: What should he do with the empty can? Many people would answer, "Recycle it!" (A) Obviously / Obscurely , recycling is good for many reasons. We can reduce the amount of trash thrown away, use less energy than we would to make new products, and conserve natural resources by recycling. However, recycling is not a perfect way to manage waste. It still (B) acquires / requires large amounts of energy to purify used resources and convert

them into new products. So, what about trying to creatively reuse, or "upcycle," them instead? This new (C) approach / reproach is becoming more popular since it is even more environmentally friendly than recycling.

9 서술형 윗글에 서술된 재활용의 장점 세 가지를 우리말로 쓰시오.

(1) _____

(2) _____

(3) _____

10 (A), (B), (C)의 각 네모 안에서 문맥에 맞는 낱말로 가장 적절한 것은?

	(A)	(B)	(C)
①	Obviously	acquires	reproach
②	Obscurely	acquires	approach
③	Obviously	requires	approach
④	Obviously	requires	reproach
⑤	Obscurely	acquires	reproach

[11~12] 다음 글을 읽고, 물음에 답하시오.

Through upcycling, a seemingly useless object can (A) transform / be transformed into something completely different that is _____ . What do you think can be done with old truck tarps, car seat belts, and bicycle inner tubes? Individually, these things look like trash, but with a little imagination the Freitag brothers, Markus and Daniel, repurpose (B) it / them for something totally new: very strong bags. These bags are perfect for bicyclists (C) go / going to work every day in all kinds of weather.

11 (A), (B), (C)의 각 네모 안에서 어법에 맞는 표현으로 가장 적절한 것은?

	(A)		(B)		(C)
①	transform	⋯	it	⋯	go
②	transform	⋯	them	⋯	go
③	be transformed	⋯	it	⋯	going
④	be transformed	⋯	them	⋯	going
⑤	be transformed	⋯	it	⋯	go

13 주관식 윗글의 빈칸 (A)와 (B)에 공통으로 들어갈 단어를 쓰시오.

14 밑줄 친 ①~⑤ 중에서 가리키는 대상이 나머지 넷과 다른 것은?

12 윗글의 빈칸에 들어갈 말로 가장 적절한 것은?

① luxurious and special
② useful for everyday life
③ comforting to your feelings
④ perfect for children to play with
⑤ helpful to improve your safety

[13~14] 다음 글을 읽고, 물음에 답하시오.

A man named Kyle Parsons and his partners have been creatively reusing old motorcycle tires from Bali, Indonesia. A shocking number of tires get thrown away there every year, and ①they are a serious environmental problem since ②they cannot decompose. ③They can't be recycled either. ___(A)___ solve this problem, Parsons and his team are turning ④them into sandal bottoms. ⑤They then use canvas and natural materials ___(B)___ make the other sandal parts. What a great reuse of resources!

[15~17] 다음 글을 읽고, 물음에 답하시오.

Along with small everyday items, ①much bigger things can also be upcycled—even old buildings that cannot be used for their original purpose anymore. The German government showed us an excellent example of this with a former steel plant that closed in 1985. Rather than destroy the plant's buildings or ②abandon the entire facility, they decided to give it new meaning as a series of useful public structures. Many of the buildings kept their original shapes, but received extra equipment and new designs in their surrounding areas. _____, old gas tanks became pools for divers. Concrete walls of iron storage towers ③were turned into ideal training fields for rock climbers. Can you believe a building for ④melting metal is now a viewing platform with a gorgeous 360-degree view? The final result is the Landscape Park Duisburg Nord. It has almost 570 acres of land ⑤to fill with gardens, cycling paths, and pretty lights at night, in addition to its creatively repurposed buildings.

15 밑줄 친 ①~⑤ 중, 어법상 틀린 것은?

16 윗글의 빈칸에 들어갈 말로 가장 적절한 것은?

① However   ② In addition

③ For instance   ④ By the way

⑤ On the contrary

17 The Landscape Park Duisburg Nord에 관한 윗글의 내용과 일치하는 것은?

① 독일 정부가 원래 용도로 쓰일 수 없는 낡은 건물을 업사이클링한 예이다.

② 원래는 1985년에 건설된 철강공장이었다.

③ 건물의 많은 부분이 부서진 후 새로운 디자인이 입혀졌다.

④ 기존의 가스탱크가 암벽등반훈련장이 되었다.

⑤ 철을 저장하던 탑이 전망대로 바뀌었다.

[18~20] 다음 글을 읽고, 물음에 답하시오.

When artists add their own creative touches, <u>대부분의 사람들이 쓰레기로 여기던 사물들이 다시 태어난다</u> as beautiful works of art. (①)The giant pictures made from trash by environmental artist Tom Deininger are one of a kind. (②) Up close, these brightly colored creations look like a mixed-up mess of broken plastic, unwanted toys, and bent wire—all things that cannot be recycled. (③) There is also an artist who shows that even disposable cups can be reused as artistic material. (④) For years, Gwyneth Leech has turned used coffee cups into brilliant art exhibits. (⑤) After a cup is used by someone, she paints a unique design on it and hangs it with many other painted cups in front of a window or pretty background. These works

from Leech and Deininger are not only pleasing to the eye, but they also naturally provoke an interest in environmental conservation in people.

18 주관식 윗글의 밑줄 친 우리말과 같은 뜻이 되도록 다음 괄호 안의 단어를 바르게 배열하시오.

(junk / are reborn / that / most people / things / consider)

19 글의 흐름으로 보아, 주어진 문장이 들어가기에 가장 적절한 곳은?

From farther away, however, they appear to blend together into marvelous landscapes or other paintings.

20 윗글에서 예술품으로 재탄생한 것들의 재료로 언급되지 <u>않은</u> 것은?

① 조각난 플라스틱   ② 버려진 장난감

③ 도자기 파편   ④ 휘어진 철사

⑤ 일회용 커피컵

[1~2] 다음 글을 읽고, 물음에 답하시오.

> Earlier today, Angela Reynolds, a senior at Garland High School, received the Good Citizen Award. A few days ago, Angela saw a young child fall off the subway platform at Park Station. She bravely rushed onto the subway tracks to rescue him. Others helped pull her and the little boy back up to safety. Because of her quick thinking, Angela _____.

1 윗글의 빈칸에 들어갈 말로 가장 적절한 것은?

① went to school on time
② showed off her bravery
③ saved a young boy's life
④ improved the subway station's service
⑤ protected the passengers of the subway

2 다음 중 Angela Reynolds에 대한 설명으로 일치하지 않는 것은?

① 고등학교 졸업반 학생이다.
② 훌륭한 시민상을 받았다.
③ 어린 아이가 지하철 승강장에서 떨어지는 것을 보았다.
④ 떨어진 아이를 구하기 위해 달려들었다.
⑤ 혼자 힘으로 아이를 구해냈다.

3 다음 대화가 자연스럽게 이어지도록 (A)~(D)를 올바른 순서로 배열하시오.

> How about joining me to help the Heritage Heroes group?

> (A) Yeah. As citizens, we should be more interested in our town.
> (B) Yes. We'd be kind of like a tour guide. We can help share our heritage with visitors through the program.
> (C) Great! It sounds like a good way to give back to our community.
> (D) Oh, I heard about that. Isn't it a volunteer program?

_____ → _____ → _____ → _____

4 다음 빈칸에 들어갈 말로 가장 적절한 것을 고르시오.

> G: These creative designs can actually change people's behavior.
> B: _____
> G: After the stairs were installed, many people started walking on them instead of riding the escalator.
> B: That's really great. Maybe other cities will copy this creative idea!

① Why did they do it?
② How do they do that?
③ Where is it taking place?
④ What's wrong with them?
⑤ Who came up with this idea?

5 다음 문장의 밑줄 친 close와 같은 의미로 쓰인 것은?

> The game was so close, but we had a bit of luck in the last two minutes of the last quarter and could beat the opposing team.

① Close your eyes—I've got a surprise for you.

② The election results are so close. We have to vote again.

③ The shop closed about five months ago.

④ He tried to bring the discussion to a close.

⑤ I don't get along with my brother, but I'm very close to my sister.

6 주관식 다음 두 문장의 빈칸에 공통으로 들어갈 말을 쓰시오.

> • I'm sorry, I won't be able to _____ _____ on Friday.
> (미안해. 나 금요일에 못 갈 것 같아.)
> • I think I can _____ _____ on time if I hurry from now.
> (지금부터 서두르면 제시간에 갈 수 있을 것 같아.)

7 다음 문장의 밑줄 친 단어와 바꿔 쓸 수 있는 것은?

> I prefer contemporary literature to classic books.

① artistic   ② helpful

③ modern   ④ typical

⑤ traditional

[8~9] 다음 문장의 밑줄 친 부분 중, 어법상 틀린 것을 고르시오.

8 ① What were you doing while I was working?

② Complaining can produce unexpected results.

③ I'm not afraid of go out alone at night.

④ It is important for you to be on time.

⑤ It is very kind of you to invite us.

9 ① I saw a new movie produced by my favorite director.

② Look at the stars shined like mini lanterns!

③ He stared at a man who was wearing a black mask.

④ We saw a small house which was made out of soil.

⑤ She grew up in a town that had a river by it.

10 다음 글의 빈칸에 들어갈 말로 가장 적절한 것은?

> With only two minutes to play, both teams were fighting for the football. It was the last home game for the seniors of Winston High, and they were _____ to win. Since it had been a close game the whole evening, the best players of each team hadn't left the

field. Once Winston High's coach finally knew that victory was theirs, all the seniors on the sidelines were allowed to play for the last few seconds. One of the seniors, Ethan, was especially happy. He had never played in any of the games before. Now, Ethan was finally getting the chance to step onto the grass.

① satisfied   ② relaxed
③ determined   ④ suspicious
⑤ exhausted

12 (A), (B), (C)의 각 네모 안에서 어법에 맞는 표현으로 가장 적절한 것은?

	(A)		(B)		(C)
①	can	…	be moving	…	cross
②	could	…	be moving	…	to cross
③	could	…	be moving	…	cross
④	could	…	have moved	…	to cross
⑤	can	…	have moved	…	cross

[11~12] 다음 글을 읽고, 물음에 답하시오.

When the rival team dropped the ball, one of our players recovered it and quickly ran down the field with it. Ethan ran right after him to catch up. As our player got closer to the end zone, he saw Ethan behind him on his left. _____ running straight ahead, the player kindly passed the ball to Ethan so that he (A)can / could score a touchdown.

All eyes were on Ethan. With the ball in his hands, everything seemed to (B)be moving / have moved in slow motion, like in a Hollywood movie. People kept their eyes on him as he made his way to the end zone. They saw him (C)cross / to cross the goal line right before the clock ran out.

11 윗글의 빈칸에 들어갈 말로 가장 적절한 것은?

① As a result of   ② In spite of
③ Speaking of   ④ Because of
⑤ Instead of

[13~14] 다음 글을 읽고, 물음에 답하시오.

Unexpectedly, everyone in the crowd leapt to their feet with their hands in the air. They were bursting with excited shouts and unending cheers for Ethan. In this moment, all of Ethan's hard work and (A)dedication / demonstration was being rewarded with glory. Ethan's touchdown didn't win the game, but it will be worth remembering. By now, you're probably wondering why.

Well, Ethan is only five feet tall, and his legs unnaturally bend away from each other. 그는 걷고, 뛰거나, 돌아다니는 게 어렵다. Because of his condition, he decided to leave his (B)crowded / uncrowded high school in the big city. He moved to our school in the middle of his first year in high school. That following summer, he asked the coach if he could join the football team as a sophomore. The coach wasn't sure at first, but in the end he allowed Ethan to come to practice. Regardless of his (C)mental / physical difficulties, Ethan worked just as hard as every other player on the team. Although he knew he would never be a valuable player in any of the team's games, he poured his heart and soul into practice every day.

13 (A), (B), (C)의 각 네모 안에서 문맥에 맞는 낱말로 가장 적절한 것은?

	(A)	(B)	(C)
①	dedication	⋯ crowded	⋯ mental
②	dedication	⋯ uncrowded	⋯ mental
③	dedication	⋯ crowded	⋯ physical
④	demonstration	⋯ uncrowded	⋯ physical
⑤	demonstration	⋯ crowded	⋯ mental

14 [주관식] 윗글의 밑줄 친 우리말과 같은 뜻이 되도록 다음 문장을 완성하시오.

It is _____

_____.

[15~17] 다음 글을 읽고, 물음에 답하시오.

Day in and day out, seeing Ethan's smile, positive attitude, and hard work lifted everyone's spirits. Right before every game, Ethan would always be in the middle of the group offering motivational words. He had a special talent for calming people down and bringing out the best in them. Ethan was also Winston High's loudest supporter. He always observed each play carefully from the sidelines. Although he wasn't the one <u>make</u> the actual plays on the field, Ethan's mind was always right there with his teammates. Everyone could sense his love for football, and the coaches admired his commitment.

15 [주관식] 다음 영영 뜻풀이에 해당하는 단어를 윗글에서 찾아 쓰시오.

the quality of being devoted to something, especially a cause or activity

16 윗글의 밑줄 친 <u>make</u>의 형태로 가장 적절한 것은?

① makes ② making
③ made ④ will make
⑤ have made

17 [서술형] 윗글에서 Ethan이 가진 특별한 재능으로 언급된 것을 찾아 30자 내외의 우리말로 쓰시오.

[18~19] 다음 글을 읽고, 물음에 답하시오.

Every day during lunch, Jamie enjoys a soft drink and has a decision to make: What should he do with the empty can? Many people would answer, "Recycle it!"

(A) Obviously, recycling is good for many reasons. We can reduce the amount of trash thrown away, use less energy than we would to make new products, and conserve natural resources by recycling.

(B) This new approach is becoming more popular since it is even more environmentally friendly than recycling. What's more, it can also be fun! Here are some inspiring examples of how people have creatively upcycled old, used things.

(C) However, recycling is not a perfect way to manage waste. It still requires large amounts of energy to purify used resources and convert them into new products. So, what about trying to creatively reuse, or "upcycle," them instead?

18 주어진 글 다음에 이어질 글의 순서로 가장 적절한 것은?

① (A) − (C) − (B)　　② (B) − (A) − (C)
③ (B) − (C) − (A)　　④ (C) − (A) − (B)
⑤ (C) − (B) − (A)

19 윗글의 목적으로 가장 적절한 것은?

① to explain the disadvantages of recycling
② to introduce a better method for managing waste
③ to demonstrate the harmful effects of soft drinks
④ to promote the necessity of conserving natural resources
⑤ to encourage people to use environmentally friendly products

[20~21] 다음 글을 읽고, 물음에 답하시오.

What do you think can be done with old truck tarps, car seat belts, and bicycle inner tubes? (①) Individually, these things look like trash, but with a little imagination the Freitag brothers, Markus and Daniel, repurpose them for something totally new: very strong bags. (②) These bags are perfect for bicyclists going to work every day in all kinds of weather. (③) A shocking number of tires get thrown away there every year, and they are a serious environmental problem since they cannot decompose or be recycled. (④) To solve this problem, Parsons and his team are turning them into sandal bottoms. (⑤) They then use canvas and natural materials to make the other sandal parts. What a great reuse of resources!

20 글의 흐름으로 보아, 주어진 문장이 들어가기에 가장 적절한 곳은?

Similarly, a man named Kyle Parsons and his partners have been creatively reusing old motorcycle tires from Bali, Indonesia.

21 주관식 윗글의 내용을 다음과 같이 요약하고자 할 때, (A), (B)의 괄호 안에 주어진 단어를 알맞게 바꿔 쓰시오.

Through upcycling, a seemingly (A)(use) object can be transformed into something completely different that is (B)(use) for everyday life.

(A) _____
(B) _____

[22~23] 다음 글을 읽고, 물음에 답하시오.

Along with small everyday items, much bigger things can also be upcycled—even old buildings that cannot be used for their original purpose anymore. The German government showed us an excellent example of this with a former steel plant that closed in 1985. Rather than destroy the plant's buildings or abandon the entire facility, (A)they decided to give it new meaning as a series of useful public structures. Many of the buildings kept their original shapes, but received extra equipment and new designs in (B) their surrounding areas. For instance, old gas tanks became pools for divers. Concrete walls of iron storage towers were turned into ideal training fields for rock climbers. Can you believe a building for melting metal is now a viewing platform with a gorgeous 360-degree view? The final result is the Landscape Park Duisburg Nord.

22 윗글의 앞에 올 내용으로 가장 적절한 것은?

① 폐기 처분된 건물의 운명
② 독일의 환경 보호 정책
③ 도심 내 공원의 필요성
④ 새로운 디자인의 중요성
⑤ 일상 용품을 업사이클한 예

23 [주관식] 밑줄 친 (A)와 (B)가 가리키는 바를 윗글에서 찾아 쓰시오.

(A) _____

(B) _____

[24~25] 다음 글을 읽고, 물음에 답하시오.

Creative thinking has the power to make many positive changes to the environment. By giving old products more value, we can ___(A)___ the amount of waste in a way that is even more eco-friendly than recycling. So what would you say to Jamie now as he decides what to do with his cans? Perhaps he could upcycle them to make lanterns, toys, or sculptures for his friends and family. The options are endless, and all he needs is a little ___(B)___ to think of them. In the same way, stop and think before you throw something out. Who knows? Maybe 당신은 그 쓰레기를 보물로 변화시킬 수 있다.

24 윗글의 빈칸 (A), (B)에 들어갈 말로 가장 적절한 것은?

	(A)		(B)
①	reduce	…	respect
②	boost	…	creativity
③	boost	…	inspiration
④	lessen	…	creativity
⑤	lessen	…	respect

25 [주관식] 윗글의 밑줄 친 우리말과 같은 뜻이 되도록 다음 괄호 안의 단어를 알맞게 배열하시오.

(turn / that trash / you / into / can / treasure)

Sound Life

Functions

- 제안·권유하기
Why don't you try eating a banana?

- 걱정, 두려움 표현하기
I'm worried about making a mistake.

Structures

- Has a painting, a movie, or a novel ever **made** you **feel** better?

- This is **what makes you special.**

Vocabulary

Words

☐ advantage [ædvǽntidʒ] 명 이점

☐ apologize [əpálədʒàiz] 동 사과하다

☐ artificial [ὰːrtəfíʃəl] 형 인공의

☐ bold [bould] 형 과감한

☐ boring [bɔ́ːriŋ] 형 지루한

☐ broaden [brɔ́ːdn] 동 넓히다

☐ cheerful [tʃíərfəl] 형 쾌활한

☐ concentrate [kánsəntrèit] 동 집중하다

☐ confidence [kánfədəns] 명 자신감

☐ contrasting [kəntrǽstiŋ] 형 대조적인

☐ courage [kə́ːridʒ] 명 용기

☐ cure [kjuər] 명 치유; 치유법, 치료제

☐ daydream [déidrìːm] 명 몽상

☐ develop [divéləp] 동 (필름을) 현상하다

☐ disappoint [dìsəpɔ́int] 동 실망시키다

☐ disturb [distə́ːrb] 동 방해하다

☐ dominant [dámənənt] 형 지배적인, 주요한

☐ dutifully [djúːtifəli] 부 충실하게

☐ embrace [imbréis] 동 포용하다

☐ engaging [ingéidʒiŋ] 형 매력 있는

☐ eruption [irʌ́pʃən] 명 폭발, 분화

☐ essential [isénʃəl] 형 필수적인

☐ existence [igzístəns] 명 존재

☐ flock [flɑk] 명 떼, 무리

☐ formation [fɔːrméiʃən] 명 (특정한) 대형[편대]

☐ irritated [íritèitid] 형 짜증이 난

☐ lack [læk] 동 …이 없다[부족하다]

☐ medicine [médəsin] 명 약

☐ opportunity [ὰpərtjúːnəti] 명 기회

☐ opposite [ápəzit] 명 반대(되는 사람·것)

☐ overcome [òuvərkʌ́m] 동 극복하다

☐ overwhelm [òuvərhwélm] 동 압도하다, 사로잡다

☐ perspective [pərspéktiv] 명 관점, 시각

☐ pressure [préʃər] 명 압박

☐ publication [pʌ̀bləkéiʃən] 명 간행물

☐ random [rǽndəm] 형 무작위의

☐ realize [ríːəlàiz] 동 깨닫다

☐ release [rilíːs] 동 (감정을) 발산하다

☐ relieve [rilíːv] 동 (걱정, 불안)을 덜어주다

☐ routine [ruːtíːn] 명 일상

☐ satisfied [sǽtisfàid] 형 만족하는

☐ seagull [síːgʌl] 명 갈매기

☐ soar [sɔːr] 동 (하늘 높이) 날아오르다

☐ substance [sʌ́bstəns] 명 물질

☐ task [tæsk] 명 일, 과업

☐ trail [treil] 명 자취

☐ unfit [ʌnfít] 형 부적합한

☐ unfortunately [ʌnfɔ́ːrtʃənitli] 부 불행하게도

☐ uplifting [ʌplíftiŋ] 형 사기를 높이는, 격려가 되는

☐ vividly [vívidli] 부 생생하게, 선명하게

Phrases

☐ be about to 막 …하려던 참이다

☐ break out 갑자기 (발진이) 잔뜩 나다

☐ carry on …을 계속하다

☐ consist of …으로 이루어지다[구성되다]

☐ deal with 다루다, 대처하다

☐ fall into place 꼭 들어맞다

☐ have trouble v-ing …하는 데에 어려움을 겪다

☐ inform A of B A에게 B를 알리다

☐ trick ... into v-ing …를 속여서 ~하게 하다

☐ work out 운동하다

Vocabulary Test

1 다음 영어는 우리말로, 우리말은 영어로 쓰시오.

(1) disappoint _____

(2) overcome _____

(3) publication _____

(4) essential _____

(5) 이점 _____

(6) 만족하는 _____

(7) 과감한 _____

(8) 집중하다 _____

2 다음 빈칸에 들어갈 알맞은 단어를 보기 에서 골라 쓰시오. 필요하다면 형태를 바꾸시오.

보기	lack	random	disturb	boring

(1) The film was _____, so I fell asleep.

(2) Do not _____ me while I'm reading.

(3) I live and work in my studio because I work at _____ hours.

(4) I think he _____ the ability to do this job properly.

3 주어진 우리말과 같은 뜻이 되도록 빈칸에 알맞은 말을 쓰시오.

(1) When I _____ _____ _____ leave, my phone rang.
(막 떠나려는데, 내 전화기가 울렸다.)

(2) I _____ _____ when I use cosmetic products.
(나는 화장품을 쓰면 뾰루지가 난다.)

(3) This class _____ _____ thirty students.
(이 학급은 30명의 학생으로 구성되어 있다.)

(4) She knows how to _____ _____ the problem.
(그녀는 그 문제를 처리하는 방법을 알고 있다.)

4 다음 영영풀이에 해당하는 단어를 보기 에서 골라 쓰시오.

보기	apologize	dominant	soar	unfit

(1) _____ : not good enough for a particular use

(2) _____ : more noticeable than the other parts

(3) _____ : to rise quickly upward to a great height

(4) _____ : to tell someone that you are sorry for doing something wrong

Communicative Functions

1 제안·권유하기

> A: I think I'm gaining weight these days.
> (나 요즘 살이 찌는 것 같아.)
> B: **Why don't you** try boxing? It's very effective for losing weight.
> (복싱을 해 보는 건 어때? 그건 살을 빼는 데 매우 효과적이야.)

••••• 어떤 일을 하도록 제안하거나 권할 때 "Why don't you ... ?"라는 표현을 사용할 수 있다. 이와 유사한 표현으로 "What/How about ... ?," "You'd better ...," "Would you like (me) to ...," "I suggest (that) we ..." 등이 있다.

2 걱정, 두려움 표현하기

> A: **I'm worried about** her health.
> (난 그녀의 건강이 걱정돼.)
> B: Don't worry. I heard that she's getting better.
> (걱정하지 마. 그녀가 좋아지고 있다고 들었어.)

••••• 어떤 일이 안심이 되지 않아 불안한 것을 나타낼 때, "I'm worried about ..." 이라는 표현을 사용할 수 있다. 이와 유사한 표현으로 "I'm anxious (about) ...," "I'm scared/frightened/terrified (to ...)" 등이 있다.

Check-up

1 주어진 우리말 뜻에 맞도록 빈칸에 알맞은 말을 쓰시오.

(1) _____ _____ _____ my presentation tomorrow.
(나는 내일 있을 발표가 걱정돼.)

(2) _____ _____ _____ stop eating snacks?
(과자를 그만 먹는 게 어때?)

2 다음 대화가 자연스럽게 이어지도록 순서대로 배열하시오.

> (A) I'd love to, but I'm worried about missing class. We have a test next week.
> (B) I've got a terrible toothache.
> (C) Sounds good. Thanks a lot.
> (D) You can borrow my notes later on. Come by this evening to pick up the notes.
> (E) Why don't you go to the dentist right away?

_____ → _____ → _____ → _____ → _____

Discovering Grammar

Point 1 「사역동사+목적어+동사원형」

▌ **Textbook** Has a painting, a movie, or a novel ever **made** you **feel** better?
(그림이나 영화, 혹은 소설로 인해 기분이 나아졌던 적이 있나요?)

✚ **Plus** Please **let** her **know** I'll call her later.
(그녀에게 제가 나중에 전화할 거라고 알려주세요.)

• '…하게 하다'라는 의미의 사역동사 let, have, make는 목적격 보어로 동사원형을 취한다. help는 사역동사에 준하는 동사로, 목적격 보어로 동사원형과 to부정사를 둘 다 취할 수 있다. 사역동사의 목적어와 목적격 보어가 수동의 관계일 때는 목적격 보어로 과거분사를 쓴다.

Point 2 관계대명사 what

▌ **Textbook** This is **what makes you special**.
(그것이 당신을 특별하게 만드는 것이다.)

✚ **Plus** **What matters** is how you deal with the mistake.
(중요한 것은 당신이 실수에 어떻게 대처하느냐이다.)

• what은 선행사를 포함하는 관계대명사로, '…하는 것'이라는 의미이며 the thing which[that]로 바꿔쓸 수 있다. what이 이끄는 관계사절은 명사절로 문장 내에서 주어, 목적어, 보어 역할을 한다. what절이 주어인 경우 주로 단수 취급한다.

Check-up

1 다음 괄호 안에서 어법상 올바른 것을 고르시오.

(1) You may take (what / which) you wish, except for this one.

(2) The smell of food made him (feel / to feel) hungry.

(3) I'd like to have my suitcase (repair/ repaired).

2 다음 우리말과 같은 뜻이 되도록 괄호 안의 말을 이용하여 문장을 완성하시오.

(1) 내 이웃이 차고 문을 고치는 것을 도와주었다. (help, fix)
→ My neighbor _____ _____ _____ my garage door.

(2) 사람들을 돕는 것은 그녀가 좋아하는 것이었다. (what, love)
→ Helping people was _____ _____ _____ to do.

1   다음 문장의 괄호 안에서 알맞은 것을 고르시오.

(1) Don't let your dog (eat / eaten) any raw potatoes.

(2) They had us (wait / waited) another hour at the hotel.

(3) He had the newspaper (deliver / delivered) to his house.

(4) I made her (promise / to promise) that she wouldn't tell a lie again.

2   다음 문장의 밑줄 친 부분을 어법에 맞게 고쳐 쓰시오.

(1) That she was looking for was her car key.

(2) He is going to tell you the thing what you have to do.

(3) Warm milk helps you slept better at night.

(4) They wouldn't let people parked in front of the building.

3   다음 문장의 빈칸에 관계대명사 that 또는 what 중 알맞은 것을 쓰시오.

(1) This is _____ I could do for you.

(2) The building _____ we work in faces a park.

(3) They're spending time doing everything _____ they want to.

(4) He uses _____ he has learned to teach fellow students.

4   주어진 우리말과 같은 뜻이 되도록 괄호 안의 단어를 배열하여 문장을 완성하시오.

(1) 내가 원하는 것은 네가 솔직해지는 것이다.

(be / what / you / is / for / I / to / want)

→ _____ honest.

(2) 우리는 지난 주말에 방을 칠했다.

(the room / painted / weekend / had / last)

→ We _____.

(3) 부모들은 아이들이 잘못된 식습관을 들이게 하지 말아야 한다.

(poor / let / eating habits / their children / develop)

→ Parents should not _____.

(4) 그들은 그 소년이 들고 있던 것을 빼앗았다.

(boy / carrying / what / was / the)

→ They took away _____.

[1~2] 다음 글을 읽고, 물음에 답하시오.

> The woman in the picture is standing in a vividly red room and is placing fruit in a bowl. She seems to be carrying on her work in silence. As you watch the woman working dutifully at her task in this red room, your anger melts away instead of getting worse.
>
> _____, the yellow fruit on the table brings out positive and cheerful emotions. At the same time, the green and blue space outside the window causes healing and relaxing feelings. The existence of these cool colors actually makes the "heaviness" of the red colors appear a bit lighter.

1 윗글의 빈칸에 들어갈 말로 가장 적절한 것은?

① On the other hand ② However ③ Otherwise

④ Still ⑤ In addition

2 윗글의 그림에 대한 설명과 일치하지 <u>않는</u> 것은?

① 그림 속 여인은 조용히 일하고 있다.
② 빨간색은 긍정적이고 활기찬 감정을 이끌어낸다.
③ 탁자 위에 노란색 과일이 있다.
④ 창 밖의 풍경이 편안한 느낌을 준다.
⑤ 시원한 색깔들이 빨간색의 무게감을 덜어준다.

[3~4] 다음 글을 읽고, 물음에 답하시오.

> Walter Mitty has developed the pictures used on the front cover of *Life* magazine for the past sixteen years. (①) However, his world is about to change: *Life* will soon become an online-only publication. (②) Unfortunately, the picture for the final cover is missing. (③) Walter decides to hit the road to find the picture. (④) He believes the photographer still has <u>it</u> and follows his trail. (⑤) This is how Walter's wild dash across Greenland, Iceland, and the Himalayas begins.

3 글의 흐름으로 보아, 주어진 문장이 들어가기에 가장 적절한 곳은?

> Other than that, he leads a boring life filled with daydreams.

4 주관식 윗글에서 밑줄 친 it이 가리키는 바를 찾아 쓰시오.

5 다음 글의 요지로 가장 적절한 것은?

> Learn from Walter. Don't sit around and dream about your next adventure—just go ahead and make it happen. Don't wait for the right moment—there is no such thing as the right moment. Create your own opportunities, and everything will fall into place. Don't worry about not being brave enough—once you begin making bold choices, courage will follow. All you need is motivation and this is already inside of you. So start living! This movie will remind you that your dreams are ready whenever you are.

① 절호의 기회가 올 때까지 기다려라.
② 목표가 있다면 망설이지 말고 당장 실행하라.
③ 모험에는 항상 위험이 따른다는 것을 명심하라.
④ 허황된 꿈은 늦기 전에 버리는 것이 이롭다.
⑤ 강한 동기를 가진 사람이 성공할 가능성이 높다.

6 주어진 글 다음에 이어질 글의 순서로 가장 적절한 것은?

> Jonathan Livingston Seagull knows that he's different from others.

(A) During one of his practices, Jonathan flies through his flock. He expects the others to praise his amazing ability.

(B) Instead, they look at him coldly as they now consider him unfit to be a part of the flock. Jonathan tries his best to rejoin the flock, but he's no longer satisfied flying in formation with the other seagulls as he knows how wonderful soaring above the clouds really feels.

(C) Instead of fighting over food with the other seagulls, Jonathan spends all his time learning about flying. Every day, he practices new skills by rolling, spinning, and diving high above the sea.

① (A) − (C) − (B)　　　② (B) − (A) − (C)　　　③ (B) − (C) − (A)
④ (C) − (A) − (B)　　　⑤ (C) − (B) − (A)

1 다음 대화를 읽고, 남자의 마지막 말에 대한 여자의 응답으로 가장 적절한 것을 고르시오.

> B: Do you want to grab something to eat?
> G: Didn't you have breakfast?
> B: No, I don't eat breakfast that often.
> G: You should eat breakfast every morning. It gives you energy and helps you concentrate during class.
> B: That's probably why I have trouble paying attention in class. What's something easy I can have in the morning?

① Actually, you should pay more attention.
② Remember you can't use your cell phone during class.
③ Don't worry. I can lend it to you.
④ Why don't you try eating a banana? You don't need to cook at all.
⑤ Maybe you'd better start exercising in the morning.

2 다음 대화가 자연스럽게 이어지도록 (A)~(D)를 올바른 순서로 배열하시오.

> What are you making flashcards for?

> (A) I've already tried that, but it's not easy to do it by myself.
> (B) Take it easy. Practice your speech over and over again until you're comfortable.
> (C) Okay, then. Come over to my house after school. I'll help you practice.

> (D) They're for a presentation I have in two days. I've done a lot of research, but I'm worried about making a mistake.

_____ → _____ → _____ → _____

3 다음 대화를 읽고, 남자가 충고하는 바로 가장 적절한 것을 고르시오.

> M: Hi, Sally. What's wrong? You look a little blue.
> G: I'm worried about the test in your class next week. I'm feeling a lot of pressure to do well on it.
> M: You know, I was once very nervous about a test like you. But when I became too stressed out, I found myself making more mistakes. So, I realized that too much worrying doesn't do any good.
> G: Hmm... You're right. I should just relax and do my best.

① 시험에 철저히 대비하라.
② 연습을 많이 하라.
③ 지나치게 걱정하지 마라.
④ 실수를 줄이도록 노력하라.
⑤ 충분한 휴식을 취하라.

4 다음 중 단어의 영영 뜻풀이가 적절하지 <u>않은</u> 것은?

① artificial: created by human beings and used instead of something natural
② opportunity: a chance to do something
③ routine: the unusual way of doing something at a particular time
④ task: something you have to do
⑤ realize: to become aware of or understand something

5 다음 글에서 잠을 방해하는 요소로 언급되지 <u>않은</u> 것은?

> Today, I want to tell you about what's really keeping you from getting enough sleep. First, staying up late texting and watching TV is a sure way to disturb your sleep. The artificial light coming from these screens tricks your brain into keeping you up later! Second, eating at random hours can throw your body off track and keep you awake. Last, exercising too late in the evening increases a stress-related substance in your blood and keeps you awake.

① 밤 늦게 TV 시청하기
② 인공조명에 노출되는 것
③ 잦은 과식
④ 불규칙적인 식사
⑤ 밤 늦게 운동하기

6 [주관식] 다음 빈칸에 공통으로 들어갈 말을 쓰시오.

> • _____ are the most popular foods in Korea?
> • I'm sorry for _____ I did to you yesterday.

[7~8] [주관식] 주어진 우리말과 같은 뜻이 되도록 빈칸에 알맞은 말을 쓰시오.

7 We need to _____ _____ the fight against this disease.
(우리는 이 질병에 맞서서 싸움을 계속해 나가야 한다.)

8 He _____ _____ _____ when he was young.
(그는 어렸을 때 읽는 데 어려움이 있었다.)

9 밑줄 친 부분의 뜻풀이로 적절하지 <u>않은</u> 것은?

① Regular exercise can <u>relieve</u> stress. (…을 덜어주다)
② The pieces of the puzzle <u>fell into place</u>. (곳곳에 떨어지다)
③ She <u>tricked</u> me <u>into</u> buying it. (…을 속여서 ~하게 하다)
④ She had <u>dutifully</u> reported it to her boss. (충실하게)
⑤ He <u>works out</u> for an hour every day. (운동하다)

10 다음 글의 빈칸에 들어갈 말로 가장 적절한 것은?

> Has a painting, a movie, or a novel ever made you feel better? Taking medicine can help you deal with your emotions and relieve your worries, but sometimes art might actually be the cure you're looking for. As you will see, the use of color, different perspectives, and engaging plots _____ _____.

① may be harmful to teens
② lead to a higher quality of life
③ will put pressure on your brain
④ can have an uplifting effect on your mind
⑤ make you understand other people's perspectives

[11~13] 다음 글을 읽고, 물음에 답하시오.

In addition, the yellow fruit on the table brings out positive and cheerful emotions. (①) At the same time, the green and blue space outside the window causes healing and relaxing feelings. (②) Although the color red is dominant, it works together with the various contrasting colors to form a harmony. (③) Seeing this balance keeps you from becoming overwhelmed by your emotions and helps you overcome your anger. (④) As the painting's title suggests, this must be the power of the harmony in red. (⑤)

11 글의 흐름으로 보아, 주어진 문장이 들어가기에 가장 적절한 곳은?

The existence of these cool colors actually makes the "heaviness" of the red colors appear a bit lighter.

12 주관식 다음 영영 뜻풀이에 해당하는 단어를 윗글에서 찾아 쓰시오.

to succeed in dealing with or controlling something difficult

13 다음 중 윗글의 밑줄 친 **to form**과 같은 용법으로 쓰인 것은?

① I was so glad to hear that news.
② Can you give me something to drink?
③ She grew up to be a famous dancer.
④ He loves to travel foreign countries.
⑤ I raised my hand to ask a question.

14 (A), (B), (C)의 각 네모 안에서 어법에 맞는 표현으로 가장 적절한 것은?

The woman in the picture is standing in a vividly red room and is placing fruit in a bowl. She seems (A) to be / being carrying on her work in silence. As you watch the woman (B) working / works dutifully at her task in this red room, your anger melts away instead of (C) getting / to get worse.

	(A)		(B)		(C)
①	to be	⋯	works	⋯	getting
②	being	⋯	works	⋯	to get
③	to be	⋯	working	⋯	getting
④	being	⋯	working	⋯	to get
⑤	to be	⋯	working	⋯	to get

[15~17] 다음 글을 읽고, 물음에 답하시오.

Walter Mitty has developed the pictures (A)(use) on the front cover of *Life* magazine for the past sixteen years. Other than that, he leads a boring life (B)(fill) with daydreams. _____, his world is about to change: *Life* will soon become an online-only publication. Unfortunately, the picture for the final cover is missing. Walter decides to hit the road to find the picture. He believes the photographer still has it and follows his trail. This is how Walter's wild dash across Greenland, Iceland, and the Himalayas begins. During this adventure, he survives a volcanic eruption and a fall from a helicopter. Although he finally finds the photographer, Walter realizes he has, more importantly, become the person he always imagined he could be.

15 [주관식] (A), (B)의 괄호 안에 주어진 단어를 알맞은 형태로 고쳐 쓰시오.

(A) _____

(B) _____

16 윗글의 빈칸에 들어갈 말로 가장 적절한 것은?

① Besides ② However

③ Therefore ④ Similarly

⑤ For example

17 윗글의 내용과 일치하지 <u>않는</u> 것은?

① Walter는 잡지 표지 사진을 현상하는 일을 했다.

② Life지는 온라인으로만 출간될 예정이었다.

③ Walter는 사진을 찾기 위해 모험을 떠났다.

④ Walter는 화산 폭발로부터 살아남았다.

⑤ Walter는 결국 사진작가를 찾지 못했다.

[18~20] 다음 글을 읽고, 물음에 답하시오.

Jonathan Livingston Seagull knows that he _____. Instead of fighting over food with the other seagulls, Jonathan spends all his time ①learning about flying. Every day, he practices new skills by rolling, spinning, and diving high above the sea. During one of his practices, Jonathan flies through his flock. He expects the others ②praise his amazing ability. Instead, they look at him ③coldly as they now consider him ④unfit to be a part of the flock. Jonathan tries his best to rejoin the flock, but he's no longer satisfied ⑤flying in formation with the other seagulls as he knows 구름 위로 치솟아 날아오르는 것이 정말로 얼마나 멋진 기분인지.

18 윗글의 빈칸에 들어갈 말로 가장 적절한 것은?

① should accept others' opinions

② is different from others

③ always wants to be a part of the flock

④ has no courage to try something new

⑤ doesn't realize what he wants

19 밑줄 친 ①~⑤ 중, 어법상 <u>틀린</u> 것은?

20 [주관식] 윗글의 밑줄 친 우리말과 같은 뜻이 되도록 다음 괄호 안의 단어를 알맞게 배열하시오.

(wonderful / soaring / really / the clouds / how / above / feels)

Toward a Better World

Functions

- 바람 표현하기
  I wish I could do more to help them.

- 선호 표현하기
  I think sharing food is better than throwing it away.

Structures

- I am so glad that this family now has a safe place **where** they can lay their heads.

- It was quite clear that this place was not big **enough to** house all the family members.

Vocabulary

Words

☐ actually [ǽktʃuəli] (부) 사실은
☐ afford [əfɔ́ːrd] (동) …할 여유가 있다
☐ annual [ǽnjuəl] (형) 연례의
☐ appearance [əpíərəns] (명) 외관
☐ assist [əsíst] (동) 돕다
☐ brick [brik] (명) 벽돌
☐ cause [kɔːz] (명) 대의, 목적
☐ celebrate [séləbrèit] (동) 축하하다, 기념하다
☐ certificate [sərtífikeIt] (명) 증서
☐ charity [tʃǽrəti] (명) 자선 단체
☐ complain [kəmpléin] (동) 불평하다
☐ construction [kənstrʌ́kʃən] (명) 건설, 공사
☐ decent [díːsnt] (형) (수준·질이) 괜찮은, 제대로 된
☐ deserve [dizə́ːrv] (동) …을 누릴 자격이 있다
☐ dig [dig] (동) (구멍 등을) 파다
☐ donate [dóuneit] (동) 기증하다
☐ doubt [daut] (명) 의심, 의문
☐ drip [drip] (동) (액체가) 똑똑 떨어지다
☐ exchange [ikstʃéindʒ] (명) 교환
☐ financial [finǽnʃəl] (형) 금융[재정]의
☐ hardly [háːrdli] (부) 거의 … 아니다
☐ hut [hʌt] (명) 오두막
☐ incredible [inkrédəbl] (형) 놀라운, 엄청난
☐ jar [dʒɑːr] (명) 단지, 항아리
☐ lay [lei] (동) 놓다, 두다

☐ leak [liːk] (동) 새다
☐ mission [míʃən] (명) 사명, 임무
☐ necessarily [nèsəsérəli] (부) 필연적으로
☐ nightmare [náitmɛər] (명) 악몽
☐ ordinary [ɔ́ːrdənèri] (형) 평범한
☐ participate [pɑːrtísəpèit] (동) 참가하다
☐ presentation [prìːzəntéiʃən] (명) 발표, 설명
☐ protect [prətékt] (동) 보호하다
☐ recommend [rèkəménd] (동) 추천하다
☐ relief [rilíːf] (명) 안도
☐ scary [skɛ́əri] (형) 무서운, 겁나는
☐ self-confidence (명) 자신감
☐ sigh [sai] (명) 한숨
☐ sour [sauər] (형) 상한
☐ starve [stɑːrv] (동) 굶주리다
☐ suspend [səspénd] (동) 연기하다, 보류하다
☐ temperature [témpərətʃər] (명) 온도
☐ thankful [θǽŋkfəl] (형) 감사하는
☐ tireless [táiərlis] (형) 지칠 줄 모르는
☐ touched [tʌtʃt] (형) 감동한
☐ treatment [tríːtmənt] (명) 치료
☐ tutor [tjúːtər] (동) 가르치다
☐ upset [ʌpsét] (형) 기분 나쁜, 화난
☐ victim [víktim] (명) 희생자
☐ volunteer [vàləntíər] (명) 자원봉사자

Phrases

☐ help out (곤란한 때에) 거들다, 도와주다
☐ let alone …는 고사하고, …커녕
☐ might as well …하는 편이 낫다
☐ reach out to …에게 다가가다[관심을 보이다]
☐ show up (예정된 곳에) 나타나다

☐ sign up 신청하다, 가입하다
☐ take apart 해체하다
☐ take ~ for granted …을 당연하게 여기다
☐ take part in …에 참가하다

1 다음 영어는 우리말로, 우리말은 영어로 쓰시오.

(1) afford _____   (5) 굶주리다 _____

(2) scary _____   (6) 자선 단체 _____

(3) tutor _____   (7) 오두막 _____

(4) doubt _____   (8) 자신감 _____

2 다음 빈칸에 들어갈 알맞은 단어를 보기 에서 골라 쓰시오. 필요하다면 형태를 바꾸시오.

보기	victim	relief	ordinary	financial

(1) This headphone is different from that _____ one.

(2) It's a(n) _____ that you've arrived at last.

(3) Although he has _____ problems, he bought an expensive car.

(4) There are many _____ as a result of the flood.

3 주어진 우리말과 같은 뜻이 되도록 빈칸에 알맞은 말을 쓰시오.

(1) Teenagers are very sensitive about their _____.
   (십 대들은 자신의 외모에 매우 민감하다.)

(2) The bridge over the river is under _____.
   (강 위에 다리가 건설 중이다.)

(3) When I was in trouble, he kindly _____ me _____.
   (내가 곤경에 처했을 때, 그는 친절하게도 나를 도와주었다.)

(4) Anyone who wants to attend the campaign should _____ _____.
   (캠페인에 참석할 사람은 누구든지 신청해야 한다.)

4 다음 영영풀이에 해당하는 단어를 보기 에서 골라 쓰시오.

보기	volunteer	suspend	exchange	annual

(1) _____ : to delay or stop something from happening for a short time

(2) _____ : giving each other something at the same time

(3) _____ : happening once a year

(4) _____ : someone who does work without being paid for it

Communicative Functions

1 바람 표현하기

> A: I can't see the end of this line of cars.
> (이 자동차 행렬의 끝이 보이지 않네요.)
> B: **I wish we could** just fly over this traffic jam.
> (이 꽉 막힌 도로를 그냥 날아서 갈 수 있으면 좋겠어요.)

• 바라는 것을 표현할 때 "I wish I could ..."라는 표현을 사용할 수 있다. 이와 유사한 표현으로는 "I want (to) ...," "I'd like ...," "I look/am looking forward to ..." 등이 있다.

2 선호 표현하기

> A: **I think** riding a bike to work **is better than** driving to work.
> (자전거를 타고 출근하는 것이 차를 타고 출근하는 것보다 나은 것 같아.)
> B: I agree! It's eco-friendly and good for your health.
> (맞아! 그건 친환경적이고 건강에 좋아.)

• 선호하는 것을 말할 때 "I think X is better than Y"라는 표현을 사용할 수 있다. 이와 유사한 표현으로 "I prefer X to Y," "I('d) prefer (to) ...," "I think X is preferable to Y" 등이 있다.

Check-up

1 주어진 우리말 뜻에 맞도록 빈칸에 알맞은 말을 쓰시오.

(1) _____ _____ _____ _____ spend more time together.
 (나는 우리가 함께 더 많은 시간을 보낼 수 있으면 좋겠어.)

(2) _____ _____ a good ending _____ _____ _____ a good beginning.
 (나는 처음보다 끝이 좋은 게 낫다고 생각해.)

2 다음 대화의 빈칸에 적절한 말을 보기 에서 고르시오.

A: _____
B: Not yet. I haven't made up my mind about where to go.
A: Time is running out. You'd better hurry up and make some plans.
B: _____
A: Well, _____

> 보기   ⓐ What if I make the wrong choice?
> ⓑ Have you booked a plane ticket for your trip?
> ⓒ I think a poor choice is better than not choosing at all.

Discovering Grammar

Point 1 관계부사

> ▐ **Textbook** I am so glad that this family now has a safe place **where** they can lay their heads.
> (나는 이 가족이 머리를 누일 수 있는 안전한 장소를 갖게 되었다는 사실이 매우 기쁘다.)
>
> ✚ **Plus** She is looking forward to the day **when** she can visit her parents.
> (그녀는 부모님을 뵐 수 있는 날을 고대하고 있다.)
> Tell me the reason **why** you're late.
> (네가 지각한 이유를 말해 봐.)

• 관계부사는 「접속사+부사」의 역할을 하며, 선행사를 수식하는 형용사절을 이끈다. 선행사가 시간을 나타낼 경우 when, 장소를 나타낼 경우 where, 이유를 나타낼 경우 why, 방법을 나타낼 경우 how를 쓴다. 선행사와 관계부사는 함께 쓰거나 둘 중 하나를 생략할 수 있는데, how의 경우 관계부사나 선행사 중 하나를 반드시 생략해야 한다.

Point 2 「형용사/부사+enough+to-v」

> ▐ **Textbook** It was quite clear that this place was not big **enough to** house all the family members.
> (이 장소가 모든 가족 구성원들을 수용하기에 충분한 공간이 아님은 명백했다.)
>
> ✚ **Plus** Ron is tall **enough to** be a basketball player.
> = Ron is so tall that he can be a basketball player.
> (Ron은 농구 선수가 될 수 있을 정도로 키가 크다.)

• 「형용사/부사+enough+to-v」는 '…하기에 충분한/충분하게'라는 의미이다. 이 구문은 「so+형용사/부사+that+주어+can」의 형태로 바꿀 수 있다.

Check-up

1 다음 괄호 안에서 어법상 올바른 것을 고르시오.

(1) I know the place (where / why) he used to play.

(2) Do you remember the day (how / when) the war broke out?

(3) My mom doesn't like (how / why) I dress.

2 주어진 우리말과 같은 뜻이 되도록 괄호 안의 말을 이용하여 문장을 완성하시오.

(1) 밧줄이 바닥에 닿을 정도로 긴지 확인하세요. (long)
→ Please make sure the rope is _____ _____ _____ reach the bottom.

(2) 숲 속에서 캠핑을 할 수 있을 정도로 충분히 따뜻하다. (warm)
→ It is _____ _____ _____ camp in the woods.

1 다음 문장의 빈칸에 알맞은 관계부사를 쓰시오.

(1) The apartment _____ he lives is very old.

(2) Wednesday is the day _____ project will be completed.

(3) _____ she approaches the problem is creative.

(4) He is tired and that's the reason _____ he can't focus in class.

2 다음 문장에서 어법상 틀린 부분을 고쳐 쓰시오.

(1) David isn't enough old to have his own car.

(2) My brother exercises so hard to he can lift 100 kilograms.

(3) I don't like the way how she talks.

(4) I see no reason when we should stay here.

3 주어진 두 문장을 괄호 안의 말을 이용하여 한 문장으로 만드시오.

(1) Her smile is bright. It can make other people happy. (enough)

→ _____

(2) He is tall. He can reach the ceiling. (enough)

→ _____

(3) She ran fast. No one could catch her. (so ... that ~)

→ _____

(4) My laptop is light. I can carry it anywhere. (so ... that ~)

→ _____

4 다음 우리말과 같은 뜻이 되도록 주어진 단어를 배열하여 문장을 완성하시오.

(1) 이 담요는 침대를 덮을 만큼 충분히 넓지 않다.

(the bed / enough / is / not / to cover / wide)

→ This blanket _____.

(2) 저곳이 그 사고가 일어난 곳이다.

(where / the place / occurred / the accident)

→ That is _____.

(3) 지금이 우리가 결단을 내려야 할 때다.

(a decision / we / the time / make / when / have to)

→ Now is _____.

[1~2] 다음 글을 읽고, 물음에 답하시오.

> Sometimes you may feel upset when you wake up suddenly from a nightmare, but you can always let out a sigh of relief. No matter how scary the dream was, at least you've woken up safe and sound in your own home. ①Things that worry you or stress you out can appear in your dreams. ②You can go back to sleep because you know your loved ones are just around the corner in their own beds. ③Your home is a special place that protects you and your family from everything.
>
> ④Unfortunately, <u>this</u> is not a reality that everyone shares. ⑤Many people around the world don't wake up in a soft and comfortable bed.

1 윗글에서 전체 흐름과 관계 없는 문장은?

2 서술형 밑줄 친 <u>this</u>의 내용을 우리말 30자 이내로 쓰시오.

3 필자에 관한 설명 중 다음 글의 내용과 일치하지 않는 것은?

> One day, I learned about a program that needed volunteers to go to different parts of the world to help build houses for the poor. After watching a presentation about it, I was really touched by the mission, so I decided to take part in the next volunteer trip. I had my doubts, though. I didn't know anything about construction, and we'd only be there for two weeks. Could we really change these people's lives as the presentation had suggested? I was going to find out soon enough.

① 가난한 사람들을 위한 집 짓기 활동에 대해 알게 되었다.
② 친구의 권유로 해외 자원봉사에 참여하게 되었다.
③ 건축에 대해 아는 바가 전혀 없었다.
④ 2주 동안 집 짓기 봉사 활동을 할 예정이었다.
⑤ 봉사 활동을 성공적으로 해낼 수 있을지 의구심을 갖고 있었다.

4 주어진 글 다음에 이어질 글의 순서로 가장 적절한 것은?

> The volunteers and I got to meet the family that would be moving into the home we were going to build the day after we arrived in Karjat, India.

(A) It was shocking to see how they were living. After meeting them, I felt even more determined to build them a beautiful home.

(B) In addition to that, there were jars everywhere to catch all the rainwater dripping from the roof. With all these jars on the floor, there was hardly any space to sit, let alone lie down.

(C) This family of five was living in a one-room hut. It was quite clear that this place was not big enough to house all the family members.

① (A) − (C) − (B) ② (B) − (A) − (C) ③ (B) − (C) − (A)
④ (C) − (A) − (B) ⑤ (C) − (B) − (A)

[5~6] 다음 글을 읽고, 물음에 답하시오.

> As I look back on this trip, I find it amazing that so many different people came together to build a house for a family they'd never met. (①) The work was hard, but not one person ever stopped smiling or even complained. (②) I'm thankful for the friendships I've made through this trip. (③) In addition, I learned so much from the other volunteers, the community members, and this family. (④) I thought I was there to give, but I received so much more in return. (⑤) This experience has inspired me to continue building houses for others. I hope it will also encourage my friends and family members to help out in the future.

5 글의 흐름으로 보아, 주어진 문장이 들어가기에 가장 적절한 곳은?

> For many of us, it was the first time we'd ever built a house.

6 윗글에 드러난 필자의 심경으로 가장 적절한 것은?

① curious ② disappointed ③ grateful
④ doubtful ⑤ embarrassed

1 다음 대화를 읽고, 남자의 마지막 말에 대한 여자의 응답으로 가장 적절한 것을 고르시오.

> B: I wish we could do something for the sick babies in developing countries.
> G: We can help them by knitting hats for them!
> B: Hmm... Tell me more. How will that help them?

① Wait. I think there's something wrong.

② Why don't you tell me about it?

③ That's great. It's a good way we can help them.

④ Those hats keep babies warm and help save their lives.

⑤ I'll think more about ways to help sick people.

2 다음 중 대화 내용과 일치하지 <u>않는</u> 것은?

> G: What will you bring to the school bazaar?
> B: I'm bringing a pair of shoes. They are too small for me. What about you?
> G: I'm bringing a hair pin. I have short hair now, so I don't need it.
> B: That's a good idea. I think selling it at the bazaar is better than keeping it.

① 학교에서 바자회가 열릴 예정이다.

② 남자는 바자회에 신발을 가져갈 것이다.

③ 남자의 신발은 그에게 너무 작아졌다.

④ 여자는 더는 머리핀이 필요하지 않다.

⑤ 남자는 바자회에 물건을 파는 것보다 집에 보관하는 것을 선호한다.

3 다음을 읽고, Wonderful Length의 캠페인에 관해 언급되지 <u>않은</u> 것을 고르시오.

> Wonderful Length will host its third annual campaign to collect hair on Saturday, November 22! On this day people nationwide will cut and donate their hair to kids who have lost their hair because of cancer treatment. Hair loss doesn't only change a child's appearance. It can also lower their self-confidence and limit their quality of life. Wonderful Length helps these children regain their confidence by providing free wigs. This is why your support is important. In order to help them, you just need to grow out your hair. Then cut it and donate it to kids. Your simple act will be of great help.

① 개최 날짜   ② 캠페인의 목적

③ 활동 내용   ④ 개최 장소

⑤ 캠페인의 효과

4 다음 중 단어의 영영 뜻풀이가 적절하지 <u>않은</u> 것은?

① decent: good or good enough

② ordinary: not unusual or different

③ complain: to say that you are not satisfied with something

④ appearance: the way that somebody or something looks on the outside

⑤ mission: a feeling of being uncertain about something or not believing something

5 밑줄 친 부분의 뜻풀이로 적절하지 <u>않은</u> 것은?

① We need to find new ways of <u>reaching out</u> to young students. (…에게 다가가다)
② He <u>showed up</u> all dressed up. (자랑하다)
③ How can I <u>sign up</u> for a membership? (가입하다)
④ We <u>took part in</u> the dance contest. (…에 참가하다)
⑤ He spent his time building and <u>taking apart</u> radios. (해체하다)

[6~7] 주관식 주어진 우리말과 같은 뜻이 되도록 빈칸에 알맞은 말을 쓰시오.

6 We _____ _____ _____ take a bus.
(우리는 버스를 타는 게 낫겠어.)

7 You must not _____ other people's help _____ _____.
(남의 도움을 당연하게 여기면 안 된다.)

[8~9] 다음 글을 읽고, 물음에 답하시오.

  Sometimes you may feel upset when you wake up suddenly from a nightmare, but you can always let out a sigh of relief. (①) No matter how scary the dream was, at least you've woken up safe and sound in your own home. (②) You can go back to sleep because you know your loved ones are just around the corner in their own beds. (③) Your home is a special place that protects you and your family from everything. (④) Many people around the world don't wake up in a soft and comfortable bed. (⑤) Instead, (A) they open their eyes and see a dirt floor or a leaking roof. I didn't realize for a long time that something I take for granted could be someone else's biggest dream.

8 글의 흐름으로 보아, 주어진 문장이 들어가기에 가장 적절한 곳은?

  Unfortunately, this is not a reality that everyone shares.

9 주관식 밑줄 친 (A)와 같은 뜻이 되도록 to부정사를 이용하여 빈칸을 채우시오.

→ they open their eyes _____ _____ a dirt floor or a leaking roof

[10~11] 다음 글을 읽고, 물음에 답하시오.

  One day, I learned about a program (A) where / that needed volunteers to go to different parts of the world to help build houses for the poor. After watching a presentation about <u>it</u>, I was really (B) touched / touching by the mission, so I decided to take part in the next volunteer trip. I had my doubts, though. I didn't know anything about construction, and we'd only be there (C) during / for two weeks. Could we really change these people's lives as the presentation had suggested?

10 (A), (B), (C)의 각 네모 안에서 어법에 맞는 표현으로 가장 적절한 것은?

	(A)		(B)		(C)
①	where	…	touched	…	for
②	where	…	touching	…	during
③	that	…	touched	…	for
④	that	…	touching	…	during
⑤	that	…	touched	…	during

11 서술형 밑줄 친 it이 가리키는 내용을 40자 내외의 우리말로 쓰시오.

12 주관식 윗글의 밑줄 친 우리말과 같은 뜻이 되도록 다음 괄호 안의 단어를 알맞게 배열하시오.

(not / house / enough / all / big / to / the family members)

13 윗글의 빈칸에 들어갈 말로 가장 적절한 것은?

① shocking   ② amusing
③ wonderful   ④ priceless
⑤ fascinating

14 윗글의 내용과 일치하지 <u>않는</u> 것은?

① 필자는 다른 사람의 집을 지어주기 위해 인도를 방문했다.
② 필자는 새로 지은 집으로 이사할 가족을 만났다.
③ 다섯 가족은 방 한 칸짜리 오두막에 살고 있었다.
④ 오두막은 5명이 겨우 누울 크기였다.
⑤ 필자는 가족을 돕겠다는 결의를 다졌다.

[12~14] 다음 글을 읽고, 물음에 답하시오.

The volunteers and I got to meet the family that would be moving into the home we were going to build the day after we arrived in Karjat, India. This family of five was living in a one-room hut. It was quite clear that this place was <u>모든 가족 구성원들을 수용하기에 충분히 크지 않은</u>. In addition to that, there were jars everywhere to catch all the rainwater dripping from the roof. With all these jars on the floor, there was hardly any space to sit, let alone lie down. It was _____ to see how they were living. After meeting them, I felt even more determined to build them a beautiful home.

[15~17] 다음 글을 읽고, 물음에 답하시오.

Under the burning sun, we carried bricks, mixed concrete, and dug holes for pipes. We had to slowly take apart the family's hut to get more bricks and other materials for the new house. Every morning, the family and their neighbors (A)<u>would</u> provide breakfast for everyone. Then, all of us—the volunteers, community members, and the family—would start working. When evening came, we were all very tired and sweaty, but we were happy.

After another week, the home was finally finished. On the last day, we had a party to celebrate the completion of the new house. (B)It was the best way to end such an incredible experience. Everyone was dancing or crying tears of joy.

15 주관식 다음 영영 뜻풀이에 맞는 단어를 윗글에서 찾아 쓰시오.

> to do something enjoyable to show that an event is special

16 다음 중 (A)의 밑줄 친 would와 같은 의미로 쓰인 것은?

① Jack said he would quit his job.
② Would you shut the window?
③ Going to the festival would be fun.
④ She would go swimming on Saturdays.
⑤ He's so stubborn. He wouldn't listen to me.

17 서술형 (B)의 밑줄 친 It이 가리키는 내용을 우리말로 쓰시오.

18 주관식 다음 글에서 어법상 틀린 표현 두 가지를 찾아 바르게 고치시오.

> As I look back on this trip, I find it amazed that so many different people came together to build a house for a

family they'd never met. For many of us, it was the first time we'd ever built a house. The work was hard, but not one person ever stopped to smile or even complained.

(1) _____ → _____
(2) _____ → _____

[19~20] 다음 글을 읽고, 물음에 답하시오.

Although two weeks may not seem like a long time, I had the chance to make new friends, learn about a different culture, and, most importantly, do something ①what makes the lives of others better. I am so glad that this family now has a safe place ②where they can lay their heads. I believe

_____.

Right now, there are still many people around the world without a place ③to live. They are the reason ④why ordinary people like me want to go out there and ⑤help put a roof over their head.

19 윗글의 빈칸에 들어갈 말로 가장 적절한 것은?

① making new friends is difficult
② everyone deserves a decent home
③ houses reflect people's culture
④ family means different things to each person
⑤ we can get design ideas from nature

20 윗글의 밑줄 친 ①~⑤ 중, 어법상 틀린 것은?

1 다음 대화의 빈칸에 들어갈 말로 가장 적절한 것은?

> A: These days, I have trouble falling asleep.
> B: Hmm... _____

① Actually, I fell asleep during class.

② Let me know if you need any help.

③ The next time you're late, you'll be in trouble.

④ That's a good idea. You should try it yourself.

⑤ Why don't you take a warm bath before going to bed?

① 여자는 플래시카드를 만들고 있다.

② 여자는 발표를 위한 조사를 많이 했다.

③ 여자는 발표 중 실수할까 봐 걱정한다.

④ 여자는 발표 연습을 여러 번 했다.

⑤ 방과 후 남자는 여자의 집에 가기로 했다.

2 다음 대화의 내용과 일치하지 <u>않는</u> 것은?

> G: Ricky, do you have a pen? I need to make flashcards.
> B: What are you making flashcards for?
> G: They're for a presentation I have in two days. I've done a lot of research, but I'm worried about making a mistake.
> B: Take it easy. Giving a presentation is all about practice. Practice your speech over and over again until you're comfortable.
> G: I've already tried that, but it's not easy to do it by myself.
> B: Okay, then. Come over to my house after school. I'll help you practice.
> G: Great! Thanks!

3 다음 대화의 주제로 가장 적절한 것은?

> G: I think there's something wrong. You paid too much.
> B: Actually, I didn't. These days I'm participating in the Suspended Coffee project.
> G: What is that?
> B: It's for those who can't afford to drink coffee, such as the homeless.
> G: So you pay for a second drink that they will pick up later?
> B: Exactly.
> G: That's really nice of you. I think I will participate in it, too.

① the health benefits of coffee

② where to get free coffee

③ how to sign up for charity events

④ the cashier's mistake at the cafe

⑤ a charity program that helps people in need

4 대화의 흐름으로 보아, 주어진 문장이 들어가기에 가장 적절한 곳은?

> Anyone who needs food can take what's there for free.

> W: You shouldn't have bought so much milk. We are going to be away for the next few weeks. (①)
>
> B: Oh... It just slipped my mind. Sorry, Mom. (②)
>
> W: That's all right. But this milk will go sour while we're gone. (③)
>
> B: Let's put it in the food-sharing fridge in the community center. (④)
>
> W: What's that?
>
> B: It's like a fridge for everyone. (⑤)
>
> W: That sounds good. I think sharing food is better than throwing it away.

5 다음 중 단어의 영영 뜻풀이가 적절하지 <u>않은</u> 것은?

① courage: the ability to be brave

② assist: to help someone or something

③ broaden: to make something include less things

④ certificate: a document that is official proof that something has happened

⑤ touched: feeling happy and grateful by what someone has done

6 밑줄 친 부분의 뜻풀이로 적절하지 <u>않은</u> 것은?

① The roof is still <u>leaking</u>. (새다)

② Many people <u>take for granted</u> our right to vote. (당연하게 여기다)

③ He always <u>has trouble waking</u> up in the morning. (…하는 데에 어려움을 겪다)

④ The book <u>consists of</u> seven chapters. (…을 계속하다)

⑤ The man <u>was about to</u> get on the train. (막 …하려던 참이다)

7 다음 빈칸에 들어갈 말로 바르게 짝지어진 것은?

> • Is there a place _____ I can buy some bread?
>
> • My brother showed me _____ he had borrowed from Jim.

① when – that   ② when – what

③ where – what   ④ where – that

⑤ when – which

[8~9] 주관식 주어진 우리말과 같은 뜻이 되도록 괄호 안의 단어를 이용하여 문장을 완성하시오.

8 이 소설은 하루 만에 끝낼 수 있을 정도로 재미있다. (interesting, finish)

→ This novel is _____ _____ _____ _____ in one day.

9 John은 내 여동생에게 꽃이 배달되게 했다. (have, deliver)

→ John _____ the flowers _____ to my sister.

[10~11] 다음 글을 읽고, 물음에 답하시오.

Has a painting, a movie, or a novel ever made you feel better? Taking medicine can help you deal with your emotions and (A) deepen / relieve your worries, but sometimes art might actually be the cure you're looking for. As you will see, the use of color, different (B) perspectives / prospective , and engaging plots can have a(n) (C) discouraging / uplifting effect on your mind, body, and soul.

10 (A), (B), (C)의 각 네모 안에서 문맥에 맞는 낱말로 가장 적절한 것은?

	(A)	(B)	(C)
①	deepen	perspectives	uplifting
②	relieve	perspectives	discouraging
③	deepen	prospective	discouraging
④	deepen	prospective	uplifting
⑤	relieve	perspectives	uplifting

[12~13] 다음 글을 읽고, 물음에 답하시오.

Many people think that they should look at (A) (calm) colors when they are angry or irritated. Because the color red excites the emotions, they may think that (B) (look) at it will make them angrier. However, this picture shows that the opposite can be true. By looking at the color red here, you can release your anger. This picture is actually

_____.

The woman in the picture is standing in a vividly red room and is placing fruit in a bowl. She seems to be carrying on her work in silence. As you watch the woman working dutifully at her task in this red room, your anger melts away instead of getting worse.

12 [주관식] (A), (B)의 괄호 안에 주어진 단어를 알맞은 형태로 고쳐 쓰시오.

(A) _____

(B) _____

11 윗글의 주제로 가장 적절한 것은?

① how to control your emotion

② ways to beat your worries

③ medicine as the key to good health

④ how to view and appreciate art

⑤ art as a way to improve emotional health

13 윗글의 빈칸에 들어갈 말로 가장 적절한 것은?

① not impressive at all

② making you angrier

③ helping you calm down

④ asking a serious question

⑤ showing pure happiness

[14~15] 다음 글을 읽고, 물음에 답하시오.

Don't sit around and dream about your next adventure—just go ahead and make it happening. Create your own opportunities, and everything will fall into place. Don't worry about not be brave enough—once you begin making bold choices, courage will follow. All you need is motivation and this is already inside of you.

14 주관식 윗글에서 어법상 **틀린** 표현 두 가지를 찾아 바르게 고치시오.

(1) _____ → _____

(2) _____ → _____

15 윗글의 내용을 한 문장으로 요약할 때, 빈칸에 들어갈 말로 가장 적절한 것은?

Believe in yourself and choose to _____ your dreams now.

① change   ② pursue

③ give up   ④ imagine

⑤ record

[16~17] 다음 글을 읽고, 물음에 답하시오.

Jonathan Livingston Seagull knows that he's different from others. (①) Instead of fighting over food with the other seagulls, Jonathan spends all his time learning about flying. (②) Every day, he practices new skills by rolling, spinning, and diving high above the sea. (③) During one of his practices, Jonathan flies through his flock. (④) He expects the others to praise his amazing ability. (⑤) Jonathan tries his best to rejoin the flock, but 그는 다른 갈매기들과 대형을 이루어 날 때 더는 만족할 수 없다 as he knows how wonderful soaring above the clouds really feels.

16 글의 흐름으로 보아, 주어진 문장이 들어가기에 가장 적절한 곳은?

Instead, they look at him coldly as they now consider him unfit to be a part of the flock.

17 주관식 윗글의 밑줄 친 우리말과 같은 뜻이 되도록 다음 괄호 안의 단어를 알맞게 배열하시오.

(no longer / flying / is / in formation / satisfied / with / he / the other seagulls)

[18~19] 다음 글을 읽고, 물음에 답하시오.

One day, I learned about a program that needed volunteers to go to different parts of the world to help build houses for the poor.

(A) I had my doubts, though. I didn't know anything about construction, and we'd only be there for two weeks.

(B) Could we really change these people's lives as the presentation had suggested? I was going to find out soon enough.

(C) After watching a presentation about it, I was really touched by the mission, so I decided to take part in the next volunteer trip.

18 주어진 글 다음에 이어질 글의 순서로 가장 적절한 것은?

① (A) − (C) − (B)　　② (B) − (A) − (C)
③ (B) − (C) − (A)　　④ (C) − (A) − (B)
⑤ (C) − (B) − (A)

19 주관식 다음 영영 뜻풀이에 해당하는 단어를 윗글에서 찾아 쓰시오.

an important job that a person or group of people is given to do

[20~22] 다음 글을 읽고, 물음에 답하시오.

There were clear skies and temperatures over 30˚C that first week. Under the ① burned sun, we carried bricks, mixed concrete, and ② dug holes for pipes. We had to slowly take apart the family's hut to get more bricks and other materials for the new house. Every morning, the family and their neighbors ③ would provide breakfast for everyone. Then, all of us—the volunteers, community members, and the family—would start ④ working. When evening came, we were all very tired and sweaty, but we were happy.

After another week, the home was finally finished. On the last day, we had a party ⑤ to celebrate the completion of the new house. It was 대단히 놀라운 경험을 마무리 짓는 가장 좋은 방법.

20 밑줄 친 ①~⑤ 중, 어법상 틀린 것은?

21 주관식 윗글의 밑줄 친 우리말과 같은 뜻이 되도록 아래 괄호 안의 단어를 알맞게 배열하시오.

(to end / incredible / such / the best way / experience / an)

22 윗글의 내용과 일치하지 않는 것은?

① 필자는 벽돌을 나르고 콘크리트를 섞었다.
② 헌 집은 해체하여 모두 폐기했다.
③ 이웃들이 아침식사를 마련했다.
④ 일이 고되었으나 모두 즐겁게 일했다.
⑤ 집 짓기를 완성한 기념으로 파티를 열었다.

[23~25] 다음 글을 읽고, 물음에 답하시오.

Although two weeks may not seem like a long time, I had the chance to make new friends, learn about a different culture, and, _____, do something that makes the lives of others better. I am so glad (A) that / why this family now has a safe place where they can lay their heads. I believe everyone (B) deserve / deserves a decent home. Right now, there are still many people around the world without a place to live. They are the reason (C) why / how ordinary people like me want to go out there and help put a roof over their head.

23 윗글의 빈칸에 들어갈 말로 가장 적절한 것은?

① as a result
② for instance
③ in other words
④ most importantly
⑤ on the other hand

24 (A), (B), (C)의 각 네모 안에서 어법에 맞는 표현으로 가장 적절한 것은?

	(A)		(B)		(C)
①	that	⋯	deserve	⋯	why
②	why	⋯	deserves	⋯	why
③	that	⋯	deserves	⋯	why
④	why	⋯	deserve	⋯	how
⑤	that	⋯	deserves	⋯	how

25 다음 중 윗글의 밑줄 친 **to live**와 쓰임이 같은 것은?

① He called me to meet for tea.
② I'm sorry to bother you.
③ She wants to help the elderly.
④ Animals have the ability to predict earthquakes.
⑤ I went to the office to find the window open.

What Matters Most

Functions

• 강조하기
It is important to be happy with who you are.

• 관심에 대해 묻기
What are you interested in?

Structures

• **Reaching** the hermit's hut, the king found the old man digging in his garden.

• **If** you **hadn't helped** me, you **would've left**, and that man **would've attacked** you.

Vocabulary

Words

- [ ] announce [ənáuns] ⑧ 발표[공표]하다, 알리다
- [ ] attack [ətǽk] ⑧ 공격하다
- [ ] bandage [bǽndidʒ] ⑧ 붕대를 감다
- [ ] beg [beg] ⑧ 간청[애원]하다
- [ ] career [kəríər] ⑲ 직업; 경력, 이력
- [ ] childish [tʃáildiʃ] ⑲ 유치한
- [ ] considerate [kənsídərit] ⑲ 사려 깊은, 배려하는
- [ ] consult [kənsʌ́lt] ⑧ 상담[상의]하다
- [ ] council [káunsəl] ⑲ 의회; 자문위원회
- [ ] decline [dikláin] ⑧ 거절[사양]하다
- [ ] demonstration [dèmənstréiʃən] ⑲ 시범
- [ ] disguise [disgáiz] ⑧ 변장하다
- [ ] effective [iféktiv] ⑲ 효과적인
- [ ] enemy [énəmi] ⑲ 적
- [ ] ensure [inʃúər] ⑧ 확실하게 하다, 보증하다
- [ ] entire [intáiər] ⑲ 전체의, 전부의
- [ ] eventually [ivéntʃuəli] ⑨ 결국, 마침내
- [ ] exhausted [igzɔ́:stid] ⑲ 기진맥진한
- [ ] folk [fouk] ⑲ 사람들
- [ ] forgive [fərgív] ⑧ 용서하다
- [ ] formal [fɔ́:rməl] ⑲ 정식의, 공식적인
- [ ] fulfill [fulfíl] ⑧ 달성하다
- [ ] generous [dʒénərəs] ⑲ 관대한, 너그러운
- [ ] greet [gri:t] ⑧ 인사하다; 맞이하다
- [ ] hermit [hə́:rmit] ⑲ 은자, 은둔자
- [ ] lately [léitli] ⑨ 최근
- [ ] merit [mérit] ⑲ 장점
- [ ] method [méθəd] ⑲ 방법
- [ ] modify [mádəfài] ⑧ 개조하다
- [ ] outgoing [áutgòuiŋ] ⑲ 외향적인, 사교적인
- [ ] peasant [pézənt] ⑲ 농부, 농민; 소작농
- [ ] personality [pə̀rsənǽləti] ⑲ 성격
- [ ] precise [prisáis] ⑲ 정확한
- [ ] property [prápərti] ⑲ 재산
- [ ] publish [pʌ́bliʃ] ⑧ 출판하다
- [ ] quality [kwáləti] ⑲ 자질
- [ ] recall [rikɔ́:l] ⑧ 회상하다, 기억해내다
- [ ] recognize [rékəgnàiz] ⑧ 알아보다, 인식하다
- [ ] remarkably [rimá:rkəbli] ⑨ 놀랍게도; 매우
- [ ] respond [rispánd] ⑧ 대답[응답]하다
- [ ] restore [ristɔ́:r] ⑧ 되돌려주다, 반환하다
- [ ] serve [sə:rv] ⑧ (사람을) 모시다, 섬기다
- [ ] sociable [sóuʃəbl] ⑲ 사교적인
- [ ] spade [speid] ⑲ 삽
- [ ] stare [stɛər] ⑧ 빤히 쳐다보다, 응시하다
- [ ] strength [streŋkθ] ⑲ 장점, 강점
- [ ] whereas [hwɛərǽz] ⑳ 반면
- [ ] wisdom [wízdəm] ⑲ 지혜
- [ ] worship [wə́:rʃip] ⑲ 예배
- [ ] wound [wu:nd] ⑲ 상처, 부상

Phrases

- [ ] as though 마치 …인 것처럼
- [ ] by oneself 혼자
- [ ] care for …를 돌보다
- [ ] come across 우연히 마주치다[발견하다]
- [ ] figure out …을 알아내다, …을 이해하다
- [ ] hang out with …와 많은 시간을 보내다
- [ ] live by (신조 · 원칙)에 따라 살다
- [ ] make fun of …를 놀리다
- [ ] make one's way to …로 나아가다
- [ ] take ... into account …을 고려하다

1 다음 영어는 우리말로, 우리말은 영어로 쓰시오.

(1) merit _____   (5) 변장하다 _____

(2) demonstration _____   (6) 결국, 마침내 _____

(3) decline _____   (7) 전체의, 전부의 _____

(4) precise _____   (8) 상처, 부상 _____

2 다음 빈칸에 들어갈 알맞은 단어를 보기 에서 골라 쓰시오.

보기	recognize	ensure	fulfill	exhausted

(1) At the end of the long interview I felt _____.

(2) He worked really hard to _____ his dream.

(3) How could you _____ her as soon as she came in?

(4) Please _____ that all lights are turned off.

3 주어진 우리말과 같은 뜻이 되도록 빈칸에 알맞은 말을 쓰시오.

(1) She behaved _____ _____ nothing had happened.
(그녀는 마치 아무 일도 일어나지 않은 것처럼 행동했다.)

(2) I _____ _____ some old books in a box.
(나는 상자에서 오래된 책들을 우연히 발견했다.)

(3) He lost all his _____ when his business failed.
(그는 사업의 실패로 자신의 모든 재산을 잃었다.)

(4) This is a simple but highly _____ treatment.
(이것은 간단하지만 매우 효과적인 치료이다.)

4 다음 영영풀이에 해당하는 단어를 보기 에서 골라 쓰시오.

보기	respond	formal	modify	sociable

(1) _____ : friendly and enjoying talking to other people

(2) _____ : to give a spoken or written answer

(3) _____ : very correct and serious rather than relaxed and friendly

(4) _____ : to change something slightly, usually in order to improve it

Communicative Functions

1 강조하기

> A: What can I do to do well on the midterm?
> (중간고사를 잘 보기 위해 무엇을 해야 할까?)
> B: Well, I think **it is important to** concentrate during class.
> (음, 내 생각에는 수업시간에 집중하는 것이 중요한 것 같아.)

• 어떤 것을 강하게 주장하거나 두드러지게 할 때, "It is important to ..."라는 표현을 사용할 수 있다. 이와 유사한 표현으로 "It is important that ...," "I want to stress ..." 등이 있다.

2 관심에 대해 묻기

> A: **What are you interested in?**
> (너는 어떤 것에 관심이 있니?)
> B: I'm interested in playing the guitar.
> (나는 기타를 치는 것에 관심이 있어.)

• 상대방이 어떤 것에 흥미를 느끼고 관심이 있는지를 물을 때, "What are you interested in?"이라는 표현을 사용할 수 있다. 이와 함께 쓸 수 있는 표현으로 "Are you interested in ... ?," "Do you find X interesting?" 등이 있다.

Check-up

1 주어진 우리말 뜻에 맞도록 빈칸에 알맞은 말을 쓰시오.

(1) ＿＿＿＿ ＿＿＿＿ ＿＿＿＿ ＿＿＿＿ have an open mind.
(열린 마음을 갖는 것이 중요하다.)

(2) What ＿＿＿＿ ＿＿＿＿ ＿＿＿＿ ＿＿＿＿ these days?
(요즘 너는 무엇에 관심이 있니?)

2 다음 대화가 자연스럽게 이어지도록 순서대로 배열하시오.

> (A) Then, why don't you join our musical club?
> (B) I don't know what club to join.
> (C) I'm interested in singing and dancing.
> (D) Hmm... What are you interested in?

＿＿＿＿ → ＿＿＿＿ → ＿＿＿＿ → ＿＿＿＿

Discovering Grammar

Point 1 분사구문

> ▌ **Textbook** **Reaching** the hermit's hut, the king found the old man digging in his garden.
> (은자의 오두막에 도착했을 때, 왕은 그 노인이 정원에서 땅을 파고 있는 것을 발견했다.)
>
> ✚ **Plus** **Driving** his car, he usually listens to the radio.
> (운전할 때, 그는 보통 라디오를 듣는다.)
> **(Being) Left** alone, the little girl began to cry.
> (홀로 남겨지자, 그 어린 소녀는 울기 시작했다.)

• 분사구문은 부사절에서 접속사와 (주절과 동일한) 주어를 생략한 형태이다. 시간, 이유, 조건, 양보, 동시동작, 연속동작 등 부사절에 있던 접속사의 의미를 담고 있으며, 주절에 대해 부가적인 정보를 제공해 준다. 부사절의 동사가 수동태로 쓰인 경우 분사구문에서는 「Being+과거분사」의 형태로 바뀌는데, 이때 Being은 생략될 수 있다.

Point 2 가정법 과거완료

> ▌ **Textbook** If you **hadn't helped** me, you **would've left**, and that man **would've attacked** you.
> (당신이 나를 돕지 않았다면, 당신은 떠났을 것이고, 그 남자가 당신을 공격했을 겁니다.)
>
> ✚ **Plus** If I **had known** the truth, I **would have called** you right away.
> (내가 진실을 알았더라면, 너에게 바로 전화했을 것이다.)

• 「If+주어+had+p.p., 주어+조동사의 과거형+have+p.p.」의 형태로, '만약 …했더라면, ~했을 텐데'라는 의미이다. 이미 벌어진 과거의 사실과 다른 가정이나 상상을 할 때 사용한다.

Check-up

1 다음 괄호 안에서 어법상 올바른 것을 고르시오.

(1) If I (have been / had been) wiser, I would have accepted the offer.
(2) If he had had more time, he could (do / have done) better.
(3) (Walked / Walking) along the street, he saw a restaurant.

2 다음 문장을 밑줄 친 부분에 유의하여 우리말로 해석하시오.

(1) <u>Listening to the radio</u>, he cooked his dinner.
(2) <u>Being caught in the rain</u>, I got a cold.

1 밑줄 친 부분을 분사구문으로 바꿔 쓰시오.

(1) When he entered the room, he threw his hat on the bed.

→ _____

(2) Because she was wounded badly, she couldn't move at all.

→ _____

(3) When he tries to comfort himself, he sings his favorite songs.

→ _____

(4) Because he had a lot of work to do, he couldn't go to the party.

→ _____

2 다음 문장의 괄호 안에서 알맞은 것을 고르시오.

(1) Grandma was watching TV, (drunk / drinking) coffee.

(2) (Written / Writing) in easy words, this book is useful for beginners.

(3) (Finished / Finishing) all my homework, I went out for a walk.

(4) (Taking / Being taken) for granted, his advice was not accepted.

3 밑줄 친 부분을 어법에 맞게 고쳐 쓰시오.

(1) I could not find the way if the child had not helped me.

(2) If she didn't join the team, we could not have completed the mission.

(3) What could I have done if I knew the facts?

4 다음 문장을 가정법 과거완료 구문을 이용하여 바꿔 쓰시오.

(1) As she wasn't there with you, she wasn't very happy.

→ _____

(2) As he didn't score a goal, he didn't feel better.

→ _____

(3) As I didn't notice the mistake, I didn't correct it.

→ _____

[1~2] 다음 글을 읽고, 물음에 답하시오.

> The hermit lived in a forest and met only ordinary folk, so the king disguised himself as a simple peasant. He ordered his bodyguards to stay behind while he went on alone to seek out the hermit.

> (A) The king worked for a long time, while the hermit watched him silently. Eventually, as the sun was setting, the king stopped and said, "I came to you for answers to my questions. If you can give me none, please let me know so that I can return home."

> (B) Reaching the hermit's hut, the king found the old man digging in his garden. The hermit greeted the king and continued digging. The king said, "I have come here to ask you three questions. How can I learn the right time to do everything? Whom do I most need to pay attention to? Finally, what is the most important thing to do?"

> (C) The hermit listened carefully but declined to respond. "You must be tired," the king said. "Let me help you with that." The hermit thanked him, handing the king his spade.

1 주어진 글 다음에 이어질 글의 순서로 가장 적절한 것은?

① (A) − (B) − (C)   ② (B) − (A) − (C)   ③ (B) − (C) − (A)
④ (C) − (A) − (B)   ⑤ (C) − (B) − (A)

2 윗글의 내용과 일치하지 <u>않는</u> 것은?

① 왕은 은자를 만나기 위해 평범한 농부로 변장했다.
② 왕은 그의 경호원들에게 뒤에 남아있으라고 명령했다.
③ 왕이 일하는 동안 은자는 조용히 왕을 바라보았다.
④ 왕이 은자를 만났을 때, 은자는 땅을 파고 있었다.
⑤ 왕의 질문에 은자는 바로 답변을 해주었다.

[3~4] 다음 글을 읽고, 물음에 답하시오.

> "Someone is running toward us," the hermit said. "Let's see who it is."
> The king turned and saw a man running out of the woods. When the man reached the king, (A)he fell down. The king could see blood flowing from a large wound in his stomach. The king washed and bandaged the wound, and then (B)he and the hermit carried the man into the hut. The man closed his eyes and fell asleep. _____ he was completely exhausted, the king also lay down and slept.

3 주관식 밑줄 친 (A), (B)가 가리키는 대상을 윗글에서 찾아 쓰시오.

(A) _____ (B) _____

4 윗글의 빈칸에 들어갈 말로 가장 적절한 것은?

① While   ② Until   ③ Although
④ Because   ⑤ Before

[5~6] 다음 글을 읽고, 물음에 답하시오.

> When he awoke in the morning, the man was staring at him.
> "Forgive me," the man begged.
> "I don't know you, and I have no reason to forgive you," the king replied.
> "You might not know me, but I know you," the man answered. "During the last war, you killed my brother and took my property. When I knew that you had gone to see the hermit, (A)I decided to kill you on your way back. However, I came across your bodyguards, who recognized me and wounded me. Although I escaped, I would have died if you hadn't saved my life. Now, my sons and I will serve you forever."
> Pleased to have made friends with his enemy so easily, the king forgave the man and promised to restore his property.

5 윗글에 나타난 왕의 심경 변화로 가장 적절한 것은?

① angry → regretful   ② confused → happy
③ relieved → scared   ④ surprised → disappointed
⑤ thankful → depressed

6 서술형 남자가 (A)와 같이 결심한 이유를 찾아 우리말로 쓰시오.

1 빈칸에 들어갈 말로 적절한 것을 보기 에서 찾아 순서대로 쓰시오.

> M: I am very happy to speak with psychologist Dr. Julie Brown. _____
>
> _____
>
> W: It's all about the importance of loving yourself.
>
> M: _____
>
> W: Well, it can help you build your self-esteem. Furthermore, it can help you learn to love others.
>
> M: I see. _____
>
> W: One effective method is to accept that you can't be perfect and focus on what you're good at.

보기
ⓐ Why is loving yourself so important?
ⓑ Please tell us about your most recent book.
ⓒ So what are some ways you can learn to love yourself?

[2~3] 다음 대화를 읽고, 물음에 답하시오.

> G: I need some help figuring out the best career for me.
> B: What are you interested in?
> G: Actually, I don't really know. I just hang out with my friends, and that's all.
> B: That's okay. If you don't know what you like to do, then you should try doing different things.
> G: Hmm... like what?
> B: How about volunteering or doing a job experience program? Sometimes when you try something new, you can find out what fits you and what doesn't.

2 남자의 조언의 내용으로 가장 적절한 것은?

① 일찍부터 자신의 진로계획을 세워라.
② 자원봉사를 통해 이웃을 도와야 한다.
③ 처음에 흥미가 없더라도 끈기 있게 임해라.
④ 한 가지 일을 끝까지 마쳐야 한다.
⑤ 관심사를 찾기 위해 다양한 경험을 쌓아라.

3 남자의 마지막 말에 대한 여자의 응답으로 가장 적절한 것은?

① Sure, I'll help you with that.
② Oh, good idea! I'll give it a try.
③ How about trying something new?
④ I have an appointment with my friends.
⑤ When was the last time you volunteered?

4 글의 흐름으로 보아, 주어진 문장이 들어가기에 가장 적절한 곳은?

> Despite his great creativity, though, he was not taken seriously for most of his career.

> Remarkably, the great artist Henri Rousseau did not start painting until he was in his early forties. (①) In addition, he never received any formal artistic instruction. (②) He studied art by himself by going to the Louvre Museum and looking at the artworks of his favorite artists. (③) He loved painting and enjoyed the entire process itself. (④) His works were even criticized for looking childish by critics but he continued to paint as he wanted. (⑤) Finally, he was recognized as a genius by a younger generation of artists, including Pablo Picasso.

5 밑줄 친 부분의 뜻풀이로 적절하지 <u>않은</u> 것은?

① It is <u>generous</u> of you to forgive her.
(관대한)

② She would someday <u>care for</u> sick people.
(조심하다)

③ Sometimes my friends <u>make fun of</u> my accent. (⋯를 놀리다)

④ I couldn't <u>figure out</u> how to open the lock. (⋯을 알아내다)

⑤ We're making every effort to <u>ensure</u> perfect quality. (확실하게 하다)

6 다음 중 단어의 영영 뜻풀이가 적절하지 <u>않은</u> 것은?

① greet: to say hello to people

② announce: to tell people about something publicly

③ stare: to look at someone or something for a long time

④ restore: to eagerly ask someone to do something

⑤ attack: to try to hurt people using physical violence

7 주관식 다음 빈칸에 들어갈 알맞은 말을 쓰시오.

> Walking in the forest, I _____ _____ a deer!
> (숲 속을 걷다가, 나는 우연히 사슴을 마주쳤다!)

8 다음 중 어법상 <u>틀린</u> 문장은?

① Watching TV, he fell asleep.

② I was sitting on the sofa, reading a book.

③ Opening the window, he felt refreshed.

④ Feeling exhausted, she decided not to go out.

⑤ Raising in the countryside, he didn't know how to take the subway.

9 주관식 주어진 문장을 다음과 같이 바꿔 쓸 때, 빈칸에 알맞은 말을 쓰시오.

Because he didn't listen to me, he lost a lot of money.

→ If he had _____, he _____ a lot of money.

[10~11] 다음 글을 읽고, 물음에 답하시오.

> The hermit listened carefully but declined to respond. "You must be tired," the king said. "Let me help you with that." The hermit thanked him, handing the king his spade.
> The king worked for a long time, while the hermit watched him silently. Eventually, as the sun was setting, the king stopped and said, "I came to you for answers to my questions. If you can give me <u>none</u>, please let me know so that I can return home."

10 밑줄 친 **none**이 의미하는 것으로 가장 적절한 것은?

① no questions ② no answers

③ no spade ④ no time

⑤ no work

11 윗글의 마지막에 나타난 왕의 심경으로 가장 적절한 것은?

① shocked ② thankful

③ relieved ④ disappointed

⑤ apologetic

[12~13] 다음 글을 읽고, 물음에 답하시오.

> The hermit lived in a forest and met only ordinary folk, so the king _____ _____. He ordered his bodyguards to stay behind while he went on alone to seek out the hermit.
> Reaching the hermit's hut, the king found the old man digging in his garden. The hermit greeted the king and continued digging.

12 윗글의 빈칸에 들어갈 말로 가장 적절한 것은?

① dressed himself to be very polite
② brought much money to please him
③ disguised himself as a simple peasant
④ wrote down his questions on the paper
⑤ went there with gifts for ordinary people

13 주관식 윗글의 밑줄 친 **Reaching the hermit's hut**과 같은 의미가 되도록 빈칸에 한 단어를 쓰시오.

→ _____ he reached the hermit's hut

[14~15] 다음 글을 읽고, 물음에 답하시오.

> "During the last war, you killed my brother and took my (A) property / priority . When I knew that you had gone to see the hermit, I decided to kill you on your way back. However, I came across your bodyguards, who (B) organized / recognized me and wounded me. Although I escaped, 당신이 제 목숨을 구해주지 않았다면, 저는 죽었을 것입니다. Now, my sons and I will serve you forever."
> (C) Embarrassed / Pleased to have made friends with his enemy so easily, the king forgave the man and promised to restore his property.

14 (A), (B), (C)의 각 네모 안에서 문맥에 맞는 낱말로 가장 적절한 것은?

	(A)	(B)	(C)
①	property	··· organized	··· Embarrassed
②	priority	··· organized	··· Pleased
③	property	··· recognized	··· Pleased
④	property	··· recognized	··· Embarrassed
⑤	priority	··· organized	··· Embarrassed

15 주관식 윗글의 밑줄 친 우리말과 같은 뜻이 되도록 다음 괄호 안의 단어를 알맞게 배열하시오.

(would / my life / you / have / saved / I / if / hadn't / died)

[16~17] 다음 글을 읽고, 물음에 답하시오.

> "For the last time, I beg you to answer my questions," the king said.
> "They've already ① been answered," said the hermit.
> "What do you mean?" the king asked.
> "If you ② hadn't helped me, you would've left, and that man would've attacked you. Therefore, the most important time was when you were digging. I was the most important person, and ③ helping me was the most important thing. Later, the most important time was when you cared for the man. If you hadn't helped him, he would've died, so he was the most important person, and helping him was the most important

thing. Remember, there is only one time ④that is important: now! The person that you are with is the most important person, and ⑤do that person good is the most important thing."

16 밑줄 친 ①~⑤ 중, 어법상 **틀린** 것은?

17 [서술형] 왕의 세 가지 질문에 대한 답을 윗글에서 찾아 우리말로 간략히 쓰시오.

　(1) 가장 중요한 때: _____

　(2) 가장 중요한 사람: _____

　(3) 가장 중요한 일: _____

[18~20] 다음 글을 읽고, 물음에 답하시오.

There was once a king who wanted to know three things: the right time to do everything, the most necessary people to pay attention to, and the most important thing to do. He thought that knowing these things would ensure his success.

He announced that he would reward anyone who could teach him these things. Many people traveled to his palace, but they all provided different answers to his questions.

Regarding the first question, some said that the king should make a detailed schedule 그가 항상 최적의 때를 알 수 있도록 to do everything. Others claimed that he should take every situation _____(A)_____ account and wait for the precise moment to act. Still others suggested that he should consult wise men.

Equally various were the answers to the second question. Some said that the members of the king's council were the most important people, while others mentioned priests, doctors, or warriors.

In response _____(B)_____ the third question, some replied that science was the most important thing, whereas others insisted that it was war or religious worship.

The king was not pleased with any of the answers. Still wishing to find the best answers to his questions, the king decided to visit an old hermit who was famous _____(C)_____ his wisdom.

18 윗글의 밑줄 친 우리말과 같은 뜻이 되도록 다음 괄호 안의 단어를 바르게 배열하시오.

(that / he / the perfect time / know / always / could / so)

19 윗글의 빈칸 (A), (B), (C)에 들어갈 말로 가장 적절한 것은?

	(A)	(B)	(C)
①	into	at	by
②	into	to	for
③	into	in	at
④	for	to	by
⑤	for	in	for

20 윗글의 내용과 일치하지 **않는** 것은?

① 왕은 성공하기 위하여 세 가지 질문에 대한 답을 알고자 했다.

② 왕은 질문에 대한 답을 가르쳐주는 이에게 보상을 약속했다.

③ 많은 사람들이 왕을 찾아왔으나 모두 비슷한 답을 내놓았다.

④ 왕은 지원자의 대답 중 마음에 드는 것을 찾지 못했다.

⑤ 왕은 질문에 대한 답을 찾고자 현자를 찾아가기로 결심했다.

Beyond the Limits

Functions

- 알고 있는지 묻기
Have you heard about the big competition that's coming up?

- 놀람 표현하기
I'm surprised that he is able to memorize so many lines then.

Structures

- With his assistance, she also studied higher mathematics and engineering **so** hard **that** she became an expert in them without ever going to college!

- **Not only did they prove** their doubters wrong, but they also achieved an accomplishment that inspired us to do the impossible.

Vocabulary

Words

- ☐ accomplishment [əkámpliʃmənt] 몡 업적, 공적
- ☐ amazement [əméizmənt] 몡 놀라움
- ☐ ambition [æmbíʃən] 몡 야망, 포부
- ☐ approximately [əpráksəmətli] 뷔 대략
- ☐ assistant [əsístənt] 톙 보조의, 보좌의
- ☐ burden [bə́rdn] 몡 (의무, 책임의) 짐, 부담
- ☐ carve [kɑːrv] 동 조각하다, 깎아서 만들다
- ☐ commuter [kəmjúːtər] 몡 통근자
- ☐ competition [kàmpətíʃən] 몡 대회, 시합
- ☐ constantly [kánstəntli] 뷔 끊임없이
- ☐ contribution [kàntrəbjúːʃən] 몡 공헌, 기여
- ☐ despite [dispáit] 전 …에도 불구하고
- ☐ destined [déstind] 톙 (to) (…할) 운명인
- ☐ disaster [dizǽstər] 몡 재난, 재해
- ☐ drain [drein] 동 물을 빼내다, 배수하다
- ☐ evidence [évidəns] 몡 증거; 흔적
- ☐ excess [éksəs] 톙 초과한, 제한 외의
- ☐ expert [ékspəːrt] 몡 전문가
- ☐ fascinated [fǽsənèitid] 톙 매혹[매료]된
- ☐ foundation [faundéiʃən] 몡 기반
- ☐ frequently [fríːkwəntli] 뷔 자주, 흔히
- ☐ including [inklúːdiŋ] 전 …을 포함하여
- ☐ infection [infékʃən] 몡 감염
- ☐ injure [índʒər] 동 부상을 입히다, 해치다
- ☐ instruction [instrʌ́kʃən] 몡 지시
- ☐ involved [inválvd] 톙 관련[연루]된, 휘말린
- ☐ landmark [lǽndmàːrk] 몡 주요 지형지물, 명소
- ☐ launch [lɔːntʃ] 동 시작[착수]하다
- ☐ obstacle [ábstəkl] 몡 장애(물)
- ☐ outstanding [àutstǽndiŋ] 톙 뛰어난
- ☐ permanently [pə́ːrmənəntli] 뷔 영구적으로
- ☐ persistence [pərsístəns] 몡 끈기, 인내심
- ☐ portable [pɔ́ːrtəbl] 톙 휴대[이동]가 쉬운
- ☐ precisely [prisáisli] 뷔 정확히
- ☐ process [práses] 몡 과정
- ☐ propose [prəpóuz] 동 제안하다
- ☐ quit [kwit] 동 그만두다, 포기하다
- ☐ rescue [réskju:] 몡 구조, 구출
- ☐ sacrifice [sǽkrəfàis] 몡 희생
- ☐ shortly [ʃɔ́ːrtli] 뷔 곧, 금방
- ☐ site [sait] 몡 현장
- ☐ succeed [səksíːd] 동 뒤를 잇다
- ☐ supervise [sjúːpərvàiz] 동 감독[관리]하다
- ☐ suspension bridge 몡 현수교
- ☐ telescope [téləskòup] 몡 망원경
- ☐ tide [taid] 몡 조수, 조류
- ☐ transport [trǽnspɔ̀ːrt] 몡 수송[운송] 수단
- ☐ unprecedented [ʌnprésidèntid] 톙 전례[유례] 없는
- ☐ unstable [ʌnstéibl] 톙 불안정한
- ☐ waterproof [wɔ́ːtərprùːf] 톙 방수가 되는

Phrases

- ☐ carry out 수행하다
- ☐ come up (행사가) 다가오다
- ☐ end up v-ing …하는 것으로 끝나다
- ☐ hold ... back …을 방해[저해]하다
- ☐ hold up 지탱하다
- ☐ in charge of 책임이 있는
- ☐ in particular 특히
- ☐ make up one's mind 결심하다
- ☐ on account of … 때문에, …으로
- ☐ see ... through …을 끝까지 해내다
- ☐ step in 돕고 나서다
- ☐ take over …을 넘겨[인계]받다

1 다음 영어는 우리말로, 우리말은 영어로 쓰시오.

(1) fascinated _____   (5) 희생 _____

(2) launch _____   (6) 장애(물) _____

(3) transport _____   (7) 끈기, 인내심 _____

(4) process _____   (8) 뒤를 잇다 _____

2 다음 빈칸에 들어갈 알맞은 단어를 보기 에서 골라 쓰시오.

보기	infection	evidence	rescue	unstable

(1) The political situation in the country remained _____ after the war.

(2) The route of _____ for this disease is not yet known.

(3) The _____ team rushed to the scene of the accident.

(4) The police officer found an important piece of _____.

3 주어진 우리말과 같은 뜻이 되도록 빈칸에 알맞은 말을 쓰시오.

(1) The population is aging at an _____ rate.
(인구는 전례 없는 속도로 고령화되고 있다.)

(2) Once I _____ _____ _____ _____, no one can stop me.
(내가 일단 결심하면 어느 누구도 나를 말릴 수 없다.)

(3) He's going to be _____ _____ _____ advertising for a while.
(그가 당분간 광고를 담당할 예정이다.)

(4) The picnic was cancelled _____ _____ _____ bad weather.
(나쁜 날씨 때문에 소풍은 취소되었다.)

4 다음 영영풀이에 해당하는 단어를 보기 에서 골라 쓰시오.

보기	landmark	excess	disaster	injure

(1) _____ : more than is needed or allowed

(2) _____ : to damage some part of a person or an animal

(3) _____ : a sudden event such as a flood, storm, or accident which causes great damage or suffering

(4) _____ : a building or feature which is easily noticed and can be used to judge your position

Communicative Functions

1 알고 있는지 묻기

> A: **Have you heard about** the new English teacher?
> (너 새로운 영어 선생님에 대해 들었어?)
> B: Yes, we'll be in his conversation class once a week.
> (응. 우리는 일주일에 한 번 그의 회화 수업을 들을 거야.)

• 상대방이 무엇을 알고 있는지 물어볼 때 "Have you heard about ... ?"이라는 표현을 사용할 수 있다. 함께 쓸 수 있는 표현으로 "Do you know about ... ?," "You know ... (, don't you)?," "Are you aware of ... ?" 등이 있다.

2 놀람 표현하기

> A: **I'm surprised that** she got married.
> (그녀가 결혼했다니 정말 놀랐어.)
> B: Me too. She looks very young.
> (나도. 그녀는 정말 어려 보여.)

• 무언가에 대해 놀랐음을 표현할 때 "I'm surprised that ..."을 쓸 수 있다. 이와 유사한 표현으로 "What a surprise!," "That's surprising!," "I can't believe this." 등이 있다.

Check-up

1 주어진 우리말 뜻에 맞도록 빈칸에 알맞은 말을 쓰시오.

(1) _____ _____ _____ _____ the new exhibition?
(새로운 전시회에 대해 들어봤니?)

(2) _____ _____ _____ he lied to us.
(나는 그가 우리에게 거짓말을 했다는 것이 놀랍다.)

2 다음 대화가 자연스럽게 이어지도록 순서대로 배열하시오.

> (A) Have you ever heard about the AI Assistant?
> (B) I'm surprised, too. Life will be much more convenient thanks to it.
> (C) No, what's that?
> (D) Wow, I'm surprised that the technology has developed so rapidly.
> (E) It is a digital personality that uses AI to help with tasks like remembering appointments.

(A) → _____ → _____ → _____ → _____

Discovering Grammar

「so+형용사/부사+that+주어+동사」

■ **Textbook** With his assistance, she also studied higher mathematics and engineering **so** hard **that** she became an expert in them without ever going to college!
(그녀는 또한 그의 도움으로 고등 수학과 공학 기술을 매우 열심히 공부해서 대학에 가지 않고도 그 분야의 전문가가 되었다!)

＋**Plus** The questions were **so** difficult **that** I could only answer just a few of them.
(그 질문들은 너무 어려워서 나는 그 중 몇 개만을 답할 수 있었다.)

•「so+형용사/부사+that+주어+동사」는 주로 결과나 정도를 나타내며 '너무 …하여 ~하다' 또는 '…할 정도로 ~하다'로 해석한다.「so+that+주어+동사」는 '…가 ~하도록'이라는 의미로 목적을 나타낸다.

부정어로 인한 도치

■ **Textbook** **Not only did they prove** their doubters wrong, but they also achieved an accomplishment that inspired us to do the impossible.
(그들은 의심하던 사람들이 틀렸다는 것을 증명했을 뿐만 아니라, 또한 우리에게 불가능한 일을 하도록 고무하는 업적을 이뤘다.)

＋**Plus** **Not only was he** a writer, but he was also a singer.
(그는 작가였을 뿐 아니라 가수이기도 했다.)
Hardly could he sleep last night.
(그는 지난 밤 잠을 거의 잘 수 없었다.)

•not only, not until, no sooner, never, little, hardly, seldom 등의 부정어(구)가 문두에 위치하면 주어와 동사가 도치된다. 이때, 동사가 be동사나 조동사일 때는 그대로 도치되지만, 일반동사일 경우에는 조동사 do를 인칭과 시제에 맞게 바꾸어 주어 앞에 삽입해야 한다.

Check-up

1 다음 괄호 안에서 어법상 올바른 것을 고르시오.

(1) Dave is (so / such) friendly that everyone likes him.
(2) We got up so late (that / which) we missed the train.
(3) Seldom (do / am) I late for school.
(4) No sooner (had / did) they seen her, they ran toward her.

2 다음 괄호 안의 단어를 알맞은 순서로 배열하여 문장을 완성하시오.

(1) The gas was (everybody / poisonous / had to / so / that) go outside.
(2) Little (I / that / dream / did) I would win the race.

1   밑줄 친 부분에 유의하여 주어진 문장을 해석하시오.

(1) She was so shocked that she could hardly speak.

(2) It was so hot yesterday that I couldn't take a walk.

(3) This frying pan is coated so that food doesn't stick to it.

(4) He was wearing a baseball cap so that nobody could recognize him.

2   주어진 우리말과 같은 뜻이 되도록 괄호 안의 단어를 배열하여 문장을 완성하시오.

(1) 그녀는 너무 바빠 이메일을 확인할 수 없었다.

(so / check / couldn't / busy / she / that / her email)

→ She was _____ .

(2) 나는 그들이 쉽게 지나가도록 옆으로 이동했다.

(so / could / that / pass by easily / they)

→ I moved aside _____ .

(3) 그는 너무나 긴장하여 무엇을 해야할지 몰랐다.

(that / he / what / nervous / so / know / didn't / do / to)

→ He was _____ .

3   밑줄 친 부분을 어법에 맞게 고쳐 쓰시오.

(1) Scarcely they had sat down at the table, when the phone rang.

(2) Little knew I it was already too late.

(3) Not only does she is kind, but she is also very humorous.

(4) Not until the next day did he came back.

4   주어진 문장을 다음과 같이 바꿔 쓸 때 빈칸에 알맞은 말을 쓰시오.

(1) She can speak not only Chinese but also Spanish.

→ Not only _____ .

(2) I never expected to meet him again.

→ Never _____ .

(3) I had no sooner gone to bed than I fell asleep.

→ No sooner _____ .

[1~2] 다음 글을 읽고, 물음에 답하시오.

> In the 1860s, the populations of Manhattan and Brooklyn were rapidly increasing, and so was the number of the commuters between them. Thousands of people took boats and ferries across the East River every day, but these forms of transport were unstable and frequently stopped by bad weather. Many New Yorkers wanted to have a bridge directly connecting Manhattan and Brooklyn because ⓐ it would make their commute quicker and safer. Unfortunately, because of the East River's great width and rough tides, it would be difficult to build anything on ⓑ it.

1 윗글의 제목으로 가장 적절한 것은?

① Reasons for the Rapid Growth of New York City
② New Yorkers Are Upset by Unstable Bridges
③ New Bridge Offers New Yorkers Safer Commute
④ The East River Bridge: An Impossible Dream in the 1860s
⑤ Boats and Ferries: Commuters' Favorite Modes of Transport

2 [주관식] 밑줄 친 ⓐ, ⓑ가 각각 가리키는 바를 윗글에서 찾아 쓰시오.

3 글의 흐름으로 보아, 주어진 문장이 들어가기에 가장 적절한 곳은?

> Considering the limited technology in those days, building such a bridge seemed impossible.

> Any bridge over the river would need to be a very high suspension bridge. (①) That is, people thought it was impossible until John Roebling, an expert at building suspension bridges, accepted the challenge. (②)
> John proposed the use of steel cables—instead of iron ones—that would be six times stronger than needed to support the bridge. (③) In addition, he planned to build two large stone towers to hold up the bridge's road and allow people to walk across it. (④) If his ideas worked, the final result would be the longest, strongest suspension bridge ever built. (⑤) John's ambition inspired people, so construction began in 1869.

4 주어진 글 다음에 이어질 글의 순서로 가장 적절한 것은?

At that time, the foundations for the bridge's two towers were being built in the East River, which was extremely difficult and dangerous work.

(A) In 1872, he developed this disease and was unable to move easily or visit the construction sites throughout the rest of the project.

(B) Other people would have quit at that point, but not Washington. He continued to supervise the bridge building for years by watching it through a telescope from his bedroom.

(C) Workers had to stay at the bottom of the river in a waterproof box with little light and constant danger. Many died or were permanently injured by a serious disease called "the bends," including Washington Roebling.

① (A) − (C) − (B) ② (B) − (A) − (C)
③ (B) − (C) − (A) ④ (C) − (B) − (A)
⑤ (C) − (A) − (B)

5 Emily Warren Roebling에 관한 다음 글의 내용과 일치하는 것은?

This time, it was Washington's wife, Emily Warren Roebling. She believed in what her family had started, and she was determined to see it through. Before marriage, she knew almost nothing about engineering. As her husband's health failed, though, Emily began passing his instructions to the assistant engineers and bringing back their construction reports. In the process, she naturally picked up a lot of information about bridge building. With his assistance, she also studied higher mathematics and engineering so hard that she became an expert in them without ever going to college!

By the time the bridge was finished in 1883, Emily was carrying out many of the chief engineer's duties, which was unprecedented for a woman in those days. Many people praised her contributions to the project, and she became the first person to cross the bridge.

① 결혼 전에 공학에 대한 지식이 풍부했다.
② 남편의 건강이 악화되자 간호에만 전념했다.
③ 대학에 진학하여 수학과 공학을 공부했다.
④ 브루클린 다리 공사가 진행되던 중 업무 수행을 중단하였다.
⑤ 브루클린 다리를 건넌 최초의 사람이 되었다.

1 (A)~(D)를 배열하여 대화를 완성하고자 할 때 가장 적절한 것은?

> (A) It's for designing robots that can help in disasters.
> (B) No. What kind of competition is it?
> (C) Oh... Do you mean the ones that enter dangerous areas people can't easily reach?
> (D) Hey, Danny. Have you heard about the big competition that's coming up?

① (A) − (C) − (B) − (D)
② (B) − (C) − (D) − (A)
③ (C) − (A) − (B) − (D)
④ (D) − (B) − (A) − (C)
⑤ (D) − (C) − (B) − (A)

2 다음 대화의 빈칸에 들어갈 말로 적절한 것은?

> A: Have you heard about a 3D printer?
> B: No. What is it?
> A: It is a machine that creates solid objects from a digital file.
> B: Wow, awesome! _____
> A: For one thing, it will increase the speed of manufacturing an item; for another, it will reduce the cost of production.

① Have you ever used a 3D printer?
② Can you help me download this file?
③ What effects will it have on our lives?
④ What can we do to lower the cost?
⑤ How did you know about 3D printers?

3 다음 대화를 읽고, 여자의 마지막 말에 대한 남자의 응답으로 가장 적절한 것을 고르시오.

> G: Believe it or not, the actor has a learning disability that makes it difficult for him to read and write.
> B: Really? I'm surprised that he is able to memorize so many lines then.
> G: Well, I heard that someone else helps him by reading them aloud.

① Can you read this aloud for me?
② We should help a friend in need.
③ Still, it must not be easy for him.
④ I think he is not a very talented actor.
⑤ I can memorize things very easily.

4 다음 빈칸에 들어갈 말로 가장 적절한 것은?

> When astronauts at the International Space Station lost a tool, they had to wait several months until another ship brought a new one. Sending up new supplies like this doesn't just take time. It's extremely expensive too, costing approximately $10,000 for every pound that gets launched into space. With a 3D printer, _____, astronauts could create new tools whenever they needed them, saving both time and money.

① however   ② therefore
③ for instance   ④ consequently
⑤ nonetheless

5 주관식 다음 빈칸에 들어갈 알맞은 말을 쓰시오.

> He is strong enough to _____ the work _____ to the end.
> (그는 그 일을 끝까지 해낼만큼 강한 사람이다.)

6 밑줄 친 부분의 뜻풀이로 적절하지 <u>않은</u> 것은?

① No matter what others say, I will <u>carry out</u> the plan. (수행하다)

② I loved him <u>despite</u> all his faults. (…을 포함하여)

③ She likes sausage pizza <u>in particular</u>. (특히)

④ Seals are lying on the rocks at low <u>tide</u>. (조수, 조류)

⑤ This will <u>permanently</u> delete the file. (영구적으로)

7 밑줄 친 부분과 바꿔 쓸 수 있는 것은?

> We will be stopping in this town for <u>about</u> half an hour.

① similarly   ② ultimately

③ simultaneously   ④ appropriately

⑤ approximately

8 다음 밑줄 친 부분 중 어법상 틀린 것은?

① I was <u>so tired that</u> I cancelled the meeting.

② Never <u>did he expect</u> that he would get the job.

③ Hardly <u>could I see</u> anything in the fog.

④ Turn off the TV <u>so that I can</u> focus on reading.

⑤ Not only <u>the movie was exciting</u> but it was also very touching.

9 주관식 다음 괄호 안의 단어를 알맞은 순서로 배열하여 문장을 완성하시오.

> The movie (so /was / he / that / interesting) didn't know how late it was.

[10~11] 다음 글을 읽고, 물음에 답하시오.

> People thought it was impossible until John Roebling, an expert at building suspension bridges, accepted the challenge.
>
> John proposed the use of steel cables—instead of iron ones—that would be six times stronger than needed to support the bridge. In addition, he planned to build two large stone towers to hold up the bridge's road and allow people to walk across it. If <u>his ideas</u> worked, the final result would be the longest, strongest suspension bridge ever built. John's ambition inspired people, so construction began in 1869. _____, he was involved in a ferry accident later that year and died of an infection not long after.

10 서술형 윗글의 밑줄 친 **his ideas**의 내용을 우리말로 쓰시오.

11 윗글의 빈칸에 들어갈 말로 가장 적절한 것은?

① Moreover   ② Therefore

③ However   ④ For example

⑤ In contrast

[12~13] 다음 글을 읽고, 물음에 답하시오.

> In the 1860s, the populations of Manhattan and Brooklyn were rapidly increasing, and so (A) was / were the number of the commuters between them.

Thousands of people took boats and ferries across the East River every day, but these forms of transport were unstable and frequently stopped by bad weather. Many New Yorkers wanted to have a bridge directly (B) connected / connecting Manhattan and Brooklyn because it would make their commute quicker and safer. Unfortunately, because of the East River's great width and rough tides, it would be difficult to build anything on it. It was also a very busy river at that time, with hundreds of ships constantly (C) sail / sailing on it.

Any bridge over the river would need to be a very high suspension bridge. Considering the limited technology in those days, _____.

12 (A), (B), (C)의 각 네모 안에서 어법에 맞는 표현으로 가장 적절한 것은?

	(A)		(B)		(C)
①	was	⋯	connected	⋯	sail
②	were	⋯	connecting	⋯	sailing
③	were	⋯	connected	⋯	sail
④	was	⋯	connecting	⋯	sail
⑤	was	⋯	connecting	⋯	sailing

13 윗글의 빈칸에 들어갈 말로 가장 적절한 것은?

① they needed a better bridge
② a new bridge was not necessary
③ people were excited to have a bridge
④ building such a bridge seemed impossible
⑤ it wouldn't be a problem to build a bridge

[14~15] 다음 글을 읽고, 물음에 답하시오.

To everyone's amazement, yet another Roebling stepped in to save the bridge. (①) This time, it was Washington's wife, Emily Warren Roebling. (②) She believed in what her family had started, and she was determined to see it through. (③) Before marriage, she knew almost nothing about engineering. (④) As her husband's health failed, though, Emily began passing his instructions to the assistant engineers and bringing back their construction reports. (⑤) With his assistance, she also studied higher mathematics and engineering so hard that she became an expert in them without ever going to college!

14 글의 흐름으로 보아, 주어진 문장이 들어가기에 가장 적절한 곳은?

In the process, she naturally picked up a lot of information about bridge building.

15 주관식 다음 영영 뜻풀이에 해당하는 표현을 윗글에서 찾아 쓰시오.

to enter into a difficult situation in order to help find a solution

[16~17] 다음 글을 읽고, 물음에 답하시오.

By the time the bridge was finished in 1883, Emily was carrying out many of the chief engineer's duties, which was unprecedented for a woman in those days. Many people praised her ①contributions to the project, and 그녀는 그 다리를 건너는 첫 번째 사람이 되었다. It was the moment she, Washington, John, and everyone else who built the bridge had worked so hard for.

To this day, the Brooklyn Bridge stands as evidence of the Roebling family's ②persistence. These amazing people made incredible sacrifices and ③overcame all obstacles to complete a project that seemed impossible to others. Not only did they prove their doubters ④right, but they also achieved an accomplishment that inspired us to do the ⑤impossible.

16 밑줄 친 ①~⑤ 중, 문맥상 단어의 쓰임이 옳지 않은 것은?

17 주관식 윗글의 밑줄 친 우리말과 같은 뜻이 되도록 다음 괄호 안의 단어를 알맞게 배열하시오.

(she / cross / bridge / first / the / to / became / person / the)

[18~20] 다음 글을 읽고, 물음에 답하시오.

Luckily, John's role as chief engineer was succeeded by ①his son, Washington Roebling. Because he had built bridges with ②his father and studied bridge construction in Europe, ③he believed in

John's dream. At that time, the foundations for the bridge's two towers were being built in the East River, which was extremely difficult and dangerous work. Workers had to stay at the bottom of the river in a waterproof box with little light and constant danger. Many died or were permanently injured by a serious disease called "the bends," including Washington Roebling. In 1872, ④he developed this disease and was unable to move easily or visit the construction sites throughout the rest of the project.

다른 사람들이라면 그 시점에서 포기했겠지만, but not Washington. ⑤He continued to supervise the bridge building for years by watching it through a telescope from his bedroom.

18 밑줄 친 ①~⑤ 중에서 가리키는 대상이 나머지 넷과 다른 것은?

19 Washington Roebling에 대한 설명으로 윗글의 내용과 일치하지 않는 것은?

① John Roebling의 아들이다.
② 아버지와 다리를 건설한 적이 있었다.
③ 유럽에서 다리 건설을 공부했다.
④ 다리 건설 중 병을 얻었다.
⑤ 다리 건설이 끝날 때까지 현장을 방문했다.

20 주관식 윗글의 밑줄 친 우리말과 같은 뜻이 되도록 괄호 안의 단어를 알맞게 바꿔 빈칸을 채우시오.

Other people _____ at that point (quit)

1 다음 빈칸에 들어갈 말로 가장 적절한 것은?

> B: He's such an amazing actor.
> G: He sure is. And his performances are even more impressive when you consider the challenges he faces.
> B: What challenges does he face?
> G: Believe it or not, he has a learning disability that makes it difficult for him to read and write.
> B: Really? _____

① I especially liked the actor's performance.
② Do you mean he didn't want to be an actor?
③ It must be easy for him to memorize the lines.
④ Doing what you love is the most important thing.
⑤ I'm surprised that he is able to memorize so many lines then.

2 다음 대화가 자연스럽게 이어지도록 (A)~(D)를 순서대로 배열하시오.

> (A) I need some help figuring out the best career for myself.
> (B) Actually, I don't really know. I just hang out with my friends, and that's all.
> (C) That's okay. If you don't know what you like to do, then you should try doing different things.
> (D) What are you interested in?

_____ → _____ → _____ → _____

3 다음 대화를 읽고, 여자의 조언으로 가장 적절한 것을 고르시오.

> B: I want to be as popular as she is, but I'm too quiet. I think I should be more like her.
> G: Well, you have your own merits. You always listen carefully to others when they are talking.
> B: Really? But I don't think that's such a great quality.
> G: Sure it is. Everyone needs a friend who is a good listener.
> B: Thank you for saying that.
> G: Try to always remember that it is important to be happy with who you are.

① 친구들을 많이 사귀는 것이 좋다.
② 타인의 말을 끝까지 경청해야 한다.
③ 자신의 모습에 만족할 수 있어야 한다.
④ 작은 일에 행복을 느낄 수 있어야 한다.
⑤ 사교적이고 외향적인 성격을 가져야 한다.

4 대화의 흐름으로 보아, 주어진 문장이 들어가기에 가장 적절한 곳을 고르시오.

> Furthermore, it can help you learn to love others.

> M: Today, I am very happy to speak with psychologist Dr. Julie Brown. Dr. Brown, please tell us about your most recent book.
> W: It's all about the importance of loving yourself. (①)

M: Why is loving yourself so important? (②)

W: Well, it can help you build your self-esteem. (③)

M: I see. So what are some ways you can learn to love yourself? (④)

W: One effective method is to accept that you can't be perfect and focus on what you're good at. (⑤)

5 다음을 읽고, Aimee Mullins를 설명하는 말로 가장 적절한 것을 고르시오.

Aimee Mullins is no stranger to challenges. She was born in 1976 with a condition that required the removal of the lower half of her legs. But Aimee hasn't let this hold her back. During high school, she found her passion in track and field. She broke many national and world records, and even competed in the 1996 Paralympic Games in Atlanta.

① generous and kind
② passionate and strong-willed
③ creative and intelligent
④ considerate and warm-hearted
⑤ diligent and honest

6 다음 빈칸에 공통으로 들어갈 말로 알맞은 것은?

• You should not _____ fun of your friend's weakness.
• I will _____ my way to the restaurant immediately after work.

① go   ② be
③ make   ④ take
⑤ hang

7 다음 문장의 밑줄 친 단어와 바꿔 쓸 수 있는 것은?

Sometimes you need help from other people to achieve your goals.

① modify   ② involve
③ propose   ④ consult
⑤ fulfill

[8~9] 주관식 다음 문장에서 밑줄 친 부분을 어법에 맞게 고치시오.

8 If she had more money, she would have booked the concert ticket.

9 Writing in a hurry, this article has a lot of mistakes.

[10~12] 다음 글을 읽고, 물음에 답하시오.

When he awoke in the morning, the man was staring at him.

"Forgive me," the man begged.

"I don't know you, and I have no reason ① to forgive you," the king replied.

"You might not know me, but I know you," the man answered. "During the last war, you killed my brother and took my property. When I knew that you ② had gone to see the hermit, I decided to kill you on your way back. _____, I came across your bodyguards, ③ who recognized me and wounded me. Although I escaped, I would have died if you ④ didn't saved my life. Now, my sons and I will serve you forever."

⑤Pleased to have made friends with his enemy so easily, the king forgave the man and promised to restore his property.

10 윗글의 빈칸에 들어갈 말로 가장 적절한 것은?

① Luckily   ② Finally
③ However   ④ In addition
⑤ Therefore

11 밑줄 친 ①~⑤ 중, 어법상 틀린 것은?

12 서술형 글의 내용과 일치하도록 주어진 문장의 빈칸을 채우시오.

According to the story, the man tried to kill the king because ＿＿＿＿＿＿＿
＿＿＿＿＿＿＿＿＿＿＿＿＿＿.

[13~14] 다음 글을 읽고, 물음에 답하시오.

The king decided to visit an old hermit who was famous for his wisdom.

The hermit lived in a forest and met only ordinary folk, so the king ＿＿(A)＿＿ himself as a simple peasant. ①He ordered his bodyguards to stay behind while ②he went on alone to seek out the hermit.

Reaching the hermit's hut, the king found the old man digging in ③his garden. The hermit greeted the king and continued digging. The king said, "I have come here to ask you three questions."

The hermit listened carefully but declined to ＿＿(B)＿＿. "You must be tired," the king said. "Let me help you with that." The hermit thanked ④him, handing the king his spade.

The king worked for a long time, while the hermit watched ⑤him silently.

13 밑줄 친 ①~⑤ 중에서 가리키는 대상이 나머지 넷과 다른 것은?

14 윗글의 빈칸 (A), (B)에 들어갈 말로 가장 적절한 것은?

	(A)		(B)
①	regarded	…	comment
②	regarded	…	respond
③	disguised	…	respond
④	disguised	…	submit
⑤	described	…	submit

[15~16] 다음 글을 읽고, 물음에 답하시오.

There was once a king who wanted to know three things: the right time to do everything, the most necessary people to pay attention to, and the most important thing to do. He thought that (A) know / knowing these things would ensure his success.

He announced that he would reward anyone (B) who / whom could teach him these things. Many people traveled to his palace, but they all provided different answers to his questions.

Regarding the first question, some said that the king should make a detailed schedule so (C) as / that he could always know the perfect time to do everything. Others claimed that 그는 모든 상황을 고려해야 한다 and wait for the precise moment to act. Still others suggested that he should consult wise men.

15 (A), (B), (C)의 각 네모 안에서 어법에 맞는 표현으로 가장 적절한 것은?

	(A)		(B)		(C)
①	know	…	who	…	as
②	know	…	whom	…	as
③	knowing	…	whom	…	that
④	knowing	…	who	…	that
⑤	knowing	…	who	…	as

16 [주관식] 윗글의 밑줄 친 우리말과 같은 뜻이 되도록 다음 괄호 안의 단어를 바르게 배열하시오.

(he / every / account / should / into / take / situation)

17 다음 글의 빈칸 (A), (B)에 들어갈 말로 가장 적절한 것은?

"If you hadn't helped me, you would've left, and that man would've attacked you. ____(A)____ , the most important time was when you were digging. I was the most important person, and helping me was the most important thing. ____(B)____ , the most important time was when you cared for the man. If you hadn't helped him, he would've died, so he was the most important person, and helping him was the most important thing."

	(A)		(B)
①	Besides	…	Earlier
②	Therefore	…	Later
③	Besides	…	Similarly
④	However	…	Later
⑤	Therefore	…	Earlier

[18~19] 다음 글을 읽고, 물음에 답하시오.

Many people praised her ①contributions to the project, and she became the first person to cross the bridge. It was the moment she, Washington, John, and everyone else who built the bridge had worked so ②hard for.

To this day, the Brooklyn Bridge stands as evidence of the Roebling family's ③impatience. These amazing people made incredible ④sacrifices and overcame all obstacles to complete a project that seemed impossible to others. They not only proved their doubters wrong, but they also achieved an ⑤accomplishment that inspired us to do the impossible.

18 밑줄 친 ①~⑤ 중, 문맥상 단어의 쓰임이 옳지 않은 것은?

19 [주관식] 윗글의 밑줄 친 문장을 다음과 같이 바꿔 쓸 때 빈칸에 알맞은 말을 쓰시오.

Not only _____
_____

[20~21] 다음 글을 읽고, 물음에 답하시오.

In the 1860s, the populations of Manhattan and Brooklyn were rapidly increasing, and so was the number of the commuters between them. Thousands of people took boats and ferries across the East River every day, but these forms of transport were unstable and frequently stopped by bad weather. Many New Yorkers wanted to have a bridge directly connecting Manhattan and Brooklyn because _____ .

Unfortunately, because of the East River's great width and rough tides, it would be difficult to build anything on it. It was also a very busy river at that time, with hundreds of ships constantly sailing on it.

20 윗글의 빈칸에 들어갈 말로 가장 적절한 것은?

① they didn't want to commute to Manhattan

② it would make their commute quicker and safer

③ at that time their building technology was the world's best

④ they wanted Manhattan to be the biggest city in the world

⑤ the bridge would make the two cities popular tourist attractions

21 다음 중 윗글의 밑줄 친 it과 쓰임이 다른 것은?

① It was an honor to talk to you.

② It is easy for him to speak in English.

③ It was the first time for her to go abroad.

④ It would be a great chance to make new friends.

⑤ It will cost a lot of money to get a new printer.

(A) By the time the bridge was finished in 1883, Emily was carrying out many of the chief engineer's duties, which was unprecedented for a woman in those days.

(B) Before marriage, she knew almost nothing about engineering. As her husband's health failed, though, Emily began passing his instructions to the assistant engineers and bringing back their construction reports.

(C) In the process, she naturally picked up a lot of information about bridge building. With his assistance, she also studied higher mathematics and engineering so hard that she became an expert in them without ever going to college!

22 주어진 글 다음에 이어질 글의 순서로 가장 적절한 것은?

① (A) - (C) - (B)   ② (B) - (A) - (C)

③ (C) - (A) - (B)   ④ (B) - (C) - (A)

⑤ (C) - (B) - (A)

[22~23] 다음 글을 읽고, 물음에 답하시오.

To everyone's amazement, yet another Roebling stepped in to save the bridge. This time, it was Washington's wife, Emily Warren Roebling. She believed in what her family had started, and she was determined to see it through.

23 [주관식] 다음 영영 뜻풀이에 해당하는 단어를 윗글에서 찾아 쓰시오.

never having happened before, or never having happened so much

[24~25] 다음 글을 읽고, 물음에 답하시오.

Considering the limited technology in those days, building such a bride seemed impossible. That is, people thought it was impossible until John Roebling, an expert at building suspension bridges, accepted the challenge.

John proposed the use of steel cables—instead of iron ones—that would be six times stronger than needed to support the bridge. (①) In addition, he planned to build two large stone towers to hold up the bridge's road and allow people to walk across it. (②) If his ideas worked, the final result would be the longest, strongest suspension bridge ever built. (③) John's ambition inspired people, so construction began in 1869. (④) It looked like his ambitious plan was destined to fail shortly after it had been launched. (⑤)

Luckily, John's role as chief engineer was succeeded by his son, Washington Roebling. Because he had built bridges with his father and studied bridge construction in Europe, he believed in John's dream.

24 글의 흐름으로 보아, 주어진 문장이 들어가기에 가장 적절한 곳은?

However, he was involved in a ferry accident later that year and died of an infection not long after.

25 윗글의 제목으로 가장 적절한 것은?

① A Tragic Accident Killed the Roeblings
② The Roeblings' Bridge Is Finally Completed
③ Father and Son Challenge the Impossible
④ How Much Money It costs to Build a Bridge
⑤ Amateur Engineers Take on Bridge Building Challenge

Finding Out the Wonders

Functions

- 설명 요청하기
  What do you mean by that?
- 의견 묻기
  What do you think of it?

Structures

- **One of *hanji*'s newest uses** is a treat for the ears.
- In addition, **the fact that** the sound will not change over time because of the strength of *hanji* makes these speakers a great purchase.

Vocabulary

Words

☐ absorb [æbzɔ́:rb] ⑧ 흡수하다

☐ adapt [ədǽpt] ⑧ 적응하다

☐ advanced [ædvǽnst] ⑱ 진보한, 앞선

☐ appreciate [əprí:ʃièit] ⑧ 진가를 알아보다[인정하다]

☐ armor [ɑ́:rmər] ⑲ 갑옷

☐ bark [bɑːrk] ⑲ 나무껍질

☐ beneficial [bènəfíʃəl] ⑱ 유익한, 이로운

☐ bleed [bli:d] ⑧ 번지다

☐ characteristic [kæriktərístik] ⑲ 특징

☐ complex [kəmpléks] ⑱ 복잡한

☐ container [kəntéinər] ⑲ 용기, 함

☐ currently [kə́:rəntli] ⑨ 현재, 지금

☐ custom [kʌ́stəm] ⑲ 관습

☐ customer [kʌ́stəmər] ⑲ 고객

☐ damaged [dǽmidʒd] ⑱ 손상된

☐ deserve [dizə́:rv] ⑧ …을 받을 만하다

☐ discovery [diskʌ́vəri] ⑲ 발견

☐ document [dɑ́kjumənt] ⑲ 문서, 서류

☐ domestic [dəméstik] ⑱ 국내의

☐ durable [djúərəbl] ⑱ 내구성 있는, 튼튼한

☐ endure [indjúər] ⑧ 지속되다, 오래가다

☐ estimate [éstəmèit] ⑧ 추정하다

☐ explore [iksplɔ́:r] ⑧ 답사하다

☐ fabric [fǽbrik] ⑲ 직물, 천

☐ function [fʌ́ŋkʃən] ⑲ 기능

☐ generation [ʤènəréiʃən] ⑲ 세대

☐ glue [glu:] ⑧ …을 (접착제로) 붙이다

☐ harmful [hɑ́:rmfəl] ⑱ 유해한, 해로운

☐ innovative [ínəvèitiv] ⑱ 혁신적인, 획기적인

☐ intense [inténs] ⑱ 강렬한

☐ invaluable [invǽljuəbl] ⑱ 매우 귀중한

☐ joint [ʤɔint] ⑱ 공동의, 합동의

☐ layer [léiər] ⑲ 층, 겹

☐ modernization [mɑ̀dərnizéiʃən] ⑲ 현대화

☐ mulberry [mʌ́lbèri] ⑲ 뽕나무

☐ outstanding [autstǽndiŋ] ⑱ 뛰어난, 특출난

☐ panel [pǽnl] ⑲ 판

☐ practical [prǽktikəl] ⑱ 실용적인

☐ probe [proub] ⑲ 우주 탐사선, 탐사용 로켓

☐ purchase [pə́:rtʃəs] ⑲ 산 물건, 구매품

☐ ray [rei] ⑲ 광선, 빛

☐ relevant [réləvənt] ⑱ 의의가 있는, 유의미한

☐ remove [rimú:v] ⑧ 이동시키다, 치우다

☐ reveal [rivíːl] ⑧ 드러내다

☐ revival [riváivəl] ⑲ 부활

☐ spacecraft [spéiskræft] ⑲ 우주선

☐ tear [tɛər] ⑧ 찢다, 뜯다

☐ treat [tri:t] ⑲ 만족[즐거움]을 주는 것[사람]

☐ vibration [vaibréiʃən] ⑲ 진동, 흔들림

☐ yarn [jɑːrn] ⑲ (직물용) 실, 방적사

Phrases

☐ break down (물질이) 분해되다

☐ cast a vote 투표하다

☐ chip off 떨어져 나가다

☐ fall apart 오래되어 허물어지다, 망가지다

☐ for the sake of …을 위해서

☐ from time to time 때때로

☐ let go of …을 버리다

☐ make waves 파장[풍파]을 일으키다

☐ packed with …로 가득한, 꽉 찬

☐ point out 지적하다

1 다음 영어는 우리말로, 우리말은 영어로 쓰시오.

(1) deserve _____   (5) 유익한, 이로운 _____

(2) appreciate _____   (6) 드러내다 _____

(3) discovery _____   (7) 추정하다 _____

(4) outstanding _____   (8) 현재, 지금 _____

2 다음 빈칸에 들어갈 알맞은 단어를 보기 에서 골라 쓰시오.

보기	advanced	remove	adapt	durable

(1) This carpet is _____, so people can use it for a long time.

(2) She struggled to _____ to the thin mountain air.

(3) Thanks to _____ technology, our lives are becoming convenient.

(4) Please _____ the battery from the device when not in use.

3 주어진 우리말과 같은 뜻이 되도록 빈칸에 알맞은 말을 쓰시오.

(1) _____ _____ _____ all your worries and enjoy yourself.
(근심 걱정은 모두 털어버리고 즐기세요.)

(2) He saved money _____ _____ _____ _____ his family.
(그는 가족을 위해서 돈을 모았다.)

(3) We eat lunch in the park _____ _____ _____ _____.
(우리는 때때로 공원에서 점심을 먹는다.)

(4) Those shoes _____ _____ after a month.
(그 신발은 한 달 만에 망가졌다.)

4 다음 영영풀이에 해당하는 단어를 보기 에서 골라 쓰시오.

보기	domestic	absorb	generation	complex

(1) _____ : being made up of many parts and therefore difficult to understand

(2) _____ : to soak up and take in something

(3) _____ : people of the same age

(4) _____ : happening in one country, not related to another country

Communicative Functions

1 설명 요청하기

> A: This issue has become a political hot potato.
>   (이 문제는 정치적인 뜨거운 감자가 되어버렸어.)
> B: A hot potato? **What do you mean by** that?
>   (뜨거운 감자? 그게 무슨 뜻이야?)

• 어떤 일이나 대상의 내용을 잘 이해할 수 있도록 설명을 요청할 때, "What do you mean by ... ?"라는 표현을 쓸 수 있다. 이와 유사한 표현으로 "What is ... (exactly)?," "Could you explain ... ?," "What does that mean?" 등이 있다.

2 의견 묻기

> A: **What do you think of** getting a pet?
>   (애완동물을 키우는 것에 대해 어떻게 생각해요?)
> B: Well, I think it makes you more relaxed.
>   (음, 저는 그것이 당신의 마음을 더 느긋하게 만들어 준다고 생각해요.)

• 특정 대상에 대해 어떠한 생각을 갖고 있는지 물어볼 때, "What do you think of ... ?"라는 표현을 사용할 수 있다. 이와 유사한 표현으로, "How do you feel about ... ?," "What is your view/opinion?" 등이 있다.

Check-up

1 주어진 우리말 뜻에 맞도록 빈칸에 알맞은 말을 쓰시오.

(1) _____ _____ _____ _____ _____ moving to a big city?

(대도시로 이사가는 것에 대해 어떻게 생각해?)

(2) _____ _____ _____ _____ _____ "at the moment"?

('지금으로선'이라니 그게 무슨 말이야?)

2 다음 대화가 자연스럽게 이어지도록 순서대로 배열하시오.

> (A) What do you mean by that?
> (B) It means, "Forget about bad things that happened in the past."
> (C) You can do better next time. Just let bygones be bygones.
> (D) I failed the math exam. I'm so depressed.

_____ → _____ → _____ → _____

Discovering Grammar

Point 1 「one of the+최상급+복수명사」

> ▌ **Textbook** **One of** *hanji*'s **newest uses** is a treat for the ears.
> (한지의 최신 용도들 중 하나는 귀에 즐거움을 주는 것이다.)
>
> ✛ **Plus** New York is **one of the busiest cities** in the world.
> (뉴욕은 세계에서 가장 붐비는 도시 중 하나이다.)

• 최상급을 이용한 표현으로 '가장 …한 것들 중 하나'라는 의미이다. the를 대신하여 소유격 표현과 같은 한정사가 올 수도 있다. 주어로 쓰였을 경우 단수인 one에 수를 일치시켜 단수동사를 써야 하는 점에 유의한다.

Point 2 동격절을 이끄는 접속사 that

> ▌ **Textbook** In addition, **the fact that** the sound will not change over time because of the strength of *hanji* makes these speakers a great purchase.
> (게다가, 한지의 내구력 덕분에 시간이 흘러도 소리가 변하지 않을 것이라는 사실은 이 스피커를 훌륭한 구매품이 되게 한다.)
>
> ✛ **Plus** I heard **the news that** he had won the contest.
> (나는 그가 대회에서 우승했다는 뉴스를 들었다.)

• 명사의 의미를 보충하거나 바꿔 설명하기 위해 명사절을 뒤에 둘 수 있다. 이때 접속사 that을 사용하며 명사와 명사절의 관계를 동격 관계라고 한다. 동격절을 이끄는 접속사 that은 생략할 수 없으며, 동격절이 나오는 주요 명사에는 fact, news, opinion, idea, thought, question 등이 있다.

Check-up

1 주어진 우리말과 같은 뜻이 되도록 빈칸에 알맞은 말을 쓰시오.

(1) We stayed in _____ of the _____ expensive rooms in this hotel.
(우리는 이 호텔에서 가장 비싼 객실 중 하나에 묵었다.)

(2) She tried to hide _____ _____ _____ she couldn't read English.
(그녀는 영어를 읽을 줄 모른다는 사실을 숨기려고 했다.)

2 다음 문장의 괄호 안에서 어법상 올바른 것을 고르시오.

(1) One of the biggest events in life (are / is) marriage.
(2) Despite the fact (that / which) he won the game, Mike didn't feel good.
(3) Swimming in the ocean is one of his biggest (pleasure / pleasures).

1 밑줄 친 부분에 유의하여 다음 문장을 우리말로 해석하시오.

(1) Sarah followed his advice in <u>the belief that</u> he would not tell a lie.

(2) <u>The thought that</u> he might miss this opportunity worried him.

(3) I don't agree with <u>the idea that</u> natural talent is more important than practice.

2 다음 문장에서 어법상 **틀린** 부분을 고쳐 쓰시오.

(1) The taxi driver took one of the fastest road to the airport.

(2) One of his greatest songs in the 1990s are "It's my life."

(3) He didn't mention the fact which she could die.

(4) I am of the opinion there should be more books in the library.

3 다음 우리말과 같은 뜻이 되도록 주어진 단어를 배열하여 문장을 완성하시오.

(1) 그것은 올해 가장 인기 있는 영화 중 하나이다.

  (popular / one / the / of / most / this year / movies)

  → It is _____.

(2) 나의 가장 친한 친구 중 한 명은 광고회사에서 일한다.

  (best / works for / friends / an advertisement company /my)

  → One of _____.

(3) 한국에서 가장 유명한 축구선수 중 한 명을 소개하겠습니다.

  (Korea / one / famous / the/ of / in / soccer players / most)

  → Let me introduce to you _____.

4 다음 우리말과 같은 뜻이 되도록 괄호 안의 말을 이용하여 문장을 완성하시오.

(1) 크리스마스는 아이들에게 가장 즐거운 때 중 하나이다. (joyful, time)

  → Christmas is _____ for children.

(2) 그녀는 그 책에서 가장 어려운 문제 중 하나를 풀었다. (difficult, problem)

  → She solved _____ in the book.

(3) 그가 금메달을 땄다는 소식에 모두 흥분했다. (news, win)

  → Everybody was thrilled at _____.

(4) 그녀가 이 지갑을 훔쳤다는 증거가 어디에 있습니까? (proof, steal)

  → Where is _____?

[1~2] 다음 글을 읽고, 물음에 답하시오.

> *Hanji* is traditionally made from the bark of the mulberry tree. Through a number of complex processes, the tree bark is made into a paper that is very durable and hard to tear. _____, Western paper, which is made from pulp, begins to fall apart and becomes unusable after 100 years. It's easy to understand why Koreans created the old saying about *hanji*: "Paper lasts a thousand years, while silk endures five hundred." In addition to lasting a long time, *hanji* keeps heat and sound in but allows air to flow through it easily. The paper also absorbs water and ink very well, so there is no bleeding.

1 윗글에서 한지의 특성으로 언급되지 <u>않은</u> 것은?

① 튼튼하고 찢어지지 않음
② 비단보다 가벼움
③ 열과 소리를 보존함
④ 공기를 잘 통과시킴
⑤ 잉크가 번지지 않음

2 윗글의 빈칸에 들어갈 말로 가장 적절한 것은?

① Therefore   ② For example   ③ In other words
④ As a result   ⑤ On the other hand

[3~4] 다음 글을 읽고, 물음에 답하시오.

> Since ancient times, they have glued this paper to the walls, door frames, and floors of their homes. Koreans have also used it to make furniture, lanterns, wedding accessories, and boxes. Due to its (A) durability / reliability , *hanji* was even used in battle. Back then, people would put many layers of *hanji* together to make suits of armor. This armor, called *jigap*, was tough enough to stop arrows. With so many uses, *hanji* is naturally considered an (B) invaluable / valueless part of Korean history and culture. Though the tide of modernization seems to have made people forget about this paper's outstanding qualities, *hanji* has endured and remains (C) relevant / irrelevant today. In recent years, finding even more functions and purposes for *hanji* has become a trend.

3 (A), (B), (C)의 각 네모 안에서 문맥에 맞는 낱말로 가장 적절한 것은?

	(A)		(B)		(B)
①	durability	…	valueless	…	relevant
②	durability	…	invaluable	…	relevant
③	durability	…	invaluable	…	irrelevant
④	reliability	…	invaluable	…	irrelevant
⑤	reliability	…	valueless	…	irrelevant

4 윗글 뒤에 이어질 내용으로 가장 적절한 것은?

① 한지의 독보적인 특성
② 해외의 한지 사용 사례
③ 한지의 새롭고 현대적인 쓰임
④ 한지 공예를 보존하고 있는 장인들
⑤ 현대 사회에서 한지의 쓰임이 감소한 이유

[5~6] 다음 글을 읽고, 물음에 답하시오.

One of *hanji*'s newest uses is a treat for the ears. Customers can now buy speakers that use vibration plates and outside panels made of *hanji*. Compared to regular speakers, the sound that comes from *hanji* speakers is stronger and sharper. The paper's thickness and ability to absorb sound help the speakers pick up the smallest vibrations. In addition, the fact that the sound will not change over time because of the strength of *hanji* makes these speakers a great purchase. Serious music lovers will really be able to _____ the great sound quality of these speakers.

5 서술형 ▶ 윗글에서 한지로 만든 스피커의 장점 세 가지를 찾아 우리말로 쓰시오.

6 윗글의 빈칸에 들어갈 말로 가장 적절한 것은?

① change   ② produce   ③ ignore
④ appreciate   ⑤ adjust

1 다음 대화의 빈칸에 들어갈 말로 가장 적절한 것은?

> B: Did you know that people didn't shake hands to be friendly in the past?
>
> G: Really? Then why did they do it?
>
> B: They would greet each other like this for safety reasons.
>
> G: _____ How would shaking hands keep you safe?
>
> B: In the past, people shook hands with each other to see if the other person was hiding a weapon.

① What do you mean by that?
② Why don't you greet each other?
③ Is there any other way to greet?
④ Safety is the most important thing.
⑤ Please tell me what you are hiding.

2 다음 대화를 읽고, 여자의 마지막 말에 대한 남자의 응답으로 가장 적절한 것을 고르시오.

> M: Hey, Joan. Did you look at the schedule for our vacation yet? What do you think of it?
>
> W: Well, it seems really packed with activities. I want to spend some time doing absolutely nothing.
>
> M: Hmm... But that sounds like a waste of time.
>
> W: Actually, it's not. It's very important for us to empty our brains from time to time. It'll help us get more done later.
>
> M: Sounds odd. Being lazy can make you more productive?

> W: Yes. It may seem boring, but our brains function better after some rest.

① I don't think that we can do all these activities.
② Then I will try to empty our fridge to keep it clean.
③ We should make the best use of our time.
④ I never saw it that way before, but that makes sense.
⑤ That's why we need to use our vacation in an effective way.

3 다음 연설의 제목으로 가장 적절한 것은?

> When was the last time you went for a walk? And I don't mean a walk to your car or to the subway station; I mean a walk just for the sake of walking. Most people don't think about walking these days, but it can be just as beneficial to your health as more intense exercise. And the risk of injury is much lower. A physical benefit of walking is that it can reduce body fat, but it has mental health benefits, too. It can be a kind of meditation, because it gives you the opportunity to empty your mind. This can help reduce stress. So give walking a try!

① Importance of Getting Some Rest
② Physical and Mental Benefits of Walking
③ Ways of Staying Fit Without Working Out
④ Healthy Eating Habits for People Today
⑤ Differences Between Walking and Running

4 다음 중 단어의 영영 뜻풀이가 적절하지 <u>않은</u> 것은?

① outstanding: easy to be noticed

② remove: to soak up something

③ endure: to continue to exist for a long time

④ bleed: to spread from one area into another

⑤ advanced: modern and recently developed

5 주관식 다음 빈칸에 들어갈 알맞은 말을 쓰시오.

> Old people _____ respect for their experience and wisdom.
> (노인들은 그들의 경험과 지혜로 존경받을 만하다.)

6 밑줄 친 부분의 뜻풀이로 적절하지 <u>않은</u> 것은?

① The swimming pool is <u>packed with</u> kids. (…로 가득찬, 꽉 찬)

② The client <u>pointed out</u> several mistakes. (수정하다)

③ This novel is <u>making waves</u> with the readers. (파장을 일으키다)

④ The foods you eat <u>break down</u> in the body's digestive system. (분해되다)

⑤ It <u>fell apart</u> after the first wash. (망가지다)

7 다음 중 어법상 틀린 것은?

① I suffered a lot from the idea that I had to play well every game.

② This is one of the highest building in New York.

③ He informed me of the fact that she was lost.

④ Brazil is one of the largest coffee producers in the world.

⑤ He was one of the most famous scientists in the 1970s.

[8~10] 다음 글을 읽고, 물음에 답하시오.

> Until 1966, no one knew that the Mugujeonggwang Daedaranigyeong, the world's oldest printed document, lay inside a container at Bulguksa Temple in Gyeongju, Korea. Experts around the world were shocked that a document printed more than 1,200 years ago could still be around. They were even more surprised when the paper was removed from the container. _____ the document was printed before 751 CE, it was still in perfect condition.
>
> This discovery proved that the paper-making technology of the Unified Silla Kingdom era (676–935) was more advanced than <u>that</u> of either Japan or China, both of which also had highly developed paper-making technology.

8 윗글의 빈칸에 들어갈 말로 가장 적절한 것은?

① When　　② If　　③ Because

④ Although　　⑤ Unless

9 다음 중 윗글의 밑줄 친 that과 쓰임이 같은 것은?

① Something <u>that</u> is given for free isn't free.

② The news <u>that</u> he got a job made us happy.

③ People were shocked <u>that</u> she won the prize.

④ The color of the shirt goes well with <u>that</u> of the pants.

⑤ Let's ask <u>that</u> boy for directions.

10 윗글의 내용과 일치하지 <u>않는</u> 것은?

① 무구정광대다라니경은 세계에서 가장 오래된 인쇄물이다.

② 경주 불국사에서 무구정광대다라니경이 발견되었다.

③ 무구정광대다라니경은 서기 751년 이전에 인쇄되었다.

④ 무구정광대다라니경은 발견 당시 손상된 상태였다.

⑤ 통일 신라 시대에 일본과 중국은 고도의 제지 기술을 보유하고 있었다.

11 윗글의 제목으로 가장 적절한 것은?

① Why *Hanji* Is Better Than Western Paper

② Korean Interior Design in Ancient Times

③ New and Modern Ways to Use *Hanji*

④ How to Make Traditional Crafts with *Hanji*

⑤ The Various Uses of *Hanji* in Ancient Korea

12 밑줄 친 ①~⑤ 중, 문맥상 단어의 쓰임이 옳지 <u>않은</u> 것은?

13 주관식 윗글의 괄호 안의 말을 바르게 배열하여 문장을 완성하시오.

[11~13] 다음 글을 읽고, 물음에 답하시오.

Because of *hanji*'s ①<u>characteristics</u>, Koreans could see early on that it was more than just something to write on. Since ②<u>ancient</u> times, they have glued this paper to the walls, door frames, and floors of their homes. Koreans have also used it to make furniture, lanterns, wedding accessories, and boxes. Due to its ③<u>durability</u>, *hanji* was even used in battle. Back then, people would put many layers of *hanji* together to make suits of armor. This armor, called *jigap*, (stop / tough / to / arrows / was / enough). With so many uses, *hanji* is ④<u>naturally</u> considered an invaluable part of Korean history and culture.

Though the tide of modernization seems to have made people ⑤<u>remember</u> about this paper's outstanding qualities, *hanji* has endured and remains relevant today.

14 글의 흐름으로 보아, 주어진 문장이 들어가기에 가장 적절한 곳은?

This blend is almost weightless and keeps its shape better than other materials.

Lately, designers have been using *hanji* to make clothes, socks, and ties. (①) The fabric these designers are using is a blend of *hanji* yarn with cotton or silk. (②) It is also washable and eco-friendly. (③) Not only is *hanji* clothing practical, but it's also making waves at domestic and international fashion shows. (④) It seems that *hanji* clothing is here to stay. (⑤)

[15~17] 다음 글을 읽고, 물음에 답하시오.

One of *hanji*'s newest ①uses is a treat for the ears. Customers can now buy speakers that use vibration plates and outside panels made of *hanji*. ②Compared to regular speakers, the sound that comes from *hanji* speakers is ③stronger and sharper. The paper's thickness and ability to absorb sound help the speakers ④picking the smallest vibrations. In addition, the fact ⑤that the sound will not change over time because of the strength of *hanji* _____ .

15 밑줄 친 ①~⑤ 중, 어법상 틀린 것은?

16 [주관식] 다음 영영 뜻풀이에 해당하는 단어를 윗글에서 찾아 쓰시오.

a continuous slight shaking movement

17 윗글의 빈칸에 들어갈 말로 가장 적절한 것을 고르시오.

① proves *hanji* speakers' popularity
② helps people to fix these speakers
③ teaches people how to protect their ears
④ shows the importance of traditional culture
⑤ makes these speakers a great purchase

[18~20] 다음 글을 읽고, 물음에 답하시오.

And now, in one of its most innovative uses yet, *hanji* may soon be traveling into outer space. Korea and the U.S. are planning to use *hanji* on robots and spacecraft through a joint project

(A) supporting / supported by NASA. The paper has special properties that will help protect spacecraft from the harmful rays of the sun. Scientists hope to use *hanji* in the future for space probes since it is less expensive and lighter than the (B) current / currently used materials.

As you can see, people keep transforming *hanji* for countless uses. Its ability to adapt to the needs of every generation (C) has / have led to the revival of this traditional paper. So long as *hanji* continues to be treasured, there may be no limit to 미래에 한지가 어떻게 사용될 것인가.

18 (A), (B), (C)의 각 네모 안에서 어법에 맞는 표현으로 가장 적절한 것은?

	(A)	(B)	(C)
①	supporting	current	have
②	supporting	currently	have
③	supporting	current	has
④	supported	currently	have
⑤	supported	currently	has

19 윗글의 내용과 일치하지 않는 것은?

① 한지를 로봇에 활용하려는 계획이 있다.
② NASA는 한국과 미국의 공동 프로젝트를 후원하고 있다.
③ 한지는 태양의 유해 광선으로부터 우주선을 보호한다.
④ 과학자들은 우주 탐사선에 한지를 활용하려 한다.
⑤ 한지는 현재 사용되는 재료들보다 가격이 비싸다.

20 [주관식] 윗글의 밑줄 친 우리말과 같은 뜻이 되도록 다음 괄호 안의 단어를 알맞게 배열하시오.

(be / the future / enjoyed / will / how / in / it)

It's Up to You!

Functions

- 생각할 시간 요청하기
  Let me think.

- 확실성 정도 표현하기
  I'm not sure about that.

Structures

- **The harder** teens work at building good habits, **the stronger** those connections in their brains will be.

- Therefore, adolescence is **not** a stage to simply get through, **but** an important stage in people's lives.

Vocabulary

Words

- [ ] adolescence [æ̀dəlésəns] 몡 청소년기
- [ ] adolescent [æ̀dəlésənt] 몡 청소년
- [ ] aim [eim] 동 목표하다
- [ ] bargain [bɑ́ːrgən] 형 헐값의, 값싼 물건의
- [ ] confirm [kənfə́ːrm] 동 확인하다, 확증하다
- [ ] connection [kənékʃən] 몡 연결, 결합
- [ ] consequence [kɑ́nsəkwèns] 몡 결과
- [ ] discount [dískaunt] 몡 할인
- [ ] dismiss [dismís] 동 일축하다, 묵살하다
- [ ] experiment [ikspérəmənt] 몡 실험
- [ ] forehead [fɔ́ːrhèd] 몡 이마
- [ ] harsh [hɑːrʃ] 형 가혹한, 냉혹한
- [ ] host [houst] 몡 (TV · 라디오 프로의) 진행자
- [ ] identify [aidéntəfài] 동 찾다, 발견하다
- [ ] immediately [imíːdiətli] 부 즉시
- [ ] inclined [inkláind] 형 …하는 경향이 있는
- [ ] indoors [indɔ́ːrz] 부 실내에서
- [ ] influence [ínfluəns] 동 영향을 미치다
- [ ] insight [ínsàit] 몡 통찰력, 식견
- [ ] instinct [ínstiŋkt] 몡 본능
- [ ] instrument [ínstrəmənt] 몡 악기
- [ ] legal [líːgəl] 형 법적인
- [ ] location [loukéiʃən] 몡 위치, 소재지
- [ ] mature [mətjúər] 동 성숙하다; 발달하다
- [ ] measure [méʒər] 동 측정하다, 평가하다

- [ ] merely [míərli] 부 단순히, 단지
- [ ] midterm [mídtə̀ːrm] 몡 중간고사
- [ ] opposing [əpóuziŋ] 형 반대의, 대립되는
- [ ] outcome [áutkʌ̀m] 몡 결과
- [ ] period [píəriəd] 몡 시기, 기간
- [ ] phase [feiz] 몡 단계, 시기
- [ ] poll [pɑl] 몡 [pl.] 투표
- [ ] predict [pridíkt] 동 예측하다
- [ ] progress [prɑ́gres] 동 진전하다, 진행하다
- [ ] reason [ríːzn] 몡 이성
- [ ] receipt [risíːt] 몡 영수증
- [ ] region [ríːdʒən] 몡 (신체의) 부분; 지역
- [ ] register [rédʒistər] 동 등록하다
- [ ] rerun [ríːrʌ̀n] 몡 재방송
- [ ] risky [ríski] 형 위험한, 무모한
- [ ] shame [ʃeim] 몡 [sing.] 애석한[아쉬운] 일
- [ ] signal [sígnəl] 몡 신호
- [ ] significant [signífikənt] 형 중요한
- [ ] slight [slait] 형 약간의, 조금의
- [ ] stage [steidʒ] 몡 단계
- [ ] strengthen [stréŋkθən] 동 강화하다
- [ ] suffer [sʌ́fər] 동 나빠지다, 악화되다
- [ ] temple [témpl] 몡 사원
- [ ] undergo [ʌ̀ndərgóu] 동 겪다
- [ ] wireless [wáiərlis] 형 무선의

Phrases

- [ ] based on …에 기반하여
- [ ] get a refund 환불받다
- [ ] get rid of …을 없애다
- [ ] get through (어려운 때를) 견뎌내다
- [ ] go through (일련의 행동 · 절차를) 거치다
- [ ] in terms of …면에서

- [ ] lose out on …을 놓치다
- [ ] make sure 확실히 하다
- [ ] make up …을 형성하다[구성하다]
- [ ] rely on …에 의존하다
- [ ] seek out …을 구하다, 찾다
- [ ] size up …에 대해 평가를 내리다

1 다음 영어는 우리말로, 우리말은 영어로 쓰시오.

(1) dismiss ＿＿＿＿＿＿＿＿＿＿ (5) 즉시 ＿＿＿＿＿＿＿＿＿＿

(2) outcome ＿＿＿＿＿＿＿＿＿＿ (6) 측정하다, 평가하다 ＿＿＿＿＿＿＿＿＿＿

(3) significant ＿＿＿＿＿＿＿＿＿＿ (7) 애석한 일 ＿＿＿＿＿＿＿＿＿＿

(4) undergo ＿＿＿＿＿＿＿＿＿＿ (8) 영수증 ＿＿＿＿＿＿＿＿＿＿

2 다음 빈칸에 들어갈 알맞은 단어를 보기 에서 골라 쓰시오. 필요하다면 형태를 바꾸시오.

보기	adolescent	identify	mature	discount

(1) Girls ＿＿＿＿＿＿ earlier than boys both physically and mentally.

(2) ＿＿＿＿＿＿ often argue with their parents.

(3) You can get a 20% ＿＿＿＿＿＿ with this coupon.

(4) The cause of the accident has not been ＿＿＿＿＿＿ yet.

3 주어진 우리말과 같은 뜻이 되도록 빈칸에 알맞은 말을 쓰시오.

(1) Please ＿＿＿＿＿＿ ＿＿＿＿＿＿ that the door is closed.
(문이 닫혔는지 반드시 확인해주세요.)

(2) Our products have no rival ＿＿＿＿＿＿ ＿＿＿＿＿＿ ＿＿＿＿＿＿ price.
(우리 제품은 가격 면에서는 경쟁자가 없다.)

(3) It is hard for poor people to ＿＿＿＿＿＿ ＿＿＿＿＿＿ the cold winter.
(가난한 사람들에게는 추운 겨울을 견뎌내는 것이 어렵다.)

(4) He is the only person I can ＿＿＿＿＿＿ ＿＿＿＿＿＿ in my company.
(그는 회사에서 내가 의존할 수 있는 유일한 사람이다.)

4 다음 영영풀이에 해당하는 단어를 보기 에서 골라 쓰시오.

보기	register	predict	instinct	rerun

(1) ＿＿＿＿＿＿ : a television program that is shown again

(2) ＿＿＿＿＿＿ : to say something might happen in the future

(3) ＿＿＿＿＿＿ : to put your name on an official list

(4) ＿＿＿＿＿＿ : a natural tendency to behave in a particular way

Communicative Functions

1 생각할 시간 요청하기

A: Excuse me. Do you know if there's a bank near here?
　(실례합니다. 이 근처에 은행이 있는지 아시나요?)
B: **Let me think**. There's one on 34th Street.
　(음… 글쎄요. 34번가에 하나 있어요.)

• 무언가를 이야기하기 전에 생각할 시간이 필요할 때 "Let me think[see]"라는 표현을 사용할 수 있다. 이와 유사한 표현으로 "Just a moment," "May I think about that for a moment?" 등이 있다.

2 확실성 정도 표현하기

A: Does he live in this town?
　(그가 이 마을에 사니?)
B: **I'm not sure**.
　(잘 모르겠어.)

• 무언가에 대해 확실하게 알지 못할 때 "I'm not sure ..."라는 표현을 사용할 수 있다. 이와 유사한 표현으로 "I'm not (quite/fairly/absolutely) certain ...," "I can't tell you for sure" 등이 있다. 반대로 무언가에 대해 확실하게 말할때는 "I have no doubt," "I'm sure ..." 등과 같은 표현을 사용할 수 있다.

Check-up

1 주어진 우리말 뜻에 맞도록 빈칸에 알맞은 말을 쓰시오.

(1) ＿＿＿＿＿ ＿＿＿＿＿ ＿＿＿＿＿ if I can make it by 7.
　(제가 7시까지 그걸 해낼 수 있을지 잘 모르겠습니다.)

(2) I know her face but ＿＿＿＿＿ ＿＿＿＿＿ ＿＿＿＿＿ ＿＿＿＿＿ her name.
　(나는 그녀의 얼굴은 알지만 이름은 잘 모르겠다.)

2 다음 대화의 빈칸에 적절한 말을 보기 에서 고르시오.

A: Do you have anything in mind for lunch?
B : ＿＿＿＿＿＿＿＿＿＿＿＿＿＿＿＿＿
A: I like it. Why don't we have it delivered?
B : ＿＿＿＿＿＿＿＿＿＿＿＿＿＿＿＿＿

> 보기　ⓐ Sounds good. But I'm not sure what the phone number is.
> ⓑ Hmm... Let me think. How about some Chinese food?
> ⓒ Thank you for bringing me lunch.

Discovering Grammar

Point 1 「the+비교급 ..., the+비교급 ~」

■ Textbook **The harder** teens work at building good habits, **the stronger** those connections in their brains will be.
(십 대들이 좋은 습관을 기르려고 더 열심히 노력할수록, 그들 뇌 안의 그러한 연결고리는 더욱 강해질 것입니다.)

✚ Plus **The bigger** the room is, **the more comfortable** we will be.
(방이 클수록, 우리가 더 편안해질 것이다.)

The hotter it gets, **the more** ice cream we sell.
(날씨가 더울수록, 우리는 아이스크림을 더 많이 판다.)

•「the+비교급 ..., the+비교급 ~」은 '...하면 할수록 더 ~하다'라는 의미이다.「the+비교급」뒤에「주어+동사」가 오는데, 의미상 혼동이 없을 때는 주어와 동사를 생략하기도 한다.

Point 2 「not A but B」

■ Textbook Therefore, adolescence is **not** a stage to simply get through, **but** an important stage in people's lives where they can develop many qualities and abilities, and shape their future.
(그러므로, 청소년기는 그저 견뎌내야 하는 단계가 아니라 삶에서 그들이 많은 자질과 능력을 발달시키고 그들의 미래를 설계하는 중요한 단계입니다.)

✚ Plus The important thing is **not** winning the race **but** finishing it.
(중요한 건 이기는 게 아니라 완주하는 것이다.)

•「not A but B」는 'A가 아니라 B'라는 의미로, 단어, 구 또는 절을 대등하게 연결한다.

Check-up

1 밑줄 친 부분에 유의하여 다음 문장을 우리말로 해석하시오.

(1) The wallet was <u>not</u> on the drawer <u>but</u> in the drawer.

(2) It is <u>not</u> me <u>but</u> John who messed up everything.

(3) They were late <u>not</u> because of the traffic jam <u>but</u> because of bad weather.

2 다음 문장을 「the+비교급」을 이용하여 바꿔 쓰시오.

(1) As I exercised harder, I lost more weight.

→ _____

(2) As we climbed higher, the air became cooler.

→ _____

Grammar Test

1 괄호 안의 단어를 올바르게 배열하여 문장을 완성하시오.

(1) The earlier you make a reservation, (can / you / the discount / the higher / get).

(2) (speak / louder / the / you), the farther your voice travels.

(3) She was disappointed (with / my grades / not) but with my attitude.

(4) He went to Japan not to attend the meeting (visit / but / to / his / grandmother).

2 다음 문장에서 어법상 틀린 부분을 고쳐 쓰시오.

(1) The thicker the dough is, the long it takes to be baked.

(2) The older I get, I should take the more responsibilities for my life.

(3) We are not busy with writing the report, but busy with prepare for the seminar.

3 다음 문장의 빈칸에 들어갈 알맞은 말을 보기 에서 골라 쓰시오.

(1) I came here not to read any books but _____.

(2) Happiness comes not from the outside but _____.

(3) I had a stomachache not because I ate too much but _____.

(4) This city is famous not for its food but _____.

| 보기 | for its scenery | from the inside | because I was nervous | to prepare for my exams |

4 주어진 우리말과 같은 뜻이 되도록 괄호 안의 말을 이용하여 문장을 완성하시오.

(1) 우리가 여행을 더 자세히 계획할수록 우리는 실수를 덜 할 것이다. (carefully, plan for, few, make, mistakes)

→ The _____, the _____.

(2) 당신이 더 열심히 공부할수록, 더 많이 배울 것이다. (hard, study, learn)

→ The _____, the _____.

(3) 그를 더 오래 기다릴수록 나는 더 화가 났다. (long, wait for, angry, get)

→ The _____, the _____.

Reading Test

[1~2] 다음 글을 읽고, 물음에 답하시오.

> Hello, everyone! Welcome to *The Dr. Brain Show*. I'm your host, Joseph Emerson. Can you think back to a time when a friend upset you? Let's imagine that you decided to write an angry message to that friend. You say some harsh things that you normally wouldn't say. You're so angry that you don't care. When you're about to push "send," you think about whether it's a good idea. Before you know it, you've sent the message anyway. Teens are more likely to make these types of decisions than adults. With the help of our guest, we'll learn why teens tend to act _____. Now, here's our guest for tonight, Dr. Jenny Clarkson! Thank you for joining us, doctor!

1 윗글의 목적으로 가장 적절한 것은?

① 방송 시간 변경을 공지하려고
② 새 방송 프로그램 편성을 홍보하려고
③ 휴대전화 사용 예절에 관해 설명하려고
④ 청소년들의 캠페인 참여를 독려하려고
⑤ 방송의 주제와 초대 손님을 소개하려고

2 윗글의 빈칸에 들어갈 말로 가장 적절한 것은?

① with confidence
② after much thought
③ against the rules
④ as if they were adults
⑤ before thinking everything through

[3~4] 다음 글을 읽고, 물음에 답하시오.

> **Dr. C:** It seems like we make decisions almost immediately, but our brain actually has to go through several steps before deciding anything. Neurons, which are special brain cells, make up different structures in our brains. These structures send signals to each other. After the structures finish evaluating all the signals, they will send out a response that will tell our body what to do.
>
> **Host:** I see. Does this process happen exactly the same way in everyone's brain?
>
> **Dr. C:** People basically go through the same decision-making process, but there is a slight difference between teens and adults. Scientists used to think that the brain was done growing by the time you turned 12 since the brain reaches its maximum size around that age. However, studies show that some parts of the brain continue to develop until the early twenties. That means teens' brains are still maturing and not completely developed. This may be why teens seem to make risky decisions.

3 윗글의 내용과 일치하지 않는 것은?

① 우리의 뇌는 무언가를 결정하기 전에 몇 가지 단계를 거친다.

② 뉴런은 특별한 뇌 세포로 우리 뇌의 각기 다른 구조를 구성한다.

③ 기본적으로 뇌에서 일어나는 의사 결정 과정은 사람마다 다르다.

④ 연구를 통해 우리의 뇌가 20대 초반까지 성장한다는 것이 밝혀졌다.

⑤ 십 대들이 위험한 결정을 하는 것은 뇌의 발달과 관련 있다.

4 서술형 밑줄 친 this가 가리키는 것을 우리말 30자 이내로 쓰시오.

5 다음 글의 빈칸에 들어갈 말로 가장 적절한 것은?

> Well, the region that controls emotions matures faster than the part of the brain that helps you think ahead and measure risk. Teens therefore rely on it heavily, which means they are influenced more by _____ than by reason when making decisions. In other words, teens are usually not inclined to consider all the consequences of their actions, so they make choices that they end up regretting.

① social media

② critical thinking

③ their knowledge

④ feelings and instincts

⑤ their parents' opinions

6 다음 글의 제목으로 가장 적절한 것은?

> If we view the adolescent period as merely a process of becoming mature, then it's easy to dismiss it as a passing phase. However, we shouldn't look at the changes that occur in teens' brains only in terms of maturity. Adolescence is also a period when significant changes happen in the brain that help new abilities appear. Therefore, adolescence is not a stage to simply get through, but an important stage in people's lives where they can develop many qualities and abilities, and shape their future.

① Adolescence: The Period of Possibility

② Various Ways to Develop Our Brains

③ Why Teens' Brains Don't Change Easily

④ The Importance of Brain Maturity

⑤ How Our Brain Controls Emotions

1 다음 대화의 빈칸에 들어갈 말로 가장 적절한 것은?

> B: Hi, Sally. Would you like to have lunch together?
>
> G: Sure, Dan. How about having Chinese food?
>
> B: Actually, I had Chinese food yesterday. How about going to the new Italian restaurant on Main Street?
>
> G: Well, I've heard it's really expensive, and I'm trying to save money these days.
>
> B: Okay. _____ Why don't we go to Burger Castle? It's pretty cheap.

① It's not fair.

② That's a relief.

③ I'm not sure.

④ Let me think.

⑤ You're right.

2 다음 대화가 자연스럽게 이어지도록 (A)~(D)를 순서대로 배열하시오.

> (A) I wouldn't worry too much. There's still plenty of time to study.
>
> (B) I'm about to go see that new superhero movie. Would you like to come?
>
> (C) I'm not sure about that. I spent too much time hanging out with friends before our exams last term, so my grades suffered.
>
> (D) I'd like to, but midterms are next week. I should go to the library instead.

_____ → _____ → _____ → _____

3 다음 대화를 읽고, 남자의 마지막 말에 대한 여자의 응답으로 가장 적절한 것을 고르시오.

> B: I bought these shoes last weekend, but actually I regret buying them.
>
> G: Why is that? I think they look nice.
>
> B: Well, I have another perfectly good pair of shoes, so I don't really need these. I wasn't thinking clearly because of the bargain price.
>
> G: I see. Why don't you return them, then? I'm pretty sure you can get a refund if you still have your receipt.
>
> B: Unfortunately, I can't return them since they were a sale item.

① Great. Let's go shopping and get some sale items.

② No problem. You can get a refund without a receipt if you don't use it.

③ I see. Then let me check if there are bigger ones that fit you.

④ That's a shame. I guess you'll remember to think more carefully next time.

⑤ In that case, I would recommend that you buy one more pair of shoes for your sister.

4 다음 중 단어의 영영 뜻풀이가 적절하지 <u>않은</u> 것은?

① legal: related to the law

② undergo: to experience or endure something

③ strengthen: to make something more powerful

④ phase: a short group of words that has a particular meaning

⑤ measure: to judge how great something is in terms of its size, amount, etc.

[5~6] 주관식 주어진 우리말과 같은 뜻이 되도록 빈칸에 알맞은 말을 쓰시오.

5

> The _____ it becomes, the _____
> people catch colds.
> (더 추워질수록, 더 많은 사람들이 감기에 걸린다.)

6

> We tried to appeal _____ to people's
> reason _____ to their emotion.
> (우리는 사람들의 이성이 아니라 그들의 감정에 호소하려고 했다.)

7 밑줄 친 부분의 뜻풀이로 적절하지 않은 것은?

① Fire fighters carry out risky jobs. (위험한)
② Survival is the most basic instinct of humans. (본능)
③ Children go through various stages of development. (적응하다)
④ This novel was written based on a true story. (…에 기반하여)
⑤ He couldn't get rid of the stain on his shirt. (…을 없애다)

[8~9] 다음 글을 읽고, 물음에 답하시오.

> Hello, everyone! Welcome to *The Dr. Brain Show*. ① I'm your host, Joseph Emerson. ② Can you think back to a time when a friend upset you? ③ Let's imagine that you decided to write an angry message to that friend. ④ Some people think they can call you at all hours of the day and night, which might irritate you a lot. ⑤ You say some harsh things that you normally wouldn't say. 당신은 너무 화가 나서 신경쓰지 않는다. When you're about to push "send," you think about whether it's a good idea. Before you know it, you've sent the message anyway.

8 윗글의 ①~⑤ 중에서 전체 흐름과 관계 없는 문장은?

9 주관식 윗글의 밑줄 친 우리말과 같은 뜻이 되도록 다음 괄호 안의 단어를 알맞게 배열하시오.

(so / care / you're / that / angry / don't / you).

[10~11] 다음 글을 읽고, 물음에 답하시오.

> **Host:** Dr. Clarkson, could you first tell us about how we make decisions?
> **Dr. C:** Sure. It seems like we make decisions almost immediately, but our brain actually has to go through several steps before (A) decide / deciding anything. Neurons, which are special brain cells, (B) make / makes up different structures in our brains. These structures send signals to each other. After the structures finish (C) to evaluate / evaluating all the signals, they will send out a response that will tell our body what to do.

10 (A), (B), (C)의 각 네모 안에서 어법에 맞는 표현으로 가장 적절한 것은?

	(A)	(B)	(C)
①	decide	⋯ make	⋯ to evaluate
②	deciding	⋯ make	⋯ to evaluate
③	deciding	⋯ make	⋯ evaluating
④	deciding	⋯ makes	⋯ evaluating
⑤	decide	⋯ makes	⋯ to evaluate

11 [주관식] 다음 영영 뜻풀이에 해당하는 단어를 윗글에서 찾아 쓰시오.

> something that gives information about something or that tells someone to do something

12 다음 글의 빈칸에 들어갈 말로 가장 적절한 것은?

> Scientists used to think that the brain was done growing by the time you turned 12 since the brain reaches its maximum size around that age. _____, studies show that some parts of the brain continue to develop until the early twenties. That means teens' brains are still maturing and not completely developed. This may be why teens seem to make risky decisions.

① Besides ② However
③ In contrast ④ As a result
⑤ For example

[13~14] 다음 글을 읽고, 물음에 답하시오.

> **Host**: Please tell us more about the relationship between teens' brains and their decision-making.
> **Dr. C**: Well, the region that controls emotions ① matures faster than the part of the brain that helps you think ahead and

② measure risk. Teens therefore rely on it heavily, ③ that means they are influenced more by feelings and instincts than by reason when ④ making decisions. In other words, teens are usually not inclined ⑤ to consider all the consequences of their actions, so they make choices that they end up regretting.

13 윗글의 밑줄 친 ①~⑤ 중, 어법상 틀린 것은?

14 [주관식] 밑줄 친 it이 가리키는 바를 윗글에서 찾아 쓰시오.

15 주어진 글 다음에 이어질 글의 순서로 가장 적절한 것은?

> That's right. However, this is not the whole story.

(A) For example, if teens aren't reading, doing experiments, or solving problems, then the brain will get rid of the connections that are related to those activities.

(B) Once those are gone, their brains will put more energy into making other connections stronger.

(C) Teens' brains are also going through other important changes. Their brains are constantly identifying and removing any weak connections between neurons.

① (A) − (C) − (B) ② (A) − (B) − (C)
③ (B) − (A) − (C) ④ (B) − (C) − (A)
⑤ (C) − (A) − (B)

[16~18] 다음 글을 읽고, 물음에 답하시오.

Host: So, do you mean that ＿＿＿＿＿＿ ＿＿＿＿＿＿＿ can shape the way their brains develop?

Dr. C: Exactly. This is why the types of activities teens choose to participate in are especially important. If a teen decides to play sports or learn an instrument, then the brain will strengthen those connections. On the other hand, if he or she chooses to surf the Internet or play online games all day long, then those connections will survive instead. 십 대들이 좋은 습관을 기르려고 더 열심히 노력할수록, the stronger those connections in their brains will be.

16 윗글의 빈칸에 들어갈 말로 가장 적절한 것은?

① things that teens should do

② the relationships that teens make

③ struggling to make wise decisions

④ the activities teens are involved in

⑤ teens who can control their feelings

17 윗글의 밑줄 친 **to participate**와 같은 용법으로 쓰인 것은?

① She lived to be 100 years old.

② He is very difficult to persuade.

③ We have a lot of things to do today.

④ We planned to go to Europe this summer.

⑤ I bought a cake to celebrate her birthday.

18 주관식 윗글의 밑줄 친 우리말과 같은 뜻이 되도록 다음 괄호 안의 단어를 알맞게 배열하시오.

(work / the / teens / harder / at / good / building / habits)

[19~20] 다음 글을 읽고, 물음에 답하시오.

Dr. C: If we view the adolescent period as merely a process of becoming mature, then it's easy to dismiss it as a passing phase. (①) Adolescence is also a period when significant changes happen in the brain that help new abilities appear. (②) Therefore, adolescence is not a stage to simply get through, but an important stage in people's lives where they can develop many qualities and abilities, and shape their future. (③)

Host: Thank you for your insight, Dr. Clarkson! (④) We hope the information you've shared will help our viewers at home make more reasonable choices in the future. (⑤) That's it for *The Dr. Brain Show* tonight. Good night, everyone!

19 글의 흐름으로 보아, 주어진 문장이 들어가기에 가장 적절한 곳은?

However, we shouldn't look at the changes that occur in teens' brains only in terms of maturity.

20 주관식 윗글에서 알맞은 단어를 찾아 요지를 완성하시오.

Adolescence is a critical period to ＿＿＿＿＿＿ new abilities.

1 다음 대화가 자연스럽게 이어지도록 (A)~(D)를 올바른 순서로 배열하시오.

> (A) Really? Then why did they do it?
> (B) What do you mean by that? How would shaking hands keep you safe?
> (C) They would greet each other like this for safety reasons.
> (D) Did you know that people didn't shake hands to be friendly in the past?

_____ → _____ → _____ → _____

2 다음 대화의 빈칸에 들어갈 말로 가장 적절한 것은?

> M: Hey, Joan. Did you look at the schedule for our vacation yet?
>
> _____
>
> W: Well, it seems really packed with activities. I want to spend some time doing absolutely nothing.
> M: Hmm... But that sounds like a waste of time.
> W: Actually, it's not. It's very important for us to empty our brains from time to time. It'll help us get more done later.

① What do you think of it?
② Is there anything I can do?
③ How can we make a reservation?
④ Why don't you try one of them?
⑤ Have you ever done that before?

3 다음 대화의 내용과 일치하지 <u>않는</u> 것은?

> B: Hi, Sally. Would you like to have lunch together?
> G: Sure, Dan. How about having Chinese food?
> B: Actually, I had Chinese food yesterday. How about going to the new Italian restaurant on Main Street?
> G: Well, I've heard it's really expensive, and I'm trying to save money these days.
> B: Okay. Let me think. Why don't we go to Burger Castle? It's pretty cheap.
> G: I've never been there before. Is the food good?
> B: It is. I'm sure you'll like it.
> G: In that case, let's go!

① 남자는 어제 중국 음식을 먹었다.
② Main Street에 새 이탈리아 음식점이 생겼다.
③ 여자는 요즘 돈을 아끼는 중이다.
④ Burger Castle의 음식은 가격이 싸다.
⑤ 여자는 Burger Castle에 가본 적이 있다.

4 다음 대화를 읽고, 여자의 마지막 말에 대한 남자의 응답으로 가장 적절한 것을 고르시오.

> G: Hi, Mark. How's it going?
> B: Good. I'm about to go see that new superhero movie. Would you like to come?
> G: I'd like to, but midterms are next week. I should go to the library instead.
> B: I see. Then I'll have to watch the movie by myself.
> G: Why don't you go to the library with me now? We can watch it together some other time.

① Sounds good. Let's go to the theater now.

② Sure. Then let me buy the popcorn and drinks.

③ Me neither. I should have kept that spot in the library.

④ Well, okay. It's a good thing I brought my bag.

⑤ Sorry, I'm afraid I can't. I have to study for the midterm.

5 다음 글의 빈칸에 들어갈 말로 가장 적절한 것은?

Life is a series of choices. In order to _____ in life, you should consider issues from many different points of view. One way to do this is to come up with several options and think about any possible negative consequences they may have. After doing this, you will feel better because you know that you have done everything to make a careful decision. It can also be helpful to seek out advice from other people. Do you know anyone who has made a similar decision in their own life? If so, ask them how they made their decision and if they think they did the right thing.

① keep good relationships

② avoid wasting your time

③ make the best decisions you can

④ deal with your negative emotions

⑤ spend time alone and find yourself

6 주관식 다음 빈칸에 공통으로 들어갈 말로 알맞은 것을 쓰시오.

• This theory is based _____ scientific facts.
(이 이론은 과학적 사실에 기반한 것이다.)

• You should rely _____ your own judgement rather than listening to others.
(다른 사람을 말을 듣기보다는 자신의 판단에 의존해야 한다.)

7 주관식 다음 우리말과 같은 뜻이 되도록 괄호 안의 단어를 이용하여 문장을 완성하시오.

그녀는 나이가 들수록 점점 더 그녀의 할머니를 닮아간다. (old, get, look like)

→ The _____, the _____.

8 다음 중 보기 의 밑줄 친 that과 같은 용법으로 쓰인 것은?

보기   The news that she was rescued made me cry.

① You must not swim that far.

② He thought that it was too expensive.

③ She gave me something that I could eat.

④ I wish I could live in a house like that.

⑤ I agree with his idea that we should leave early.

9 다음 중 단어의 영영 뜻풀이로 적절하지 않은 것은?

① invaluable: not useful or important

② region: a part of the body

③ appreciate: to understand the worth of something

④ instrument: a tool used for producing music

⑤ confirm: to show that something is true or correct

10 밑줄 친 부분의 뜻풀이로 적절하지 <u>않은</u> 것은?

① My car is <u>falling apart</u> after the accident. (망가지다)

② I don't want to <u>let go of</u> this opportunity. (…을 쟁취하다)

③ Tropical rainforests <u>make up</u> around 80 percent of the Amazon region. (…를 구성하다)

④ This type of jobs are very good <u>in terms of</u> salary. (…에 관해서는)

⑤ That should <u>get rid of</u> your thirst. (없애다)

11 다음 글의 주제로 가장 적절한 것은?

> Until 1966, no one knew that the Mugujeonggwang Daedaranigyeong, the world's oldest printed document, lay inside a container at Bulguksa Temple in Gyeongju, Korea. Experts around the world were shocked that a document printed more than 1,200 years ago could still be around. They were even more surprised when the paper was removed from the container. Although the document was printed before 751 CE, it was still in perfect condition.

① great experts who studied old documents

② how documents were printed in ancient times

③ famous old documents from around the world

④ why ancient people kept important documents at temples

⑤ the discovery of the world's oldest printed document

[12~13] 다음 글을 읽고, 물음에 답하시오.

> *Hanji* is traditionally made from the bark of the mulberry tree. Through a number of complex processes, the tree bark is made into a paper that is very durable and ① hard to tear. On the other hand, Western paper, which is made from pulp, begins to fall apart and becomes ② usable after 100 years. It <u>왜 한국인들이 그 옛말을 만들었는지는 이해하기가 쉽다</u> about *hanji*: "Paper lasts a thousand years, while silk ③ endures five hundred." In addition to lasting a long time, *hanji* keeps heat and sound in but allows air to flow through it ④ easily. The paper also ⑤ absorbs water and ink very well, so there is no bleeding.

12 밑줄 친 ①~⑤ 중, 문맥상 낱말의 쓰임이 적절하지 <u>않은</u> 것은?

13 주관식 윗글의 밑줄 친 우리말과 같은 뜻이 되도록 다음 괄호 안의 단어를 바르게 배열하시오.

(Koreans / understand / easy / why / is / created / to / the old saying)

[14~16] 다음 글을 읽고, 물음에 답하시오.

> Because of *hanji*'s characteristics, Koreans could see early on that it was more than just something to write ① on. Since ancient times, they have glued this paper to the walls, door frames, and floors of their homes. Koreans have also used it to make furniture, lanterns, wedding accessories,

and boxes. _____ its durability, *hanji* was even used in battle. Back then, people ②would put many layers of *hanji* together to make suits of armor. This armor, called *jigap*, was ③tough enough to stop arrows. With so many uses, *hanji* is naturally considered an invaluable part of Korean history and culture.

Though the tide of modernization seems ④to have made people forget about this paper's outstanding qualities, *hanji* has endured and remains relevant today. In recent years, ⑤find even more functions and purposes for *hanji* has become a trend.

14 밑줄 친 ①~⑤ 중, 어법상 틀린 것은?

15 윗글의 빈칸에 들어갈 말로 가장 적절한 것은?

① In spite of
② According to
③ Due to
④ With regard to
⑤ By means of

16 윗글에서 한지를 활용하여 만들 수 있는 것으로 언급되지 <u>않은</u> 것은?

① 가구
② 혼례 장신구
③ 상자
④ 갑옷
⑤ 화살

[17~18] 다음 글을 읽고, 물음에 답하시오.

Lately, designers have been using *hanji* to make clothes, socks, and ties.

(A) It is also washable and eco-friendly. Not only is *hanji* clothing practical, but it's also making waves at domestic and international fashion shows. It seems that *hanji* clothing is here to stay.

(B) The fabric these designers are using is a blend of *hanji* yarn with cotton or silk. This blend is almost weightless and keeps its shape better than other materials.

(C) One of *hanji*'s ⓐ(new) uses is a treat for the ears. Customers can now buy speakers that use vibration plates and outside panels ⓑ(make) of *hanji*.

17 주어진 글 다음에 이어질 글의 순서로 가장 적절한 것은?

① (A) − (B) − (C)
② (B) − (A) − (C)
③ (B) − (C) − (A)
④ (A) − (C) − (B)
⑤ (C) − (B) − (A)

18 주관식 ⓐ, ⓑ의 괄호 안에 주어진 단어를 어법에 맞게 바꿔 쓰시오.

ⓐ _____   ⓑ _____

19 글의 흐름으로 보아, 주어진 문장이 들어갈 위치로 가장 적절한 곳은?

> These structures send signals to each other.

> **Host**: Dr. Clarkson, could you first tell us about how we make decisions? (①)
> **Dr. C**: Sure. (②) It seems like we make decisions almost immediately, but our brain actually has to go through several steps before deciding anything. (③) Neurons, which are special brain cells, make up different structures in our brains. (④) After the structures finish evaluating all the signals, they will send out a response that will tell our body what to do. (⑤)

20 다음 글에서 전체 흐름과 관계 없는 문장은?

> **Host**: I see. Does this process happen exactly the same way in everyone's brain?
> **Dr. C**: ① People basically go through the same decision-making process, but there is a slight difference between teens and adults. ② Adults usually hesitate to do something before starting what they have not experienced before. ③ Scientists used to think that the brain was done growing by the time you turned 12 since the brain reaches its maximum size around that age.
> ④ However, studies show that some parts of the brain continue to develop until the early twenties. ⑤ That means teens' brains are still maturing and not completely developed. This may be why teens seem to make risky decisions.

[21~23] 다음 글을 읽고, 물음에 답하시오.

> **Dr. C**: That's right. However, this is not the whole story. Teens' brains are also going through other important changes. Their brains are constantly identifying and removing any weak connections between neurons. For example, if teens (A) aren't / weren't reading, doing experiments, or solving problems, then the brain will get rid of the connections that are related to those activities. Once those are gone, their brains will put more energy into making other connections stronger.
> **Host**: So, do you mean that the activities teens are involved in can shape the way their brains develop?
> **Dr. C**: Exactly. This is why the types of activities teens choose to participate in (B) is / are especially important. If a teen decides to play sports or learn an instrument, then the brain will strengthen those connections. _____, if he or she chooses to surf the Internet or play online games all day long, then those connections will survive instead. The harder teens work at building good habits, the (C) strong / stronger those connections in their brains will be.

21 (A), (B), (C)의 각 네모 안에서 어법에 맞는 표현으로 가장 적절한 것은?

	(A)		(B)		(C)
①	aren't	⋯	are	⋯	strong
②	aren't	⋯	is	⋯	stronger
③	aren't	⋯	are	⋯	stronger
④	weren't	⋯	are	⋯	stronger
⑤	weren't	⋯	is	⋯	strong

22 [서술형] 밑줄 친 those가 가리키는 것을 찾아 우리말로 쓰시오.

23 윗글의 빈칸에 들어갈 말로 가장 적절한 것은?

① In addition
② For example
③ As a result
④ In other words
⑤ On the other hand

[24~25] 다음 글을 읽고, 물음에 답하시오.

Dr. C: If we view the adolescent period as merely a process of becoming mature, then it's easy to dismiss it as a passing phase. However, we shouldn't look at the changes that occur in teens' brains only in terms of maturity. Adolescence is also a period when significant changes happen in the brain that help new abilities appear. Therefore, adolescence is not a stage to simply get through, but an important stage in people's lives where they can _____, and shape their future.

24 윗글의 빈칸에 들어갈 말로 가장 적절한 것은?

① think about their future career
② become mature and responsible
③ spend much time with their friends
④ learn how their brains function
⑤ develop many qualities and abilities

25 [주관식] 다음 영영 뜻풀이에 해당하는 단어를 윗글에서 찾아 쓰시오.

to decide that something is not important and not worth thinking or talking about

정답 및 해설

Lesson 1. The Part You Play

Vocabulary Test

p. 7

1. (1) 영광   (2) 육체의, 신체의   (3) 존경하다
   (4) 동기를 부여하다   (5) contribute
   (6) determined   (7) unexpectedly   (8) senior

2. (1) crowded   (2) worth   (3) passion
   (4) apologize

3. (1) drop, by   (2) hang, out, with
   (3) instead, of   (4) show, off

4. (1) excel   (2) defeat   (3) intelligence
   (4) observe

Communicative Functions

p. 8

1. (1) I'm, going, to   (2) we, should   **2.** ⓑ, ⓒ

Discovering Grammar

p. 9

1. (1) standing   (2) eating   (3) protecting
2. (1) hard for him to read Chinese characters
   (2) impossible for me to finish it by tomorrow

Grammar Test

p. 10

1. (1) say → saying (2) work → working (3) drive →
driving (4) finish → finishing   **2.** (1) being (2) failing
(3) listening (4) closing   **3.** (1) 너는 그 모임에 참석할
필요가 있다. (2) 그녀는 충분히 자는 것이 중요하다. (3) 그가
그녀의 제안을 거절하기는 어려웠다.   **4.** (1) dangerous
for children to climb that mountain (2) unusual for
the weather to be so cold (3) very important for us
to get to know each other (4) strange for him to be
out so late

1 전치사는 명사에 준하는 형태를 목적어로 취하므로, 전치사 뒤
   의 동사를 동명사의 형태로 바꾸어 써야 한다.

2 전치사의 목적어가 되어야 하므로, 괄호 안에서 동명사의 형태
   로 된 것을 찾는다.

---

3 「for+목적격」을 to부정사구의 동작의 주체인 의미상 주어로,
   to부정사구를 진주어로 하여 해석한다. 이때 가주어 it은 해석
   하지 않는 점에 유의한다.

4 「It+be동사+보어+for+목적격+to-v」의 어순이 되도록 배열한
   다.

Reading Test

pp. 11~12

1. ①   **2.** ①   **3.** ③   **4.** ③   **5.** 다리가 부자연스럽
게 휘어서 걷거나 뛰거나 돌아다니기 어려운 것   **6.** ④

1 뒤에 '그는 이전에 어떤 경기에서도 뛰어본 적이 없었다. 이제,
   Ethan은 마침내 잔디를 밟을 기회를 얻게 된 것이었다.'라는
   내용이 이어지는 것으로 보아, 빈칸에는 ① '행복한'이 들어가
   는 것이 가장 적절하다.
   오답 ② 안도한   ③ 짜증난
         ④ 실망한   ⑤ 우울한

2 경기 종료가 2분 밖에 남지 않았다고 한 부분, 헐리우드 영화
   같았다고 묘사한 부분, 경기 종료 직전에 골라인을 통과했다
   고 한 부분 등에서 ① '극적인' 분위기를 느낄 수 있다.
   오답 ② 좌절감을 주는   ③ 겁나게 하는
         ④ 고독한   ⑤ 위로가 되는

3 승리가 확실해졌을 때 사이드라인에 있던 모든 4학년생 선수
   들이 마지막 몇 초간 경기에서 뛸 수 있도록 허락 받았다고 했
   다.

4 'his condition'이 구체적으로 지칭하는 바가 앞에 서술되어
   있고, 대도시에 있는 학교를 떠나 우리 학교로 전학 왔다는 내
   용이 뒤에 이어지는 ③에 들어가는 것이 가장 적절하다.

5 두 번째 문단의 앞부분에 나와 있다.

6 (A) 'Ethan이 그들(선수들)에게 동기를 부여하고 격려한 것'이
   '그들(선수들)이 그(Ethan)의 가장 열정적인 팬이 된 것'의 이
   유이므로 Because(…이기 때문에)가 가장 적절하다.
   (B) '그(Ethan)가 경기장에서 실제 플레이를 하는 선수가 아니
   었던 것'과 'Ethan의 마음은 항상 같은 팀 선수들과 함께한
   것'은 역접의 관계를 가지므로 Although(…에도 불구하고)가
   가장 적절하다.

1. ④   **2.** ⑤   **3.** ②   **4.** ③   **5.** ②   **6.** ③
7. was necessary for him to take   **8.** ⑤   **9.** ③
10. the ball   **11.** ④   **12.** reward   **13.** ①
14. ④   **15.** ⑤   **16.** ④   **17.** ③   **18.** ①
19. putting all his efforts into trying to be the team's best player   **20.** ②

1 B가 앞으로의 계획을 말하고 있으므로, A는 계획을 묻는 질문을 해야 한다. ④ '우리 학교에 대해 어떻게 생각해?'는 의견을 묻는 말이다.

2 좋은 아들이자 오빠이지 못했다는 걸 깨닫고 이제부터 잘 하겠다는 계획을 표현하고 있으므로, ⑤ '더 좋은 아들, 더 좋은 오빠가 될게요.'가 가장 적절하다.

오답
① 이제부터 더 좋은 학생이 되려고 노력할게요.
② 모든 가족행사에 참석하겠다고 약속해요.
③ 친구들과 주말을 보내서 미안해요.
④ 더는 게임 하지 않을게요.

3 쓰레기가 버려진 것을 보고 이에 대해 말하는 ⓑ, 쓰레기를 치워야겠다고 하는 ⓒ, 동의하며 자신의 의견을 말하는 ⓐ, 함께 치우러 가자고 제안하는 ⓓ의 순서로 이어지는 것이 가장 적절하다.

4 ③ valuable은 '귀중한'이라는 의미이다. '무언가를 성취하기 위해 필요한 신체적 혹은 정신적 활동'을 의미하는 단어는 effort이다.

오답
① 헌신: 어떤 것이 중요하기 때문에 이에 많은 시간과 에너지를 기꺼이 들이는 마음
② 붐비는: 너무 많은 사람이나 물건으로 가득 찬
④ 격려하다: 누군가에게 지지, 자신감, 또는 희망을 주다
⑤ 영감: 무언가를 하도록 아이디어를 주는 사람이나 사물

5 문맥상 '답례로'라는 의미의 ②가 들어가는 것이 가장 적절하다.

오답 ① 재고가 있는   ③ 한눈에
     ④ 혹시   ⑤ 우연히

6 문맥상 '…을 끌어내다, 발휘하게 하다'라는 의미의 ③이 들어가는 것이 가장 적절하다.

오답 ① 자랑하다 ② 다 되다 ④ 야기하다 ⑤ 따라잡다

7 「It+be동사+보어+for+목적격+to-v」의 어순이 되도록 써야 한다.

8 the seniors에 대한 언급이 나오는 (C), 그들 중 한 명인 Ethan이 언급되는 (B), Ethan이 경기에 참여할 기회를 얻었다는 내용이 나오는 (A)의 순서로 이어지는 것이 가장 적절하다.

9 공을 집어 뛰던 선수가 Ethan을 발견한 후이면서, Ethan이 공을 들고 달리며 모두의 시선을 받게 되기 전인 ③에 들어가는 것이 가장 적절하다.

10 주절에 나온 2개의 it은 모두 the ball을 가리킨다.

11 모든 노고와 헌신이 ④ '절망'으로 보상받는다는 것은 부자연스럽다.

12 '좋은 일 혹은 도움이 되는 일을 했거나 그 일을 위해 노력했기 때문에 그 사람에게 무언가를 주다'라는 영영 뜻풀이에 해당하는 단어는 reward이다.

13 (A) to부정사의 의미상의 주어는 「for+목적격」으로 나타낸다. 「of+목적격」을 쓰는 것은 사람의 성격을 나타낼 때로 한정된다.
(B) 「allow+목적어+to-v」는 '…가 ~하도록 허락하다'라는 의미이다.
(C) 양보의 의미를 갖는 Although(비록 …이지만)와 Despite(…에도 불구하고) 중, 뒤에 절이 오는 것은 접속사 Although이다. Despite는 전치사이므로 뒤에 명사가 온다.

14 ①, ②, ③, ⑤는 모두 Ethan을 가리키는 반면, ④는 the coach를 가리킨다.

15 신체적 한계와는 ⑤ '상관없이' (장애가 없는) 다른 선수들만큼 열심히 연습했다고 하는 것이 자연스럽다.

오답 ① …와는 반대로   ② … 덕분에
     ③ …을 제외하고   ④ …에 더해서

16 ④ 출전 못한 선수들을 위로하는 것과 관련된 내용은 글에 나와있지 않다.

17 ③ 전치사 for의 목적어로 온 동명사 calming과 and로 병렬 연결된 부분이므로 bringing이 되어야 한다.

18 단락 앞부분에서 Ethan이 팀에 어떻게 기여했는지 나오고, 바로 앞 문장에서 '팀원 모두가 풋볼을 향한 Ethan의 사랑을 느낄 수 있었다'고 하고 있으므로, 그의 헌신을 ① '존경했다'고 하는 것이 자연스럽다.

오답 ② 결정했다 ③ 요청했다 ④ 표현했다 ⑤ 무시했다

19 Instead of 뒤에는 전치사의 목적어로 동명사 형태가 와야 하며, '…에 노력을 들이다'라는 의미의 「put efforts into」가 쓰였다는 점에 유의하여 순서를 배열한다.

20 앞에서 '팀에서의 역할이 작지라도 모두가 팀의 성공을 위

해 중요하다', '팀을 더 좋게 만들기 위해 할 수 있는 모든 걸 했다'는 내용, 뒤에서 '다른 사람들이 빛나도록 도와주는 것'이란 말로 미루어, ② '우리 주변 사람들의 기운을 북돋워주는 것'이 들어가는 것이 가장 적절하다.

오답

① 서로를 신뢰하는 것

③ 다른 사람들에 대해 동정심을 갖는 것

④ 세부적인 것들에 주의를 기울이는 것

⑤ 작은 역할에 만족하는 것

Lesson 2. The Power of Creativity

Vocabulary Test

1. (1) (보기좋게) 조합되다, 조합하다 (2) 전시물 (3) 장비
   (4) 현대의 (5) facility (6) storage (7) sculpture
   (8) decompose
2. (1) disposable (2) heritage (3) abandon
   (4) flexible
3. (1) takes, place (2) came, up, with (3) in, place, of
   (4) tear, down
4. (1) provoke (2) repurpose (3) install (4) magnificent

Communicative Functions
p. 20

1. (1) Maybe[Perhaps/Probably], he, will   (2) It, seems,
   to, me
2. (C), (D), (A), (B)

Discovering Grammar
p. 21

1. (1) who   (2) which   (3) that
2. (1) pictures, drawn (2) applicants, showing

Grammar Test
p. 22

1. (1) talking (2) covered (3) holding (4) invited
2. (1) living (2) involved (3) building (4) injured
3. (1) My grandfather who[that] had been suffering from cancer passed away last week. (2) The people who[that] have membership cards can get tickets for free. (3) That is the road which[that] leads to the airport. (4) I bought an oven which[that] is suitable for baking and cooking. 4. (1) The woman who is sitting at the desk is (2) picked up a doll which lay on the ground (3) the boy that was playing in the park

1 (1) 문맥상 the man과 talk가 능동의 관계이므로 현재분사 talking이 알맞다.
   (2) 문장 전체의 동사는 took이고 the mountain과 cover가 수동의 관계이므로 과거분사 covered가 알맞다.
   (3) 문맥상 the man과 hold가 능동의 관계이므로 현재분사 holding이 알맞다.
   (4) 문맥상 the people과 invite는 수동의 관계이므로 과거분사 invited가 알맞다.

2 (1) 문맥상 the people과 live가 능동의 관계이므로 현재분사 living을 써야 한다.
   (2) 문맥상 the people과 involve가 수동의 관계이므로 과거분사 involved를 써야 한다.
   (3) 문맥상 a child와 build가 능동의 관계이므로 현재분사 building을 써야 한다.
   (4) 문맥상 soldiers와 injure가 수동의 관계이므로 과거분사 injured를 써야 한다.

3 (1) My grandfather를 선행사로 하고 그 뒤에 주격 관계대명사 who[that]를 써서 두 문장을 연결한다.
   (2) The people을 선행사로 하고 그 뒤에 주격 관계대명사 who[that]를 써서 두 문장을 연결한다.
   (3) the road를 선행사로 하고 그 뒤에 주격 관계대명사 which[that]를 써서 두 문장을 연결한다.
   (4) an oven을 선행사로 하고 그 뒤에 주격 관계대명사 which[that]를 써서 두 문장을 연결한다.

4 (1) 주격 관계대명사 who를 이용해 선행사 The woman을 수식하는 관계대명사절을 만든다.
   (2) 주격 관계대명사 which를 이용해 선행사 a doll을 수식하는 관계대명사절을 만든다.
   (3) 주격 관계대명사 that을 이용해 선행사 the boy를 수식하는 관계대명사절을 만든다.

128   정답 및 해설

1. ①   **2.** ④   **3.** ③   **4.** 원래 용도로 더는 사용될 수 없는 오래된 건물들조차도 업사이클될 수 있다는 것   **5.** ⑤
6. (1) 작품을 감상하는 사람의 눈을 즐겁게 해준다. (2) 자연스럽게 환경보존에 대한 사람들의 관심을 유발한다.

1 문맥상 재활용을 함으로써 쓰레기의 양을 줄일 수 있다는 내용이 되어야 하므로 ① increase 대신 reduce가 오는 것이 적절하다.

2 upcycling의 장점을 덧붙여 설명하고 있으므로 ④ '게다가'가 들어가는 것이 가장 적절하다.
　오답 ① 그 결과 　　② 예를 들어
　　　　③ 다시 말해서 　　⑤ 반면에

3 주어진 문장이 For instance를 사용하여 철강 공장의 시설이 어떻게 변화됐는지에 대한 사례를 처음 서술하고 있으므로 사례들이 언급되는 부분 앞인 ③에 들어가는 것이 가장 적절하다.

4 바로 앞 문장에서 this가 가리키는 바를 찾는다.

5 Tom Deininger와 Gwyneth Leech 모두 창의적인 아이디어로 쓰레기를 예술 작품으로 만들었기 때문에 ⑤ '그들의 창의적인 손길을 더하다'가 들어가는 것이 가장 적절하다.
　오답
　① 큐레이터의 역할을 맡다
　② 갤러리와 갈등을 빚다
　③ 자연으로부터 영감을 얻다
　④ 환경운동가와 작업하다

6 윗글의 마지막 문장에 나타나 있다.

1. ②   **2.** ③   **3.** ⑤   **4.** ④   **5.** original   **6.** ①
7. designing → designed   **8.** what → which[that]
9. (1) 버려지는 쓰레기의 양을 줄여준다. (2) 새 제품을 만드는 데 쓰는 것보다 더 적은 에너지를 사용할 수 있다. (3) 천연자원을 절약할 수 있다.   **10.** ③   **11.** ④   **12.** ②
13. To[to]   **14.** ⑤   **15.** ⑤   **16.** ③   **17.** ①
18. things that most people consider junk are reborn   **19.** ③   **20.** ③

1 주어진 문장이 어떻게 멀티탭이 구부러질 수 있는지에 대해 묻고 있으므로 이에 대한 대답의 앞인 ②에 들어가는 것이 가

장 적절하다.

2 작은 변화로 개선된 제품을 만들어내는 것에 대해 놀라워하고 있으므로 두 사람의 심경으로는 ③ '감명받은'이 가장 적절하다.
　오답 ① 짜증이 난 　　② 부러워하는
　　　　④ 무관심한 　　⑤ 겁먹은

3 예술가들이 주민들의 사기를 높이기 위해 벽화를 그림으로써 마을이 멋진 곳이 됐다는 내용이므로, ⑤ '예술가들이 이 지역에 새 생명을 불어넣은 것 같아.'가 들어가는 것이 가장 적절하다.
　오답
　① 거리의 예술가들이 벽과 집에 그림을 그리는 것은 옳지 않아.
　② 주민들이 예술가들과 함께 지역사회를 위해 작업한 것은 멋지다고 생각해.
　③ 벽화는 벽에 생긴 균열을 숨기기에 훌륭한 도구라고 생각해.
　④ 이 동네를 관광지로 바꾸는 것은 옳은 일이 아닌 것 같아.

4 ④ '무언가를 있는 그대로 유지하다'라는 뜻을 가진 단어는 preserve이다. abandon은 '버리다'라는 뜻이다.
　오답
　① 정화하다: 무언가를 순수하게 만들기 위해 나쁜 물질을 제거하다
　② 개조하다: 형태나 성격을 바꾸다
　③ 현대의: 현대의, 현재와 관련된
　⑤ 분해되다, 부패하다: 화학적으로 변화되거나 썩기 시작하다

5 '원래의'라는 뜻을 가지고 있는 단어는 original이다.

6 one of a kind는 '독특한 사람[것]'이라는 뜻이다.
　① 너의 조각품은 분명 독특한 것이 될 거야.
　오답
　② 그녀는 성공하기 전에 일련의 고난들을 겪었다.
　③ 그는 새 상품을 홍보할 좋은 아이디어를 생각해냈다.
　④ 너는 짠 음식을 줄일 필요가 있다.
　⑤ 그는 동료들과 더불어 부당한 명령을 따르는 것을 거부했다.

7 문맥상 library와 design이 수동의 관계이므로 과거분사 designed를 써야 한다.

8 선행사가 a good restaurant이므로 주격 관계대명사 which[that]를 써야 한다.

9 윗글 6~10행에 나타나 있다.

10 (A) 문맥상 '분명히'라는 의미의 Obviously가 적절하다. Obscurely는 '애매하게, 모호하게'라는 의미이다.
　(B) 문맥상 '필요로 하다'라는 의미의 requires가 적절하다.

acquire는 '얻다, 획득하다'라는 의미이다.

(C) 문맥상 '접근법'이라는 의미의 approach가 적절하다. reproach는 '비난, 책망'이라는 의미이다.

11 (A) object와 transform이 수동의 관계이므로 be transformed가 적절하다.

(B) 'old truck tarps, car seat belts, and bicycle inner tubes'를 가리키는 대명사가 들어가야 하므로 복수인 them 이 적절하다.

(C) 문장 전체의 동사로 쓰인 것은 are이고, bicyclists와 go 는 능동의 관계이므로 현재분사 going이 적절하다.

12 앞부분에 '쓸모 없어 보이는 물건이 완전히 다른 것으로 변신할 수 있다'고 서술되어 있고, 글의 뒷부분에서 매일 사용할 수 있는 튼튼한 가방이 된다고 했으므로 ② '일상생활에 유용한'이 들어가는 것이 가장 적절하다.

오답

① 호화롭고 특별한

③ 당신에게 위안을 주는

④ 아이들이 가지고 놀기 좋은

⑤ 당신의 안전을 개선하는 데 도움이 되는

13 문맥상 '…하기 위해서'라는 의미의 부사적 용법(목적)의 to부정사가 되어야 하므로 (A), (B)에 공통으로 들어갈 단어는 to이다.

14 ①~④는 모두 tires를 가리키는 반면, ⑤는 Parsons and his team을 가리킨다.

15 ⑤ land와 fill이 수동의 관계이고 문장 전체의 동사는 has이므로 과거분사 filled로 고쳐야 한다.

16 앞에서 언급한 추가 장비나 새로운 디자인이 적용된 사례를 구체적으로 제시하는 내용이 이어지므로, ③ '예를 들어'가 들어가는 것이 가장 적절하다.

오답 ① 하지만   ② 게다가
      ④ 그런데   ⑤ 그와 반대로

17 오답

② 철강공장은 1985년에 문을 닫았다.

③ 건물의 많은 부분이 원래의 모습을 유지했다.

④ 기존의 가스탱크는 다이버들을 위한 풀이 되었다.

⑤ 전망대로 바뀐 것은 금속을 녹이던 건물이다.

18 문장의 주어는 things, 동사는 are reborn이다. 목적격 관계대명사 that을 이용해 선행사 things를 수식하는 절을 만든다.

19 주어진 문장에 접속사 'however(그러나)'가 나오므로, 바로 앞에 주어진 문장과 상반된 내용이 나오는 ③에 들어가는 것이 가장 적절하다.

20 ③ '도자기 파편'은 언급되지 않았다.

1 Angela Reynolds는 지하철 선로에 뛰어들어 위험에 처한 소년을 구했으므로 ③ '어린 소년의 생명을 구했다'가 들어가는 것이 가장 적절하다.

오답

① 학교에 제시간에 갔다

② 그녀의 용기를 자랑했다

④ 지하철 역의 서비스를 개선시켰다

⑤ 지하철의 탑승객들을 보호했다

2 ⑤ 다른 사람들이 Angela Reynolds와 소년을 끌어당겨 주었다고 했다.

3 주어진 글에서 언급된 Heritage Heroes group에 대해 들어 봤다고 말하는 (D), 프로그램의 구체적인 활동을 설명하는 (B), 활동에 관심을 표하는 (C), (C)의 말에 동의하는 (A)의 순서로 이어지는 것이 자연스럽다.

4 빈칸 뒤에서 해당 계단이 어떻게 사람들의 행동을 변화시켰는지 말하고 있으므로 ② '어떻게 그렇게 하지?'가 들어가는 것이 가장 적절하다.

오답

① 그들이 왜 그걸 했지?

③ 그건 어디에서 개최되고 있니?

④ 그들에게 무슨 문제가 있니?

⑤ 누가 이 아이디어를 생각해 냈니?

5 주어진 문장과 ② '선거결과가 너무 막상막하이다. 우리는 재

투표를 해야 한다.'에서 close는 '우열을 가리기 힘든, 막상막하의'라는 뜻이다.

오답

① 눈 감아 ─ 네가 놀랄 만한 선물이 있어.

③ 그 가게는 약 다섯 달 전에 문을 닫았다.

④ 그는 토론을 끝내려고 했다.

⑤ 나는 오빠와는 잘 어울리지 못하지만, 언니와는 매우 친하다.

6 '(모임 등에) 가다'라는 뜻을 가진 말은 make it이다.

7 '나는 고전보다 현대 문학을 선호한다'라는 뜻으로, ③ modern과 바꿔 쓸 수 있다.

오답 ① 예술적인   ② 유익한

④ 전형적인   ⑤ 전통적인

8 전치사 of 뒤에는 목적어로 명사 형태가 와야 하므로, go를 동명사 going으로 고쳐야 한다.

③ 나는 밤에 혼자 나가는 것이 두렵지 않다.

오답

① 내가 일하고 있을 때 너는 뭐하고 있었니?

② 불평하는 것은 예기치 못한 결과를 가져올 수 있다.

④ 네가 정시에 오는 것이 중요하다.

⑤ 저희를 초대해 주시다니 정말 친절하시군요.

9 stars와 shine은 능동의 관계이므로 shined를 현재분사 shining으로 고쳐야 한다.

② 작은 등불처럼 빛나는 별들 좀 봐!

오답

① 나는 내가 좋아하는 감독이 제작한 새 영화를 봤다.

③ 그는 검은 마스크를 쓰고 있는 남자를 쳐다보았다.

④ 우리는 흙으로 만든 작은 집을 보았다.

⑤ 그녀는 옆에 강이 있는 마을에서 자랐다.

10 이 경기가 윈스턴 고등학교 4학년 학생들에게 있어서 마지막 홈 경기였다는 내용으로 미루어, (이기려는) ③ '의지가 확고했다'가 들어가는 것이 가장 적절하다.

오답 ① 만족스러운   ② 느긋한

④ 미심쩍은   ⑤ 지친

11 원래 공을 들고 뛰던 선수가 자신이 직접 할 수 있는 일을 Ethan이 할 수 있도록 기회를 준 내용이므로 ⑤ '… 대신에'가 가장 적절하다.

오답 ① …의 결과로서   ② …에도 불구하고

③ …에 관해 말하자면   ④ … 때문에

12 (A) 문장이 과거시제이므로 could가 적절하다.

(B) seemed와 move가 같은 시점이고, 현재 진행중인 경기 상황을 생생하게 묘사하고 있으므로 be moving이 적절하다.

(C) 지각동사 see의 목적격 보어가 들어갈 자리이므로 동사원

형 cross가 적절하다.

13 (A) 문맥상 Ethan의 '헌신'이라는 의미의 dedication이 적절하다. demonstration은 '시위; 설명; 입증'이라는 뜻이다.

(B) 문맥상 '붐비는'이라는 의미의 crowded가 적절하다.

(C) 문맥상 '신체적인'이라는 의미의 physical이 적절하다. mental은 '정신적인'이라는 뜻이다.

14 가주어 It으로 시작하는 문장이므로 의미상 주어(for+목적격)와 진주어(to부정사구)를 넣어 문장을 만든다.

15 '특히 목적이나 활동 같은 무언가에 헌신하는 자질'을 의미하는 단어는 commitment이다.

16 the one을 수식하는 현재분사 형태인 ② making이 가장 적절하다.

17 윗글의 문장 'He had a special talent for calming people down and bringing out the best in them.'에 언급되어 있다.

18 주어진 단락 마지막에 언급된 재활용의 장점을 서술한 (A), 이와 대비되는 재활용의 단점을 서술한 (C), (C)의 마지막에 언급된 업사이클링을 'This new approach'로 받아 그에 관한 설명을 이어가는 (B)의 순서로 이어지는 것이 가장 적절하다.

19 쓰레기를 처리하는 방식으로 재활용보다 더 환경친화적이면서 재미까지 있는 업사이클링을 소개하고 있으므로 ② '쓰레기를 처리하는 더 나은 방식을 소개하려고'가 가장 적절하다.

오답

① 재활용의 단점을 설명하려고

③ 청량음료의 해로운 영향을 보여주려고

④ 천연자원 보존의 필요성을 홍보하려고

⑤ 사람들이 환경친화적 제품을 사용하도록 권장하려고

20 주어진 문장이 Similarly로 시작하므로, 앞에서 낡은 물건을 창의적으로 재사용한 한 가지 사례에 대한 설명이 끝나고, 새로운 예에 대한 설명이 이어지는 ③에 들어가는 것이 가장 적절하다.

21 글에 언급된 두 가지 사례로 미루어 겉보기에는 '쓸모 없는 (useless)' 물건이 일상생활에 '유용한(useful)' 것으로 변형된다고 요약할 수 있다.

22 첫 문장에서 '작은 일상 용품과 더불어, 더 커다란 것들도 업사이클될 수 있다'고 했으므로 그 전에는 작은 일상 용품들이 업사이클된 사례가 나오는 것이 가장 적절하다.

23 (A)는 철강 공장의 용도를 변경하기로 결정한 주체인 'The German government'를, (B)는 같은 문장의 앞에 언급된 'Many of the buildings'를 가리킨다.

24 (A) 문맥상 쓰레기의 양을 '줄이다'라는 의미의 reduce나 lessen이 적절하다.

(B) 단락의 맨 앞에서 언급한 'Creative thinking'으로 미루어 '창의성'이라는 의미의 creativity가 들어가는 것이 가장 적절하다.

25 'turn ... into ~(…를 ~로 바꾸다)'를 활용하여 순서에 맞게 배열한다.

Lesson 3. Sound Life

Vocabulary Test   p. 37

1. (1) 실망시키다 (2) 극복하다 (3) 간행물 (4) 필수적인
(5) advantage (6) satisfied (7) bold (8) concentrate
2. (1) boring (2) disturb (3) random (4) lacks
3. (1) was, about, to (2) break, out (3) consists, of
(4) deal, with
4. (1) unfit (2) dominant (3) soar (4) apologize

Communicative Functions   p. 38

1. (1) I'm, worried, about (2) Why, don't, you
2. (B), (E), (A), (D), (C)

Discovering Grammar   p. 39

1. (1) what (2) feel (3) repaired
2. (1) helped, me, fix (2) what, she, loved

Grammar Test   p. 40

1. (1) eat (2) wait (3) delivered (4) promise **2.** (1) What she was looking for (2) what 또는 the thing (that[which]) (3) helps you (to) sleep (4) let people park **3.** (1) what (2) that (3) that (4) what **4.** (1) What I want is for you to be (2) had the room painted last weekend (3) let their children develop poor eating habits (4) what the boy was carrying

1 (1) 목적어와 목적격 보어가 능동의 관계이므로 동사원형 eat이 알맞다.

(2) 목적어와 목적격 보어가 능동의 관계이므로 동사원형 wait이 알맞다.

(3) 목적어와 목적격 보어가 수동의 관계이므로 과거분사 delivered가 알맞다.

(4) 목적어와 목적격 보어가 능동의 관계이므로 동사원형 promise가 알맞다.

2 (1) 문장의 주어 역할을 하는 명사절을 이끌며 선행사를 포함하는 관계대명사 what이 필요하다.

(2) tell의 직접목적어 역할을 하는 명사절을 이끄는 관계대명사 what이 와야 한다. 또는 tell의 직접목적어 the thing과 목적격 관계대명사 that[which]이 와야 한다. 이때 that[which]은 생략 가능하다.

(3) 준사역동사 help의 목적격 보어로는 to부정사나 동사원형이 와야 한다.

(4) 목적어와 목적격 보어가 능동의 관계이므로 목적격 보어로 동사원형이 와야 한다.

3 (1) 선행사를 포함하고 문장의 보어 역할을 하는 명사절을 이끄는 관계대명사 what이 필요하다.

(2) The building을 선행사로 하는 목적격 관계대명사 that이 필요하다.

(3) everything을 선행사로 하는 목적격 관계대명사 that이 필요하다.

(4) 선행사를 포함하고 uses의 목적어 역할을 하는 명사절을 이끄는 관계대명사 what이 필요하다.

4 (1) 관계대명사 what이 이끄는 명사절이 문장의 주어 역할을 한다.

(2)~(3) 「사역동사+목적어+목적격 보어」의 어순으로 문장을 만든다.

(4) 관계대명사 what이 이끄는 명사절이 took away의 목적어 역할을 한다.

1. ⑤   **2.** ②   **3.** ①   **4.** the picture (for the final cover)   **5.** ②   **6.** ④

1 그림의 또 다른 요소가 심적 안정과 치유에 도움을 준다는 설명을 추가하고 있으므로 빈칸에 ⑤ '게다가'가 들어가는 것이 적절하다.

    오답 ① 반면에 ② 그러나 ③ 그렇지 않으면 ④ 그런데도

2 ② 긍정적이고 활기찬 감정을 이끌어낸다고 서술된 것은 노란색이다.

3 주어진 문장의 that이 가리키는 Walter의 일이 언급되는 문장 뒤면서 접속사 However(그러나)를 사용해 주어진 문장과 반대되는 내용을 서술하고 있는 문장 앞인 ①에 들어가는 것이 가장 적절하다.

4 바로 앞의 두 문장에서 it이 가리키는 바를 찾을 수 있다.

5 앉아서 모험을 꿈만 꾸지 말고 바로 지금 나아가 실현시키라고 했으므로 ②가 가장 적절하다.

6 Jonathan이 다른 갈매기들과 다름을 서술한 주어진 글 다음에 Jonathan이 다른 갈매기들과 어떻게 다른지를 설명하는 (C), (C)에 언급된 연습을 하는 도중에 무리를 만났다는 내용의 (A), (A)에 언급된 Jonathan의 기대와는 다른 갈매기들의 반응을 나타낸 (B)의 순서로 이어지는 것이 적절하다.

1. ④   **2.** (D), (B), (A), (C)   **3.** ③   **4.** ③   **5.** ③
6. what   **7.** carry, on   **8.** had, trouble, reading
9. ②   **10.** ④   **11.** ②   **12.** overcome   **13.** ③
14. ③   **15.** (A) used (B) filled   **16.** ②   **17.** ⑤
18. ②   **19.** ②   **20.** how wonderful soaring above the clouds really feels

1 남자가 아침으로 간단히 먹을 수 있는 것을 물어보았으므로 ④ '바나나를 먹어보는 건 어때? 조리할 필요가 전혀 없잖아.'가 여자의 응답으로 적절하다.

    오답
    ① 사실, 너는 좀 더 집중해야 해.
    ② 수업 중에는 휴대전화를 사용할 수 없다는 걸 명심해.
    ③ 걱정 마. 내가 그걸 네게 빌려줄게.
    ⑤ 아마 너는 아침에 운동하는 것을 시작해보는 게 좋겠어.

2 주어진 질문에 따라 flashcards의 용도를 설명하고 자신의 걱정을 언급하는 (D), 발표 걱정에 대해 격려하고 연습을 더 하라고 권유하는 (B), 연습을 해봤지만 혼자 하기 힘들다는 (A), 연습하는 것을 도와주겠다는 (C)의 순서로 대화가 이어지는 것이 적절하다.

3 ③ 남자는 자신의 경험담을 들려주며 지나친 걱정이 이로울 게 없다는 충고를 해 주고 있다.

4 routine(일상)의 올바른 뜻풀이는 'the usual way of doing something at a particular time(특정 시간에 어떤 일을 하는 일상적인 방식)'이다.

    오답
    ① 인공적인: 사람에 의해 만들어져 자연적인 것 대신 사용되는
    ② 기회: 어떤 것을 할 수 있는 기회
    ④ 일, 과업: 해야 하는 어떤 것
    ⑤ 깨닫다: 어떤 것을 알게 되거나 이해하다

5 ③ 과식에 대한 내용은 언급되지 않았다.

6 첫 번째 문장에는 '무엇'을 뜻하는 의문사 what이, 두 번째 문장에는 for의 목적어 역할을 하는 명사절을 이끄는 관계대명사 what이 와야 한다.

7 carry on: …을 계속하다

8 have trouble v-ing: …하는 데 어려움을 겪다

9 fall into place는 '꼭 들어맞다'라는 의미이다.
    ② 퍼즐 조각들이 꼭 들어맞았다.

    오답
    ① 규칙적인 운동은 스트레스를 덜어줄 수 있다.
    ③ 그녀는 나를 속여서 그것을 사게 했다.
    ④ 그녀는 충실하게 그것을 상사에게 보고했다.
    ⑤ 그는 매일 한 시간씩 운동한다.

10 예술이 감정을 치유해줄 수 있다는 내용의 글이므로 빈칸에는 ④ '당신의 마음에 사기를 높이는 영향을 미칠 수 있다'가 들어가는 것이 적절하다.

    오답
    ① 십 대에게 유해할 수 있다
    ② 더 높은 질의 삶으로 이끈다
    ③ 당신의 뇌에 스트레스를 줄 것이다
    ⑤ 당신이 다른 사람의 관점을 이해하게 해 준다

11 주어진 문장의 these cool colors가 지칭하는 'the green and blue space'가 나오는 문장 바로 뒤인 ②에 들어가는 것이 적절하다.

12 '무언가 어려운 일에 대처하거나 그것을 조정하는 데 성공하

다'라는 의미를 가진 단어는 overcome(극복하다)이다.

13 윗글의 밑줄 친 to form은 결과의 의미를 나타내는 부사적 용법의 to부정사이다.

③ 그녀는 자라서 유명한 댄서가 되었다.

오답

① 나는 그 소식을 듣고 매우 기뻤다. (감정의 원인을 나타내는 부사적 용법)

② 마실 것 좀 주실 수 있나요? (형용사적 용법)

④ 그는 외국 여행하는 것을 좋아한다. (명사적 용법)

⑤ 나는 질문을 하기 위해 손을 들었다. (목적을 나타내는 부사적 용법)

14 (A) seem to-v: …인 것 같다

(B) 지각동사(watch)의 목적격 보어로 동사원형(work)이나 현재분사(working)를 써야 한다.

(C) 전치사의 목적어로는 동명사 형태가 오는 것이 적절하다.

15 (A) the pictures와 use가 수동의 관계이므로 과거분사 used를 써야 한다.

(B) a boring life와 fill이 수동의 관계이므로 과거분사 filled를 써야 한다.

16 빈칸 뒤에 앞부분과 상반된 내용이 이어지고 있으므로 ② '하지만'이 들어가는 것이 적절하다.

오답 ① 게다가 ③ 그러므로 ④ 비슷하게 ⑤ 예를 들어

17 ⑤ 윗글 16~17행에서 사진작가를 찾았다고 했다.

18 빈칸 뒤에 Jonathan이 다른 갈매기들과 다르게 행동하는 모습을 서술한 내용이 이어지므로 빈칸에는 ② '남들과 다르다'가 들어가는 것이 적절하다.

오답

① 다른 이들의 의견을 수용해야 한다

③ 항상 무리의 일원이 되고 싶어한다

④ 새로운 것을 시도할 용기가 없다

⑤ 자신이 무엇을 원하는지 깨닫지 못한다

19 ② '…가 ~하기를 기대하다'라는 의미를 나타내려면 「expect+목적어+to-v」 구문을 써야 한다.

20 동사 knows의 목적어로 쓰인 의문사절 형태가 되어야 하므로, 「의문사+주어+동사」의 어순이 되도록 배열한다.

Lesson 4. Toward a Better World

Vocabulary Test   p. 49

1. (1) …할 여유가 있다　(2) 무서운, 겁나는　(3) 가르치다
(4) 의심, 의문　(5) starve　(6) charity　(7) hut
(8) self-confidence

2. (1) ordinary　(2) relief　(3) financial　(4) victims

3. (1) appearance　(2) construction　(3) helped, out
(4) sign, up

4. (1) suspend　(2) exchange　(3) annual　(4) volunteer

Communicative Functions   p. 50

1. (1) I, wish, we, could　(2) I, think, is, better, than

2. ⓑ, ⓐ, ⓒ

Discovering Grammar   p. 51

1. (1) where　(2) when　(3) how

2. (1) long, enough, to　(2) warm, enough, to

Grammar Test   p. 52

1. (1) where　(2) when　(3) How　(4) why　**2.** (1) enough old → old enough　(2) to he → that he (3) the way how → the way 또는 how　(4) when → why　**3.** (1) Her smile is bright enough to make other people happy.　(2) He is tall enough to reach the ceiling.　(3) She ran so fast that no one could catch her.　(4) My laptop is so light that I can carry it anywhere.　**4.** (1) is not wide enough to cover the bed　(2) the place where the accident occurred (3) the time when we have to make a decision

1 (1) 선행사가 장소를 나타내는 The apartment이므로 관계부사 where가 알맞다.

(2) 선행사가 때를 나타내는 the day이므로 관계부사 when이 알맞다.

(3) 문맥상 방법을 나타내는 관계부사 How가 알맞다.

(4) 선행사가 이유를 나타내는 the reason이므로 관계부사 why가 알맞다.

2 (1) enough가 부사로 쓰일 때 「형용사/부사+enough+to-v」의 어순이 되어야 한다.

(2) '매우 …하여 ~할 수 있다'라는 의미의 「so+형용사/부사+that+주어+can」을 써야 한다.

(3) 방법을 나타내는 선행사 the way와 관계부사 how는 같이 쓸 수 없으므로 둘 중 하나를 생략해야 한다.

(4) 이유를 나타내는 reason을 선행사로 하고 관계사절 안에서 부사 역할을 하므로 관계부사 why가 와야 한다.

3 (1)~(2) '…하기에 충분히 ~한/하게'라는 의미의 「형용사/부사+enough+to-v」을 이용한다.

(3)~(4) '매우 …하여 ~할 수 있다'라는 의미의 「so+형용사/부사+that+주어+can」을 이용한다.

4 (1) 「형용사/부사+enough+to-v」의 어순에 유의한다.

(2) 관계부사 where를 이용해 선행사 the place를 수식하는 관계부사절을 만든다.

(3) 관계부사 when을 이용해 선행사 the time을 수식하는 관계부사절을 만든다.

Reading Test

pp. 53~54

1. ① **2.** 집이 자신과 가족을 모든 것으로부터 지켜주는 특별한 공간인 것 **3.** ② **4.** ⑤ **5.** ① **6.** ③

1 ① 스트레스의 원인과 꿈의 관계에 대한 설명은 글의 전체 흐름과 관련이 없다.

2 바로 앞 문장에서 this의 내용을 알 수 있다.

3 ② 봉사에 대한 발표를 보고 감동을 받아 참여했다.

4 집을 지어 줄 가족을 만났다는 주어진 글 다음에, 이 가족이 살고 있는 오두막에 대한 내용인 (C), 오두막에 대해 추가로 묘사하는 (B), 그에 대한 필자의 심경인 (A)의 순서로 이어지는 것이 적절하다.

5 주어진 문장의 us가 가리키는 바가 앞에 제시되어 있고, 뒤에 일이 힘들었다는 내용이 이어져 집을 지어본 경험이 없었다는 주어진 문장과 자연스럽게 이어지는 ①에 들어가는 것이 가장 적절하다.

6 집 짓기 봉사활동을 마친 후 여러 가지 배운 점이 많았다고 했으므로 ③ '감사하는'이 적절하다.

오답 ① 궁금해하는   ② 실망한
④ 의심스러운   ⑤ 당황한

단원평가
pp. 55~58

1. ④ **2.** ⑤ **3.** ④ **4.** ⑤ **5.** ② **6.** might, as, well **7.** take, for, granted **8.** ④ **9.** to, see **10.** ③ **11.** 가난한 사람들을 위한 집을 짓는 것을 돕기 위해 세계의 여러 곳으로 갈 자원봉사자를 필요로 하는 프로그램 **12.** not big enough to house all the family members **13.** ① **14.** ④ **15.** celebrate **16.** ④ **17.** 새로운 집의 완성을 축하하기 위해 파티를 연 것 **18.** (1) amazed → amazing (2) to smile → smiling **19.** ② **20.** ①

1 모자 뜨기가 아픈 아기들에게 어떻게 도움이 될 수 있는지 묻고 있으므로 이에 대해 설명하는 ④ '그 모자가 아기들을 따뜻하게 해주고 목숨을 구해줄 수 있어.'가 응답으로 가장 적절하다.

오답
① 잠깐만. 뭔가 잘못된 것 같아.
② 그것에 대해 나한테 이야기해 줄래?
③ 멋지다. 그건 그들을 도울 수 있는 좋은 방법이야.
⑤ 아픈 사람들을 도울 방법에 대해 더 생각해 봐야겠어.

2 ⑤ 마지막에 남자가 물건을 그냥 가지고 있는 것보다 바자회에서 파는 게 낫다고 말하고 있다.

3 ④ 개최 장소는 언급되지 않았다.

4 ⑤ '어떤 것을 믿지 않거나 확신이 없는 감정'이라는 의미가 있는 단어는 doubt(의심, 의문)이다. mission은 '임무'라는 의미이다.

오답
① 괜찮은, 제대로 된: 좋거나 충분히 괜찮은
② 평범한: 특이하거나 다르지 않은
③ 불평하다: 어떤 것에 대해 만족하지 않는다고 말하다
④ 외모: 어떤 사람이나 무언가가 겉으로 보이는 방식

5 show up은 '나타나다'라는 뜻이다.
② 그는 차려 입고 나타났다.

오답
① 우리는 어린 학생들에게 다가갈 새로운 방법을 모색해야 한다.
③ 어떻게 회원 가입을 할 수 있죠?
④ 우리는 댄스 대회에 참가했다.
⑤ 그는 라디오를 조립하고 분해하며 시간을 보냈다.

6 might as well: …하는 편이 낫다

7 take ... for granted: …을 당연시하다

8 주어진 문장에서 '불행하게도 이는 모든 사람에게 공통되는

정답 및 해설 **135**

상황은 아니다.'라고 했으므로, 앞에는 긍정적인 상황이 나오고 뒤에는 많은 사람들이 처한 불행한 현실이 제시되는 ④에 들어가는 것이 가장 적절하다.

9 결과를 나타내는 부사적 용법의 to부정사로 바꿔쓸 수 있다.

10 (A) a program을 선행사로 하고 관계사절 안에서 주어 역할을 하므로 관계대명사 that이 적절하다.
(B) 주어 I가 '감동을 받는' 것이므로 과거분사 touched가 적절하다.
(C) 숫자를 포함하는 구체적인 기간이 올 때는 '…동안'이라는 의미를 나타내기 위해 전치사 for를 사용한다.

11 바로 앞 문장에서 it이 가리키는 바를 찾을 수 있다.

12 「형용사/부사+enough+to-v」의 어순에 유의하여 배열한다.

13 가족이 살고 있던 집의 상태가 너무 열악했으므로 빈칸에 ① '충격적인'이 들어가는 것이 가장 적절하다.
오답 ② 즐거운   ③ 멋진
④ 가치를 따질 수 없는 ⑤ 매혹적인

14 ④ 오두막은 눕기는커녕 앉을 자리도 거의 없을 정도의 크기였다고 했다.

15 '어떤 일이 특별하다는 것을 보여주기 위해 즐거운 무언가를 하다'라는 영영 뜻풀이에 맞는 단어는 celebrate(축하하다)이다.

16 (A)의 would는 과거의 반복된 동작이나 습관(…하곤 했다)을 나타낸다.
④ 그녀는 토요일마다 수영을 하러 가곤 했다.
오답
① Jack은 일을 그만둘 것이라 말했다. (시제 일치를 위해 쓰인 will의 과거형)
② 창문을 닫아주시겠어요? (요청, 제안)
③ 그 축제에 가는 것은 재미있을 것이다. (추측)
⑤ 그는 고집이 세다. 그는 내 말을 듣지 않을 것이다. (강한 의지)

17 바로 앞 문장에 It이 가리키는 내용이 나와 있다.

18 (1) 목적어 it이 감정을 유발하는 것이므로 능동의 의미를 나타내는 현재분사 amazing을 써야 한다.
(2) '…하는 것을 멈추다'라는 의미를 나타내려면 「stop v-ing」를 써야 한다. 「stop to-v」는 '…하기 위해 멈추다'라는 의미이다.

19 빈칸 뒤에서 살 곳이 없는 많은 사람들이 집을 지어 주고 싶게 하는 이유라고 했으므로, ② '모든 사람이 제대로 된 집에서 살 자격이 있다'가 들어가는 것이 가장 적절하다.

오답
① 새 친구를 사귀는 것은 어렵다
③ 집은 사람들의 문화를 반영한다
④ 사람들에게 가족은 다양한 것을 의미한다
⑤ 우리는 자연으로부터 디자인 아이디어를 얻을 수 있다

20 ① something을 선행사로 하는 주격 관계대명사가 들어가야 하므로 that으로 고쳐야 한다.

1학기 기말고사   pp. 59~64

1. ⑤   **2.** ⑤   **3.** ⑤   **4.** ⑤   **5.** ③   **6.** ④
7. ③   **8.** interesting, enough, to, finish   **9.** had, delivered   **10.** ⑤   **11.** ⑤   **12.** (A) calming (B) looking   **13.** ③   **14.** (1) happening → happen (2) not be brave → not being brave   **15.** ②   **16.** ⑤
17. he is no longer satisfied flying in formation with the other seagulls   **18.** ④   **19.** mission   **20.** ①
21. the best way to end such an incredible experience   **22.** ②   **23.** ④   **24.** ③   **25.** ④

1 고민을 말하는 상대방에게 해결책을 제안하는 ⑤ '자기 전에 따뜻한 물에 목욕을 해 보지 그래?'가 들어가는 것이 자연스럽다.
오답
① 사실, 나 수업 중에 잠들었어.
② 도움이 필요하면 내게 알려줘.
③ 다음에 늦으면 큰일 날 줄 알아.
④ 그거 좋은 생각이다. 너도 그걸 한번 해봐.

2 ⑤ 남자는 여자에게 자기 집으로 오라고 했다.

3 커피를 마실 형편이 되지 않는 사람들을 돕는 Suspended Coffee(맡겨 둔 커피) 운동에 대해 이야기하고 있으므로, 대화의 주제로 ⑤ '도움이 필요한 사람들을 돕는 자선 프로그램'이 가장 적절하다.
오답
① 커피의 건강상의 이점
② 무료 커피를 받을 수 있는 곳
③ 자선 행사에 신청하는 방법

④ 카페 계산원의 실수

4 주어진 문장은 food-sharing fridge가 무엇인지에 대해 설명하는 부분에 들어가야 하므로 ⑤가 가장 적절하다.

5 ③ broaden의 영영 뜻풀이는 'to make something include more things(어떤 것이 더 많은 것을 포함하게 하다)'가 되어야 한다.

[오답]
① 용기: 용감해지는 능력
② 돕다: 누군가를 또는 무언가를 돕다
④ 증서: 어떤 일이 일어났다는 공식적인 증거가 되는 문서
⑤ 감동한: 누군가가 한 일에 의해 행복해하고 감사하는

6 consist of는 '…으로 이루어지다[구성되다]'라는 의미이다.
④ 그 책은 일곱 개의 장으로 구성되어 있다.

[오답]
① 지붕이 계속 새고 있다.
② 많은 사람들이 투표할 권리를 당연하게 여긴다.
③ 그는 항상 아침에 일어나는 데에 어려움을 겪는다.
⑤ 그 남자는 열차에 막 올라타려던 참이었다.

7 • 장소를 나타내는 a place를 선행사로 하고 관계사절 안에서 부사 역할을 해야 하므로 관계부사 where가 들어가야 한다.
• 선행사가 없고 관계사절 안에서 목적어 역할을 해야 하므로 선행사를 포함한 관계대명사 what이 들어가야 한다.

8 「형용사/부사+enough+to-v」: …할 정도로 ~한[하게]

9 사역동사의 목적어와 목적격 보어가 수동의 관계일 때는 목적격 보어로 과거분사를 쓴다.

10 (A) 문맥상 걱정을 '덜어준다'는 의미가 되어야 하므로 relieve가 적절하다. deepen은 '깊게 하다; 심화시키다'라는 의미이다.
(B) 문맥상 다양한 '관점'이라는 의미가 되어야 하므로 perspectives가 적절하다. prospective는 '장래의, 유망한'이라는 의미이다.
(C) 문맥상 '사기를 높이는' 효과라는 의미가 되어야 하므로 uplifting이 적절하다. discouraging은 '낙담시키는'이라는 의미이다.

11 예술이 감정을 치유해 줄 수 있다는 내용의 글이므로 주제로는 ⑤ '정신 건강을 향상시키는 방법으로서의 예술'이 적절하다.

[오답]
① 감정을 조절하는 방법
② 걱정거리를 날려버리는 방법
③ 건강의 비결인 약
④ 예술을 바라보고 감상하는 방법

12 (A) '진정시키는'이라는 능동의 의미이므로 현재분사의 형태가 되어야 한다.
(B) 절 안에서 주어 역할을 해야 하므로 동명사의 형태가 되어야 한다.

13 바로 앞 문장에서 이 그림의 빨간색을 보면 화를 발산할 수 있다고 했고, 두 번째 단락 끝부분에서 화가 심해지지 않고 차츰 사라진다고 한 것으로 보아 ③ '마음을 진정시키는 데 도움이 된다'가 빈칸에 가장 적절하다.

[오답]
① 전혀 인상적이지 않다
② 당신을 더 화나게 만든다
④ 심각한 질문을 던진다
⑤ 순수한 행복을 보여준다

14 (1) 사역동사 make의 목적격 보어로는 동사원형이 와야 한다.
(2) 전치사 about의 목적어 역할을 해야 하므로 동명사의 형태가 되어야 한다.

15 윗글에서 모험을 꿈만 꾸지 말고 앞으로 나아가 실현시키라고 했으므로 '당신 자신을 믿고 지금 당신의 꿈을 <u>추구하도록</u> 하라.'는 내용이 되는 것이 가장 적절하다.

[오답]
① 바꾸다 　　　 ③ 포기하다
④ 상상하다 　　 ⑤ 기록하다

16 주어진 문장은 Jonathan이 동료들로부터 냉대를 받았다는 내용이며 Instead(대신에)라는 표현으로 보아 앞에 이와 상반된 내용이 나오는 것이 적절하므로, 동료들로부터 비행 실력을 칭찬받을 것이라 기대했다는 문장 뒤인 ⑤에 들어가는 것이 적절하다.

17 '더는 만족할 수 없다'는 내용 뒤에 때를 나타내는 분사구문이 이어지는 형태임을 감안하여 적절히 순서를 배열한다.

18 주어진 글에서 언급한 봉사활동에 참여하기로 했다는 (C), though라는 표현을 사용해 상반된 내용을 이야기하는 (A), (A)에서 언급된 의문에 대해 이어서 말하는 (B)의 순서로 이어지는 것이 가장 적절하다.

19 '어떤 사람이나 한 무리의 사람들에게 하도록 주어지는 중요한 일'를 의미하는 단어는 mission(사명, 임무)이다.

20 ① '불타는, 뜨거운'이라는 능동의 의미를 나타내야 하므로 현재분사 burning이 되어야 한다.

21 형용사적 용법의 to부정사구가 the best way를 수식하고, 「such+a[an]+형용사+명사」 구문이 쓰인다는 점에 유의하여 순서를 배열한다.

22 ② 헌 집의 일부를 새집의 재료로 사용했다고 했다.

23 빈칸 앞뒤로 the chance를 수식하는 말들이 나열되고 있으므로, 문맥상 ④ '가장 중요하게는'이 가장 적절하다.

오답 ① 그 결과로 　　② 예를 들어
　　③ 다시 말하면 　　⑤ 반면에

24 (A) 이유를 나타내는 절을 이끄는 접속사 that이 적절하다.
(B) everyone은 단수 취급하므로 deserves가 적절하다.
(C) 이유를 나타내는 the reason을 선행사로 하는 관계부사 why가 적절하다.

25 밑줄 친 to live는 형용사적 용법의 to부정사이다.
④ 동물들은 지진을 예측하는 능력을 갖고 있다.

오답
① 그는 차를 마시러 만나자고 나에게 전화했다. (목적을 나타내는 부사적 용법)
② 방해해서 미안해요. (감정의 원인을 나타내는 부사적 용법)
③ 그녀는 노인들을 돕고 싶어한다. (명사적 용법)
⑤ 나는 사무실에 갔는데 창문이 열려있는 것을 발견했다. (결과를 나타내는 부사적 용법)

Lesson 5. What Matters Most

Vocabulary Test
p. 67

1. (1) 장점　 (2) 시범　 (3) 거절[사양]하다　 (4) 정확한
(5) disguise　 (6) eventually　 (7) entire　 (8) wound
2. (1) exhausted　 (2) fulfill　 (3) recognize　 (4) ensure
3. (1) as, though　 (2) came, across　 (3) property
(4) effective
4. (1) sociable　 (2) respond　 (3) formal　 (4) modify

Communicative Functions
p. 68

1. (1) It, is, important, to　 (2) are, you, interested, in
2. (B), (D), (C), (A)

Discovering Grammar
p. 69

1. (1) had been　 (2) have done　 (3) Walking
2. (1) 라디오를 들으면서, 그는 저녁 식사를 준비했다.
(2) 비를 맞았기 때문에, 나는 감기에 걸렸다.

Grammar Test
p. 70

1. (1) Entering the room　 (2) (Being) Wounded badly
(3) Trying to comfort himself　 (4) Having a lot of
work to do　 **2.** (1) drinking　 (2) Written　 (3) Finishing
(4) Being taken　 **3.** (1) I could not have found the
way　 (2) she had not joined the team　 (3) I had known
the facts　 **4.** (1) If she had been there with you,
she would have been very happy.　 (2) If he had
scored a goal, he would have felt better.　 (3) If I had
noticed the mistake, I would have corrected it.

1 부사절을 분사구문으로 만들 때는 접속사와 주어를 생략하고 동사를 주어와의 관계에 따라 현재분사 또는 과거분사로 바꿔 준다.
(1) 접속사(When)와 주어(he)를 생략하고 entered를 현재분사로 바꾼다.
(2) 접속사(Because)와 주어(she)를 생략하고 was를 현재분사로 바꾼다. Being은 생략할 수 있다.
(3) 접속사(When)와 주어(he)를 생략하고, tries를 현재분사로 바꾼다.
(4) 접속사(Because)와 주어(he)를 생략하고, had를 현재분사로 바꾼다.

2 (1) 주어 Grandma와 drink가 능동의 관계이므로 현재분사가 적절하다.
(2) 주어 this book과 write가 수동의 관계이므로 과거분사가 적절하다.
(3) 주어 I와 finish가 능동의 관계이므로 현재분사가 적절하다.
(4) 주어 his advice와 take가 수동의 관계이므로 과거분사가 적절하다.

3 (1) if절의 had not helped로 보아 가정법 과거완료임을 알 수 있으므로, 주절의 동사를 「조동사의 과거형+have+p.p.」로 고쳐야 한다.
(2) 주절의 could not have completed로 보아 가정법 과거 완료임을 알 수 있으므로, if절의 동사를 「had+p.p.」로 고쳐야 한다.

(3) 주절의 could have done으로 보아 가정법 과거완료임을 알 수 있으므로, if절의 동사를 「had+p.p.」로 고쳐야 한다.

4 「If+주어+had+p.p., 주어+조동사의 과거형+have+p.p.」의 형태를 활용하되, 과거 사실과 반대되는 내용을 표현해야 하므로 부정문을 긍정문으로 바꿔야 한다는 점에 유의한다.

Reading Test
pp. 71~72

1. ③ **2.** ⑤ **3.** (A) the man (B) the king **4.** ④
5. ② **6.** 지난 전쟁에서 왕이 남자의 형제를 죽이고 재산을 앗아갔기 때문

1 왕이 은자를 찾아 떠났다는 내용의 주어진 글 다음에, 은자의 오두막에 도착한 (B), 은자가 (B)에서 언급된 질문에 답하기를 거부하는 (C), 왕이 자신의 질문에 답해줄 수 없다면 알려달라고 말하는 (A)의 순서로 이어지는 것이 가장 적절하다.

2 ⑤ 은자는 왕의 질문을 주의 깊게 들었지만 대답하기를 거절했다.

3 해당 문장의 앞부분에서 각각의 he가 가리키는 대상을 알 수 있다.

4 완전히 지친 것은 왕이 누워서 잠든 것의 원인이므로, ④ '…때문에'가 가장 적절하다.
오답 ① …하는 동안 ② …까지
③ …이긴 하지만 ⑤ …하기 전에

5 아침에 눈을 뜨자 남자가 용서를 구하지만 왕은 그 이유를 알 수 없어 혼란스러워했다. 이후 남자의 설명을 듣고 적을 친구로 만들어 기뻤다는 내용이 나오므로 ② '혼란스러운 → 행복한'이 가장 적절하다.
오답 ① 화가 난 → 후회하는 ③ 안도한 → 겁에 질린
④ 놀란 → 실망한 ⑤ 고마워하는 → 우울한

6 바로 앞 문장에서 (A)의 이유를 찾을 수 있다.

단원평가
pp. 73~76

1. ⓑ, ⓐ, ⓒ **2.** ⑤ **3.** ② **4.** ④ **5.** ②
6. ④ **7.** came, across **8.** ⑤ **9.** listened to me, would not have lost **10.** ② **11.** ④ **12.** ③
13. When[As] **14.** ③ **15.** I would have died if you hadn't saved my life **16.** ⑤ **17.** (1) 지금 (2) 지금 같이 있는 사람 (3) 그 사람(지금 같이 있는 사람)에게 좋은 일을 하는 것 **18.** so that he could always know the perfect time **19.** ② **20.** ③

1 여자의 다음 답변이 It's all about ~인 것으로 보아, 첫 번째 빈칸에는 책의 내용을 묻는 말인 ⓑ가 들어가는 것이 적절하다. 두 번째 빈칸에는 책의 주제를 듣고 주제에 대해 질문하는 ⓐ, 마지막 빈칸에는 방법을 묻는 ⓒ가 들어가는 것이 적절하다.

2 ⑤ 자신의 관심분야를 확신하지 못하는 여자에게 봉사활동 등 다양한 경험을 쌓으라고 조언하고 있다.

3 새로운 경험을 하다 보면 자신에게 맞는 것과 맞지 않는 것을 알게 될 수 있다는 남자의 제안에 대해 여자가 할 수 있는 말로는 ② '아, 좋은 생각이네! 시도해볼게.'가 가장 적절하다.
오답
① 물론, 내가 그 일을 도와줄게.
③ 뭔가 새로운 일을 시도해보는 건 어때?
④ 나 친구들이랑 약속이 있어.
⑤ 마지막으로 봉사활동했던 게 언제였어?

4 주어진 문장에 역접의 의미를 나타내는 Despite와 though가 쓰인 것으로 보아, 앞에 긍정적인 내용이 나온 후 많은 비판을 받았다는 상반된 내용이 그 뒤에 이어지는 ④에 들어가는 것이 가장 적절하다.

5 care for는 '…를 돌보다'라는 의미이다.
② 그녀는 언젠가 병자들을 돌보게 될 것이다.
오답
① 그녀를 용서하다니 너는 참 관대하다.
③ 가끔 내 친구들은 내 억양을 놀린다.
④ 나는 그 자물쇠를 어떻게 여는지 알아낼 수 없었다.
⑤ 저희는 완벽한 품질을 보증하기 위해 모든 노력을 다하고 있습니다.

6 ④ '누군가에게 간절히 무언가를 해달라고 요청하다'라는 영영 뜻풀이에 맞는 단어는 beg(간청하다)이다. restore는 '되돌려주다'라는 의미이다.
오답
① 인사하다: 사람들에게 인사하다

② 발표[공표]하다: 사람들에게 무언가에 대해 공식적으로 말하다

③ 빤히 쳐다보다: 사람이나 사물을 오랫동안 바라보다

⑤ 공격하다: 물리적 폭력을 써서 사람들을 다치게 하려고 하다

7 come across: 우연히 마주치다

8 주어 he와 raise는 수동의 관계이므로 과거분사 Raised가 되어야 한다.

⑤ 시골에서 자랐기 때문에, 그는 지하철을 타는 법을 몰랐다.

오답

① TV를 보다가 그는 잠들었다.

② 나는 책을 읽으면서 소파에 앉아있었다.

③ 창문을 열자 그는 상쾌함을 느꼈다.

④ 기진맥진하게 느껴, 그녀는 밖에 나가지 않기로 했다.

9 과거에 실제로 일어난 일을 그와 반대되는 가정으로 바꿔 쓰는 것이므로, 가정법 과거완료 구문을 쓴다.

10 앞 문장에서 답을 얻으려 왔다고 했으므로 none이 의미하는 것은 ② no answers이다.

11 왕은 은자에게 질문에 대한 답을 구하러 갔으나 해가 질 때까지 답을 얻지 못했으므로 ④ '실망한'이 가장 적절하다.

오답 ① 충격받은　　② 감사하는

　　　③ 안도한　　　⑤ 미안해하는

12 앞에서 은자는 평범한 사람만 만났다는 내용이 언급되었으므로, ③ '평범한 농부로 변장했다'는 내용이 들어가는 것이 가장 적절하다.

오답

① 매우 예의 바른 옷차림을 차려입었다

② 그를 기쁘게 하기 위해 많은 돈을 가져갔다

④ 그의 질문을 종이에 적었다

⑤ 평민들을 위한 선물들을 갖고 그곳에 갔다

13 문맥상 때를 나타내는 분사구문이므로, 부사절로 바꿀 때 접속사 When[As]을 써야 한다.

14 (A) 문맥상 '재산'이라는 의미의 property가 적절하다. priority는 '우선 사항'이라는 의미이다.

(B) 문맥상 '알아보다'라는 의미의 recognize가 적절하다. organize는 '조직하다, 정리하다'라는 의미이다.

(C) 문맥상 '기쁜'이라는 의미의 Pleased가 적절하다. Embarrassed는 '당황스러운, 어색한'이라는 의미이다.

15 과거 사실과 반대되는 내용을 나타내는 가정법 과거완료 문장이므로, 「주어+조동사의 과거형+have+p.p. if+주어+had+p. p.」의 순서로 배열하도록 한다.

16 ⑤ 접속사 and 뒤에 오는 절에서 주어 역할을 하는 구를 이끌고 있으므로 동명사 doing이 되어야 한다.

17 지문 하단의 Remember, ... 이후의 문장에 은자가 왕에게 주는 답이 나와있다.

18 '…가 ~할 수 있도록'이라는 의미를 표현하기 위해 「so that+주어+can[could]」 순으로 배열해야 한다.

19 (A) take ... into account: …을 고려하다

(B) in response to ...: …에 대한 응답으로

(C) be famous for ...: …로 유명하다

20 ③ 왕의 질문에 대해 다양한 대답이 나왔다고 했다.

Lesson 6. Beyond the Limits

Vocabulary Test　　　　　　p. 79

1. (1) 매혹[매료]된　(2) 시작[착수]하다　(3) 수송[운송] 수단

(4) 과정　(5) sacrifice　(6) obstacle　(7) persistence

(8) succeed

2. (1) unstable　(2) infection　(3) rescue　(4) evidence

3. (1) unprecedented　(2) make, up, my, mind

(3) in, charge, of　(4) on, account, of

4. (1) excess　(2) injure　(3) disaster　(4) landmark

Communicative Functions　　　　p. 80

1. Have, you, heard, about　**2.** I'm, surprised, that

3. (C), (E), (D), (B)

Discovering Grammar　　　　　p. 81

1. (1) so　(2) that　(3) am　(4) had

2. (1) so poisonous that everybody had to

(2) did I dream that

1. (1) 그녀는 너무 놀라서 거의 말할 수 없었다. (2) 어제는 너무 더워서 나는 산책을 할 수 없었다. (3) 이 프라이팬은 음식이 달라붙지 않도록 코팅되어 있다. (4) 그는 아무도 그를 알아보지 못하도록 야구모자를 쓰고 있었다. **2.** (1) so busy that she couldn't check her email (2) so that they could pass by easily (3) so nervous that he didn't know what to do **3.** (1) had they sat down (2) did I know (3) is she kind (4) did he come back **4.** (1) can she speak Chinese but also Spanish (2) did I expect to meet him again (3) had I gone to bed than I fell asleep

1 「so+형용사+that+주어+동사」 구문은 '너무 …하여 ～하다'로 해석하며, 「so+that+주어+동사」 구문은 '…가 ～하도록'으로 해석한다.

2 (1), (3) '너무 …하여 ～하다'라는 의미를 나타내야 하므로 「so+형용사+that+주어+동사」 순으로 배열한다.
(2) '…가 ～하도록'이라는 의미를 나타내야 하므로 「so+that+주어+동사」 순으로 배열한다.

3 (1) '거의 …하지 않는'이라는 의미를 갖는 부정어 Scarcely가 문두에 왔으므로 주어(they)와 조동사(had)를 도치시켜야 한다.
(2) 부정어 Little이 문두에 왔고 knew는 일반동사이므로 주어(I) 앞에 조동사(did)를 삽입해야 한다. 주어 뒤에는 동사원형(know)이 온다.
(3) 부정어 Not only가 문두에 왔고 be동사 is가 사용되었으므로 does를 빼고 주어(she)와 be동사(is)를 도치시켜야 한다.
(4) 부정어구 Not until the next day가 문두에 왔고 조동사 did가 쓰였으므로 came을 동사원형 come으로 고쳐야 한다.

4 (1) 부정어 Not only가 문두에 왔으므로 주어(she)와 조동사(can)를 도치시켜야 한다.
(2) expected는 일반동사이므로 「조동사(did)+주어+동사원형」의 순서가 되어야 한다.
(3) 부정어 No sooner가 문두에 왔으므로 주어(I)와 조동사(had)를 도치시켜야 한다.

1. ④ **2.** ⓐ a bridge (directly connecting Manhattan and Brooklyn) ⓑ the East River **3.** ① **4.** ⑤ **5.** ⑤

1 1860년대 도시가 성장하여 교통량이 늘었으나 다리를 건설하기에 힘든 여건이었음을 설명하는 단락이다. 따라서 제목으로 가장 적절한 것은 ④ 'East River 다리: 1860년대의 불가능한 꿈'이다.

[오답]
① 뉴욕시의 빠른 성장의 이유
② 뉴요커들이 불안정한 다리들 때문에 언짢아하다
③ 새로운 다리가 뉴요커들에게 더 안전한 통근을 제공하다
⑤ 보트와 연락선: 통근자들이 가장 좋아하는 운송 수단

2 각 문장의 앞부분에서 it이 가리키는 바를 찾을 수 있다.

3 주어진 문장의 such a bridge가 문맥상 첫 문장의 a very high suspension bridge를 의미하고, That is(즉)로 시작하는 문장은 주어진 문장에 대한 부연 설명에 해당하므로 ①에 들어가는 것이 가장 적절하다.

4 어렵고 위험한 작업이 진행중이었다는 주어진 글 다음에, 구체적으로 어떤 위험이 있었는지 설명한 (C), (C)에 언급된 Washington의 병세에 대해 설명하는 (A), 그럼에도 불구하고 Washington이 건설 감독을 계속했다는 (B)의 순서로 이어지는 것이 가장 적절하다.

5 [오답]
① 결혼 전에는 공학에 대해 아는 바가 없었다.
② 남편의 건강이 악화되자 직접 건설 작업을 돕고 나섰다.
③ 대학에 진학하지 않고도 수학과 공학의 전문가가 되었다.
④ 브루클린 다리 공사가 끝날 때까지 업무를 수행했다.

1. ④ **2.** ③ **3.** ③ **4.** ① **5.** see, through **6.** ② **7.** ⑤ **8.** ⑤ **9.** was so interesting that he **10.** 철제 대신 강철 케이블을 사용하는 것, 다리의 도로를 떠받치고 그 위로 사람들이 걸어서 건널 수 있게 하기 위해 두 개의 거대한 석탑을 건설하는 것 **11.** ③ **12.** ⑤ **13.** ④ **14.** ⑤ **15.** step in **16.** ④ **17.** she became the first person to cross the bridge **18.** ① **19.** ⑤ **20.** would have quit

1 개최할 대회에 대해 아는지를 묻는 (D), 어떤 대회인지 정보를 묻는 (B), 그에 대한 답인 (A), 들은 내용을 재확인하는 (C)의 순서로 이어지는 것이 가장 적절하다.

2 마지막 문장에서 3D 프린터가 가져올 영향에 대해 설명하고 있으므로 ③ '그게 우리 삶에 어떤 영향을 미칠까?'가 가장 적절하다.

　오답
① 3D 프린터를 사용해본 적 있니?
② 이 파일 다운로드 하는 것 좀 도와줄래?
④ 비용을 줄이기 위해 무엇을 할 수 있을까?
⑤ 3D 프린터에 대해 어떻게 알게 됐니?

3 글을 읽고 쓰지 못하는 배우가 누군가 읽어주면 이를 토대로 대사를 외웠다는 내용이므로, 응답으로는 ③ '그래도 그에게는 그것(누군가 읽어주는 것을 듣고 대사를 외우는 일)도 쉽지 않을 거야.'가 가장 적절하다.

　오답
① 나를 위해 이것 좀 소리 내서 읽어줄래?
② 우리는 어려움에 처한 친구를 도와야 해.
④ 내 생각에 그는 그다지 재능 있는 배우가 아닌 것 같아.
⑤ 나는 무언가를 아주 쉽게 외울 수 있어.

4 우주공간에서 도구를 잃어버렸을 때에는 비싼 경비를 치러야 한다는 내용 후에 3D 프린터를 이용하면 시간과 비용을 절약할 수 있다는 상반된 내용이 이어지므로 ① '그러나'가 빈칸에 들어가는 것이 적절하다.

　오답　② 따라서　　　　③ 예를 들면
　　　　④ 결과적으로　　⑤ 그럼에도 불구하고

5 see ... through: …을 끝까지 해내다

6 despite는 '…에도 불구하고'라는 의미이다.
② 나는 그의 모든 결점에도 불구하고 그를 사랑했다.

　오답
① 다른 사람들이 뭐라고 말하든 간에, 나는 그 계획을 수행할 것이다.
③ 그녀는 소시지 피자를 특히 좋아한다.
④ 바다표범들은 낮은 조수(썰물)때에 바위 위에 누워 있다.
⑤ 이것은 파일을 영구적으로 삭제할 것입니다.

7 제시된 문장에서 about은 '대략'이라는 의미로 사용되었고, 이와 같은 뜻을 가진 단어는 ⑤ approximately이다.

　오답　① 비슷하게　　　　② 궁극적으로
　　　　③ 동시에　　　　　④ 적절하게

8 부정어 Not only가 문두에 왔으므로 주어(the movie)와 동사 (was)를 도치시켜야 한다.

⑤ 그 영화는 흥미로울 뿐 아니라 또한 매우 감동적이었다.

　오답
① 나는 너무나 피곤하여 회의를 취소했다.
② 그는 자신이 그 일자리를 얻게 될 것을 결코 예상하지 못했다.
③ 나는 안개 속에서 거의 아무것도 볼 수 없었다.
④ 내가 독서에 집중할 수 있도록 TV를 꺼라.

9 문맥상 '너무 …하여 ~하다'라는 의미를 나타내야 하므로 「so+형용사+that+주어+동사」 구문을 쓰는 것이 적절하다.

10 앞의 두 문장에 his ideas의 내용이 서술되어 있다.

11 사람들을 고무시켜 공사가 시작되었다는 내용 뒤에, 이와 상반되게 연락선 사고에 휘말려 사망했다는 내용이 이어지고 있으므로 빈칸에는 ③ '그러나'가 들어가는 것이 가장 적절하다.

12 (A) so가 문두에 와서 도치된 문장으로, 주어가 단수(the number)이므로 was를 써야 한다.
(B) a bridge를 뒤에서 수식하는 형용사구로, 문맥상 a bridge와 connect가 능동의 관계이므로 현재분사 connecting을 써야 한다.
(C) 「with+명사+분사」는 '…가 ~한[된] 채로'라는 뜻으로, 부대상황을 나타내는 분사구문이다. 여기서는 hundreds of ships와 sail이 의미상 능동의 관계이므로 현재분사 sailing을 써야 한다.

13 앞 문장에서 매우 높은 현수교의 필요성을 언급했고, 그러한 필요성과 대비되는 당시의 제한된 기술에 대해 언급하고 있는 문장이므로 빈칸에는 ④ '그런 다리를 건설하는 것은 불가능해 보였다'가 들어가는 것이 가장 적절하다.

　오답
① 그들은 더 좋은 다리가 필요했다
② 새로운 다리는 필요하지 않았다
③ 사람들은 다리를 갖게 되어 흥분했다
⑤ 다리를 건설하는 것은 문제가 아닐 것이었다

14 주어진 문장이 'In the process'로 시작하므로, 그녀가 교량 건설에 대한 지식을 습득할 수 있었던 과정이 언급된 문장 뒤인 ⑤에 들어가는 것이 가장 적절하다.

15 '해결책을 찾는 것을 돕기 위해 어려운 상황에 개입하다'라는 영영 뜻풀이에 해당하는 표현은 step in이다.

16 문맥상 의심하는 사람들이 '틀렸음'을 증명했다는 내용이 되어야 하므로 ④는 wrong이 되어야 한다.

17 뒤에서 명사를 수식하는 형용사적 용법의 to부정사구를 활용하여 순서에 맞게 배열한다.

18 ①은 John을, 나머지 넷은 모두 Washington을 가리킨다.

19 ⑤ 남은 건설 기간 내내 공사 현장을 방문할 수 없었다고 했다.

20 가정법 과거완료의 주절에 해당하는 문장이므로, 「조동사+have+p.p.」의 형태가 되어야 한다.

2학기 중간고사 · pp. 89~94

1. ⑤　**2.** (A), (D), (B), (C)　**3.** ③　**4.** ③　**5.** ②
6. ③　**7.** ⑤　**8.** had had　**9.** Written　**10.** ③
11. ④　**12.** the king killed the man's brother and took his property　**13.** ③　**14.** ③　**15.** ④　**16.** he should take every situation into account　**17.** ②
18. ③　**19.** did they prove their doubters wrong
20. ②　**21.** ④　**22.** ④　**23.** unprecedented
24. ④　**25.** ③

1 배우가 학습장애에도 불구하고 놀라운 연기를 보여준다는 말에 대한 적절한 응답은 ⑤ '근데 그가 그렇게 많은 대사를 암기할 수 있다는 게 놀랍네.'이다.
오답
① 나는 그 배우의 연기가 특히 좋았어.
② 그가 배우가 되고 싶지 않아 했다는 말이야?
③ 그가 대사를 외우는 것은 틀림없이 쉬울거야.
④ 네가 좋아하는 일을 하는 것이 중요해.

2 자신에게 맞는 직업을 찾고 싶다는 고민을 말하는 (A)가 먼저 오고, 흥미를 물어보는 (D), 잘 모르겠다고 대답하는 (B), 그렇다면 여러 가지를 시도해보라는 (C)의 순서로 이어지는 것이 자연스럽다.

3 여자의 마지막 말에 조언하는 내용이 나와있다.

4 앞서 한 말에 내용을 덧붙이는 문장이므로 비슷한 내용이 언급되는 ③에 들어가는 것이 가장 적절하다.

5 신체적인 어려움에도 불구하고 육상에서 기록을 갱신했다고 했으므로 ② '열정적이고 강한 의지를 가진'이 가장 적절하다.
오답
① 너그럽고 친절한
③ 창의적이고 지적인

④ 사려깊고 따뜻한 마음을 가진
⑤ 부지런하고 정직한

6 • make fun of: …를 놀리다
• make one's way to ...: …로 나아가다

7 '가끔 당신은 목표를 달성하기 위해 다른 사람들의 도움을 필요로 한다.'라는 뜻으로, ⑤ fulfill과 바꿔 쓸 수 있다.
오답 ① 변경하다　② 수반하다
③ 제안하다　④ 상담하다

8 주절의 「would have p.p.」 형태에 맞춰 if절에도 가정법 과거완료 「had p.p.」를 써야 한다.

9 this article과 write가 수동의 관계에 있으므로 과거분사를 써야 한다.

10 빈칸의 앞에는 남자가 왕을 죽일 계획을 했다는 내용이, 뒤에는 경호원을 만나 계획에 실패한 내용이 전개되고 있으므로 빈칸에는 역접의 뜻을 가진 ③ '그러나'가 들어가는 것이 가장 적절하다.
오답 ① 운 좋게도　② 마침내
④ 게다가　⑤ 따라서

11 ④ 주절의 「would have p.p.」 형태에 맞춰 if절에도 가정법 과거완료, 즉 hadn't를 써야 한다.

12 남자의 세 번째 대사에서 그가 왕을 죽이려고 한 이유가 언급되고 있다.

13 ①, ②, ④, ⑤는 모두 왕을 가리키는 반면, ③은 은자를 가리킨다.

14 (A) 왕이 신분을 숨기기 위해 농부로 '위장했다'는 내용이 되는 것이 문맥상 자연스러우므로 disguised가 가장 적절하다.
(B) 왕의 말을 들었지만 '대답하지' 않았다는 내용이 되는 것이 문맥상 자연스러우므로 respond가 가장 적절하다.

15 (A) that절의 주어 역할을 하는 동명사 형태가 와야 하므로 knowing이 적절하다.
(B) anyone을 선행사로 하는 주격 관계대명사가 와야 하므로 who가 적절하다.
(C) 뒤에 절이 이어지므로 that이 적절하다. so as는 보통 「so as to-v」의 형태로 쓰인다.

16 'take ... into account(…을 고려하다)'를 활용하여 순서에 맞게 배열한다.

17 (A) 빈칸 앞의 내용을 근거로 하여 뒤에서 그로부터 얻은 결론을 말하고 있으므로 '따라서, 그러므로'가 적절하다.
(B) 시간적으로 나중에 일어난 사건에 대해 언급하고 있으므로 '나중에'가 적절하다.

18 ③ 문맥상 브루클린 다리는 Roebling 가문의 '끈기 (persistence)'의 증거라고 서술되는 것이 자연스럽다. impatience는 '조바심, 성급함'이라는 의미이다.

19 부정어인 Not only가 문두에 나왔으므로 주어와 동사가 도치되어 「Not only+do[does/did]+주어+동사원형」의 어순이 되어야 한다.

20 앞 문장에서 New Yorker들이 통근 시 이용하던 교통수단은 불안정하고 자주 운행이 중단되었다고 했으므로, ② '그것(다리)이 통근을 더 빠르고 안전하게 해줄 것이었다'가 가장 적절하다.

> **오답**
> ① 그들은 맨해튼으로 통근하기를 원치 않았다
> ③ 그 당시에 그들의 건설 기술이 세계 최고였다
> ④ 그들은 맨해튼이 세계에서 가장 큰 도시가 되기를 바랐다
> ⑤ 다리가 두 도시를 인기있는 관광지로 만들어줄 것이었다

21 윗글의 밑줄 친 it은 가주어이며, ④ '그것은 새 친구를 만들 좋은 기회가 될 것이다.'에서 It은 앞에서 언급된 대상을 가리키는 대명사로 쓰였다.

> **오답**
> ① 당신과 대화하는 것은 영광이었습니다.
> ② 그는 영어로 말하는 것이 쉽다.
> ③ 그녀는 해외로 가는 것이 처음이었다.
> ⑤ 새 프린터를 사는 것은 돈이 많이 들 것이다.

22 주어진 글에는 Emily가 다리 공사를 돕기 위해 나섰다는 내용이 나와 있다. 이후 결혼 전 Emily에 대해 서술한 (B), (B)의 뒷부분에 나온 Emily가 남편을 도운 과정을 'In the process'로 지칭하고 있는 (C), 다리가 완공되었을 때를 서술한 (A)의 순서로 이어지는 것이 가장 적절하다.

23 '전에 일어난 적이 없거나, 그리 자주 일어나지 않는'이라는 영영 뜻풀이에 해당하는 단어는 unprecedented이다.

24 However라는 연결어로 보아, 제시된 문장은 야심차게 시작된 다리 건설이 난관에 부딪치게 되는 내용이 언급되기 시작한 ④에 들어가는 것이 가장 적절하다.

25 사람들에게 불가능하게 여겨지던 브루클린 다리 건설이 시작되었다가 공사를 시작한 아버지가 건강을 잃고, 아들이 뒤를 잇는다는 내용이므로, 제목으로 가장 적절한 것은 ③ '아버지와 아들이 불가능에 도전하다'이다.

> **오답**
> ① 비극적 사고로 Roebling 가문 사람들이 죽었다
> ② Roebling 가문의 다리가 마침내 완성되다
> ④ 다리 하나를 건설하는 데 얼마나 많은 비용이 드는가
> ⑤ 아마추어 엔지니어들이 다리 건설이라는 도전을 맡다

Lesson 7. Finding Out the Wonders

Vocabulary Test
p. 97

1. (1) …을 받을 만하다   (2) 진가를 알아보다[인정하다]
(3) 발견   (4) 뛰어난, 특출난   (5) beneficial   (6) reveal
(7) estimate   (8) currently

2. (1) durable   (2) adapt   (3) advanced   (4) remove

3. (1) Let, go, of   (2) for, the, sake, of
(3) from, time, to, time   (4) fell, apart

4. (1) complex   (2) absorb   (3) generation
(4) domestic

Communicative Functions
p. 98

1. What, do, you, think, of   **2.** What, do, you, mean, by
3. (D), (C), (A), (B)

Discovering Grammar
p. 99

1. (1) one, most   (2) the, fact, that
2. (1) is   (2) that   (3) pleasures

Grammar Test
p. 100

1. (1) Sarah는 그가 거짓말을 하지 않을 거라는 믿음에서 그의 조언을 따랐다.   (2) 이 기회를 놓칠지도 모른다는 생각이 그를 걱정하게 했다.   (3) 나는 선천적인 재능이 연습보다 더 중요하다는 생각에 동의하지 않는다.   **2.** (1) road → roads   (2) are → is   (3) which → that   (4) opinion there → opinion that there   **3.** (1) one of the most popular movies this year   (2) my best friends works for an advertisement company   (3) one of the most famous soccer players in Korea   **4.** (1) one of the most joyful times   (2) one of the most difficult problems   (3) the news that he had won the gold medal   (4) the proof that she stole this wallet

1   (1) 명사 the belief를 부연 설명하기 위한 동격의 that절이 쓰여 '…라는 믿음'으로 해석한다.

(2) 명사 The thought를 부연 설명하기 위한 동격의 that절이 쓰여 '…라는 생각'으로 해석한다.

(3) 명사 the idea를 부연 설명하기 위한 동격의 that절이 쓰여 '…라는 생각'으로 해석한다.

2 (1) 「one of the+최상급+복수명사」 구문이 쓰였으므로 road를 roads로 고쳐야 한다.

(2) 문장의 주어가 one이므로 are를 단수동사 is로 고쳐야 한다.

(3) 명사 the fact를 부연 설명하기 위한 동격절이므로 which를 접속사 that으로 고쳐야 한다.

(4) 명사 the opinion을 부연 설명하기 위한 동격절이 이어지므로 접속사 that이 들어가야 한다.

3 「one of the+최상급+복수명사」의 어순에 유의하여 단어를 배열한다.

4 (1)~(2) 「one of the+최상급+복수명사」의 구문을 사용한다.
(3)~(4) 명사를 부연 설명하기 위한 동격의 that절을 사용한다.

Reading Test
pp. 101~102

1. ② **2.** ⑤ **3.** ② **4.** ③ **5.** 일반 스피커보다 더 강하고 선명한 소리를 내고, 작은 진동까지 포착하며, 시간이 지나도 소리가 변하지 않는다. **6.** ④

1 ② 한지가 비단보다 더 오래 간다는 속담은 언급되었으나, 비단보다 가볍다는 내용은 나오지 않았다.

2 한지의 내구성을 언급한 후 이와 대비되는 서양의 종이에 대한 내용이 이어지므로 ⑤ '반면에'가 들어가는 것이 적절하다.
오답 ① 그러므로　　　② 예를 들어
③ 다시 말해서　　　④ 결과적으로

3 (A) 전장에서까지 사용할 수 있다는 뒤의 내용으로 미루어 'durability(내구성)'가 적절하다. reliability는 '믿음직함, 신뢰도'라는 의미이다.
(B) 다양한 용도로 활용되었다는 내용으로 보아 'invaluable(매우 귀중한)'이 적절하다. valueless는 '무가치한'이라는 의미이다.
(C) 한지의 기능과 용도를 찾는 것이 유행이라고 했으므로 'relevant(유의미한)'가 적절하다. irrelevant는 '무관한'이라는 의미이다.

4 글의 마지막에서 요즘에는 한지의 더 많은 기능과 용도를 찾는 것이 유행이라고 했으므로 ③이 이어지는 것이 가장 적절

하다.

5 윗글의 3~5행에 한지 스피커의 장점이 나와 있다.

6 글의 앞부분에서 한지로 만든 스피커의 장점에 대해 말하고 있고, 빈칸 뒷부분에 스피커의 훌륭한 음질이라는 내용이 나오므로 문맥상 ④ '진가를 알아보다[인정하다]'가 들어가는 것이 가장 적절하다.
오답 ① 바꾸다　　　② 생산하다
③ 무시하다　　　⑤ 조정하다

단원평가
pp. 103~106

1. ① **2.** ④ **3.** ② **4.** ② **5.** deserve **6.** ②
7. ② **8.** ④ **9.** ④ **10.** ④ **11.** ⑤ **12.** ⑤
13. was tough enough to stop arrows **14.** ②
15. ④ **16.** vibration **17.** ⑤ **18.** ⑤ **19.** ⑤
20. how it will be enjoyed in the future

1 빈칸 뒷부분에서 남자가 한 말의 내용을 언급하며 그 내용의 의미를 묻고 있으므로, ① '그게 무슨 말이야?'가 들어가는 것이 가장 적절하다.
오답
② 서로 인사하는 게 어때?
③ 인사하는 다른 방법이 있니?
④ 안전은 가장 중요한 거야.
⑤ 네가 무엇을 숨기고 있는지 말해줘.

2 아무것도 안 하면서 시간을 좀 보내고 싶다는 여자의 말에 남자가 의아해했고, 이후 여자가 뇌는 휴식 후에 더 잘 기능한다고 설명했으므로 ④ '그렇게 생각해 본 적은 없지만, 일리가 있네.'가 남자의 응답으로 가장 적절하다.
오답
① 나는 우리가 이 모든 활동을 할 수 있을 거라고 생각하지 않아.
② 그러면 내가 냉장고를 비워서 그걸 깨끗하게 유지하도록 노력해볼게.
③ 우리는 시간을 최대한 활용해야만 해.
⑤ 그게 바로 우리가 휴가를 효과적인 방식으로 써야 하는 이유야.

3 사람들이 미처 몰랐던 ② '걷기의 신체적, 정신적 이점'에 대한 연설이다.
오답
① 휴식을 취하는 것의 중요성
③ 운동하지 않고 건강을 유지하는 법

④ 현대인을 위한 건강한 식습관

⑤ 걷기와 달리기의 차이점

4 ② remove는 '이동시키다, 치우다'라는 의미이다. 'to soak up something(무언가를 빨아들이다)'이라는 영영 뜻풀이에 맞는 단어는 absorb이다.

오답

① 뛰어난, 두드러진: 눈에 잘 띄는

③ 지속되다, 오래가다: 오랫동안 계속 존재하다

④ 번지다: 한 곳에서 다른 곳으로 퍼지다

⑤ 앞선, 진보의: 현대적이고 최근에 개발된

5 deserve: …을 받을 만하다

6 point out은 '지적하다'라는 의미이다.
② 그 고객은 몇몇 실수를 지적했다.

오답

① 수영장은 아이들로 가득 차 있다.

③ 그 소설은 독자들에게 파장을 일으키고 있다.

④ 당신이 먹는 음식은 몸의 소화 기관에서 분해된다.

⑤ 그것은 첫 번째 세탁 후에 망가졌다.

7 「one of the+최상급+복수명사」 구문을 사용하며, 이때 최상급 highest 뒤에는 복수명사 buildings가 와야 한다.
② 이것은 뉴욕에서 가장 높은 건물 중 하나이다.

오답

① 나는 매 경기 잘해야 한다는 생각에 많이 시달렸다.

② 그는 그녀가 길을 잃었다는 사실을 나에게 알려줬다.

④ 브라질은 세계 최대의 커피 생산국 중 하나이다.

⑤ 그는 1970년대의 가장 유명한 과학자 중 한 명이었다.

8 문서가 서기 751년 이전에 인쇄되었다는 내용 이후 여전히 완벽한 상태라는 대조적인 내용이 이어지므로 ④ '(비록) …이긴 하지만' 이 들어가는 것이 가장 적절하다.

오답 ① (…하는) 때에 ② (만약) …면
③ … 때문에 ⑤ …하지 않는 한

9 밑줄 친 that은 the paper-making technology 을 가리키는 대명사이므로, ④에서 the color를 가리키는 대명사 that과 쓰임이 같다.
④ 그 셔츠의 색은 그 바지의 색과 잘 어울린다.

오답

① 공짜로 주어진 것은 공짜가 아니다. (주격 관계대명사)

② 그가 일자리를 얻었다는 소식은 우리를 행복하게 만들었다. (동격절을 이끄는 접속사)

③ 사람들은 그녀가 상을 타서 충격을 받았다. (이유를 나타내는 명사절을 이끄는 접속사)

⑤ 저 소년에게 길을 물어보자. (지시형용사)

10 ④ 11~12행에 무구정광대다라니경이 발견 당시 여전히 완벽한 상태였다고 나와 있다.

11 과거에 한국인들이 한지를 어떻게 사용했는지 여러 사례를 언급하고 있으므로 제목으로 가장 적절한 것은 ⑤ '고대 한국에서 한지의 다양한 쓰임'이다.

오답

① 서양의 종이보다 한지가 나은 이유

② 고대 한국의 실내 장식

③ 한지를 사용하는 새롭고 현대적인 방식

④ 한지로 전통 공예품을 만드는 법

12 문맥상 현대화로 인해 사람들이 한지의 우수성을 '잊게' 되었다는 내용이 되어야 하므로 ⑤는 forget이 되어야 한다.

13 '…하기에 충분히 ~한'이라는 의미를 표현하기 위해 「형용사+enough+to-v」순으로 배열해야 한다.

14 주어진 문장의 This blend가 가리키는 내용이 나타나 있는 문장 뒤인 ②에 들어가는 것이 가장 적절하다.

15 ④ 준사역동사 help의 목적격 보어로 to pick 혹은 pick이 와야 한다.

16 '지속적인 약간의 흔들리는 움직임'이라는 영영 뜻풀이에 맞는 단어는 vibration(진동)이다.

17 한지로 만든 스피커의 여러 장점을 언급한 후 덧붙여 시간이 지나도 소리가 변하지 않는다는 장점을 말했으므로 문맥상 ⑤ '이 스피커를 훌륭한 구매품이 되게 한다'가 들어가는 것이 적절하다.

오답

① 한지 스피커의 인기를 증명한다

② 사람들이 이 스피커를 고치는 것을 돕는다

③ 사람들에게 귀를 보호하는 법을 가르친다

④ 전통 문화의 중요성을 보여준다

18 (A) project와 support가 수동의 관계이므로 과거분사 supported가 적절하다.

(B) used를 수식하는 부사가 와야 하므로 currently가 적절하다.

(C) 문장의 주어가 Its ability이므로 단수동사 has가 적절하다.

19 ⑤ 한지는 현재 사용되는 재료들보다 덜 비싸고 가볍다고 했다.

20 전치사 to의 목적어 역할을 하는 의문사절이 되어야 하므로, 「의문사+주어+동사」의 어순에 유의하여 배열한다.

Lesson 8. It's Up to You!

Vocabulary Test

p. 109

1. (1) 일축하다, 묵살하다 (2) 결과 (3) 중요한 (4) 겪다
(5) immediately (6) measure (7) shame (8) receipt
2. (1) mature (2) Adolescents (3) discount
(4) identified
3. (1) make, sure (2) in, terms, of (3) get, through
(4) rely, on
4. (1) rerun (2) predict (3) register (4) instinct

Communicative Functions

p. 110

1. (1) I'm, not, sure (2) I'm, not, sure, about
2. ⓑ, ⓐ

Discovering Grammar

p. 111

1. (1) 그 지갑은 서랍 위가 아니라 서랍 안에 있었다.
(2) 내가 아니라 John이 모든 것을 망쳤다.
(3) 그들은 교통 체증 때문이 아니라 악천후 때문에 지각했다.
2. (1) The harder I exercised, the more weight I lost.
(2) The higher we climbed, the cooler the air became.

Grammar Test

p. 112

1. (1) the higher the discount you can get (2) The louder you speak (3) not with my grades (4) but to visit his grandmother **2.** (1) long → longer (2) I should take the more responsibilities → the more responsibilities I should take (3) prepare → preparing **3.** (1) to prepare for my exams (2) from the inside (3) because I was nervous (4) for its scenery **4.** (1) more carefully we plan for the trip, fewer mistakes we will make (2) harder you study, more you will learn (3) longer I waited for him, angrier I got

1 (1)~(2) 「the+비교급 ..., the+비교급 ∼」의 형태가 되도록 배열한다. 비교급이 명사를 수식하는 경우 「the+비교급+명사(구)+주어+동사」의 어순이 되는 점에 유의한다.
(3)~(4) 「not A but B」의 형태가 되도록 배열한다. A와 B는 대등하게 연결되므로 형태가 일치해야 하는 점에 유의한다.

2 (1) 「the+비교급 ..., the+비교급 ∼」 구문의 형식에 맞게 고쳐야 한다.
(2) 비교급이 명사를 수식하므로 「the+비교급+명사(구)+주어+동사」의 어순이 되어야 한다.
(3) 「not A but B」 구문에서 A와 B는 대등하게 연결되므로 형태를 일치시켜야 한다.

3 「not A but B」 구문에서 A와 B는 대등하게 연결되므로 일치하는 형태를 찾는다.

4 「the+비교급 ..., the+비교급 ∼」 구문을 활용하여 문장을 완성한다.

Reading Test

pp. 113~114

1. ⑤ **2.** ⑤ **3.** ③ **4.** 십 대들의 뇌가 여전히 자라는 중이고 완전히 발달하지 않았다는 것 **5.** ④ **6.** ①

1 한 프로그램의 시작 부분으로, 오늘 방송의 주제와 초대 손님을 소개하고 있다.

2 심한 말이 담긴 문자메시지에 대해 깊이 생각하지 않고 그냥 보내 버리는 십 대에 대한 이야기가 나왔으므로 ⑤ '모든 것을 충분히 고려하기 전에'가 빈칸에 들어가는 것이 가장 적절하다.
오답 ① 자신감 있게 ② 많은 생각 끝에
③ 규칙에 반하여 ④ 마치 성인인 것처럼

3 ③ 윗글 7행에서 모든 사람들이 뇌 안에서 겪는 의사 결정 과정은 기본적으로 같다고 했다.

4 바로 앞 문장에서 this가 가리키는 바를 찾는다.

5 감정에 관련된 영역이 더 빨리 성숙한다고 했고, 바로 뒤에 언급된 by reason과 대조되는 표현이 나와야 하므로 빈칸에 들어갈 말로는 ④ '감정과 본능'이 가장 적절하다.
오답 ① 소셜 미디어 ② 비판적인 사고
③ 그들의 지식 ⑤ 그들 부모님의 의견

6 청소년기는 새로운 재능이 나타나도록 돕는 중요한 변화가 뇌 안에서 일어나고, 그를 바탕으로 미래를 설계한다고 했으므로 글의 제목으로는 ① '청소년기: 가능성의 시기'가 가장 적절하다.

단원평가   pp. 115~118

1. ④   **2.** (B), (D), (A), (C)   **3.** ④   **4.** ④   **5.** colder, more   **6.** not, but   **7.** ③   **8.** ④   **9.** You're so angry that you don't care.   **10.** ③   **11.** signal   **12.** ②   **13.** ③   **14.** the region that controls emotions   **15.** ⑤   **16.** ④   **17.** ④   **18.** The harder teens work at building good habits   **19.** ①   **20.** develop

1 여자가 남자의 제안을 거절한 후 남자가 또 다른 제안을 하기 전에 들어갈 말이므로, 생각할 시간을 요청하는 ④ '어디 보자.'가 가장 적절하다.

오답 ① 이건 불공평해.   ② 다행이다.
    ③ 잘 모르겠어.   ⑤ 네 말이 맞아.

2 영화를 같이 보러 갈 것을 제안하는 (B)가 오고, 중간고사가 있어 거절하는 (D), 중간고사까지 아직 시간이 많다는 (A), (A)에 반대 의견을 나타내는 (C)의 순서로 이어지는 것이 가장 자연스럽다.

3 충동구매한 남자의 사정을 들은 여자의 반응으로 ④ '그거 안 됐구나. 다음에는 네가 더 신중히 생각할 것을 기억할 것 같네.'가 오는 것이 가장 적절하다.

오답
① 좋아. 쇼핑하러 가서 할인 상품을 좀 사자.
② 문제 없어. 사용하지 않았다면 영수증이 없어도 환불 받을 수 있어.
③ 알겠습니다. 그럼 당신에게 맞는 더 큰 게 있는지 확인해 볼게요.
⑤ 그런 경우라면 나는 여동생을 위해서 신발을 한 켤레 더 사는 것을 추천해.

4 phase는 '단계'라는 의미이다. ④ '특정한 의미를 지닌 단어들의 짧은 그룹'이라는 영영 뜻풀이에 맞는 단어는 phrase이다.

오답
① 법적인: 법과 관련된
② 겪다: 어떤 것을 경험하거나 견디다
③ 강화하다: 어떤 것을 더 강력하게 만들다

⑤ 측정하다: 어떤 것이 크기나 양 등에서 얼마나 큰지를 판단하다

5 '…할수록 더 ~하다'라는 의미의 「the+비교급 …, the+비교급 ~」 구문을 사용한다.

6 'A가 아니라 B'라는 의미의 「not A but B」 구문을 사용한다.

7 go through는 '(일련의 행동 · 절차를) 거치다'라는 뜻이다.
③ 아이들은 다양한 발달 단계를 거친다.

오답
① 소방관들은 위험한 업무를 수행한다.
② 생존은 인간의 가장 기본적인 본능이다.
④ 이 소설은 실제 이야기에 기반하여 쓰였다.
⑤ 그는 그의 셔츠 위의 얼룩을 없앨 수 없었다.

8 화가 나서 친구에게 문자메시지를 보내는 상황을 묘사하고 있으므로, 시도 때도 없이 전화를 거는 사람들에 관한 문장인 ④는 전체 흐름과 관계가 없다.

9 '너무 …해서 ~하다'라는 의미의 「so+형용사+that+주어+동사」 구문을 사용하여 배열한다.

10 (A) 전치사의 목적어이므로 동명사 deciding이 와야 한다.
(B) 주어가 Neurons로 복수이므로 make가 와야 한다.
(C) 동사 finish는 목적어로 동명사를 취한다.

11 '무언가에 대한 정보를 주거나 누군가에게 무엇을 하라고 알려주는 어떤 것'이라는 영영 뜻풀이에 해당하는 단어는 signal(신호)이다.

12 과학자들이 과거에 생각했던 내용과 최근 연구 내용이 상반되므로 ② '그러나'가 들어가는 것이 가장 적절하다.

오답 ① 게다가   ③ 대조적으로
    ④ 결과적으로   ⑤ 예를 들어

13 ③ 계속적 용법에서는 that을 쓰지 않으므로, which로 바꿔야 한다.

14 바로 앞의 문장에서 it이 가리키는 바를 찾을 수 있다.

15 앞서 언급한 내용이 전부가 아니라는 주어진 문장 뒤에, 십 대의 뇌에서 일어나는 다른 중요한 변화를 언급하는 (C), 그 변화의 내용을 사례를 들어 설명하는 (A), 그러한 변화들의 결과를 언급하는 (B)의 순서로 이어지는 것이 가장 적절하다.

16 이어지는 박사의 대답에서 십 대들이 참여하는 활동이 중요한 이유에 대해 부연 설명하고 있으므로 ④ '십 대들이 참여하고 있는 활동'이 들어가는 것이 가장 적절하다.

오답
① 십 대들이 해야 하는 것들
② 십 대들이 형성하는 관계

③ 현명한 결정을 내리려는 노력

⑤ 자신의 감정을 조절할 수 있는 십 대들

17 윗글의 밑줄 친 to participate는 choose의 목적어로 쓰인 명사적 용법의 to부정사이므로, planned의 목적어로 쓰인 ④의 to go와 용법이 같다.

④ 우리는 이번 여름에 유럽에 가기로 계획했다.

[오답]

① 그녀는 100세까지 살았다. (결과를 나타내는 부사적 용법)

② 그는 설득하기 매우 어렵다. (한정을 나타내는 부사적 용법)

③ 우리는 오늘 할 일이 많다. (형용사적 용법)

⑤ 나는 그녀의 생일을 축하하기 위해 케이크를 샀다. (목적을 나타내는 부사적 용법)

18 '…할수록 더 ~하다'라는 의미의 「the+비교급 …, the+비교급 ~」 구문을 사용하여 배열한다.

19 주어진 문장은 However(하지만)로 시작하는 것으로 보아 앞 문장과 상반된 내용이며 청소년기의 뇌에서 일어나는 변화를 성숙이라는 관점에서만 보아서는 안 된다고 하고 있으므로 청소년기를 성숙해 가는 과정으로만 볼 경우의 문제점을 언급한 문장 뒤인 ①에 들어가는 것이 가장 적절하다.

20 윗글에서 청소년기가 많은 자질과 능력을 발달시키는 중요한 시기라고 했으므로 develop이 들어가는 것이 적절하다.

2학기 기말고사

pp.119~124

1. (D), (A), (C), (B) **2.** ① **3.** ⑤ **4.** ④ **5.** ③
6. on **7.** older she gets, more she looks like her grandmother **8.** ⑤ **9.** ① **10.** ② **11.** ⑤
12. ② **13.** is easy to understand why Koreans created the old saying **14.** ⑤ **15.** ③ **16.** ⑤
17. ② **18.** ⓐ newest ⓑ made **19.** ④ **20.** ②
21. ③ **22.** 그러한 활동(독서나 실험, 문제해결)과 관련된 연결들 **23.** ⑤ **24.** ⑤ **25.** dismiss

1 악수의 유래를 아는지 물어보는 (D), 그럼 악수를 왜 했는지 묻는 (A), 이에 대해 대답하는 (C), 추가적인 설명을 요청하는 (B)의 순서로 이어지는 것이 자연스럽다.

2 휴가 일정에 관한 여자의 의견이 이어지는 것으로 보아, 빈칸에는 ① '어떻게 생각해?'가 들어가는 것이 적절하다.

[오답]

② 내가 도울 수 있는 게 있을까?

③ 우리가 어떻게 예약할 수 있지?

④ 그 중 하나를 시도해 보는 게 어때?

⑤ 전에 그것을 해본 적이 있어?

3 ⑤ 여자는 Burger Castle에 가본 적이 없다고 했다.

4 영화를 보는 대신 도서관에 가자는 여자의 제안에 대한 응답으로는 ④ '음, 그래. 가방 가져오길 잘했네.'가 적절하다.

[오답]

① 그거 좋겠다. 지금 극장에 가자.

② 물론이지. 그럼 내가 팝콘과 음료를 살게.

③ 나도야. 도서관에 그 자리를 맡아놨어야 했어.

⑤ 미안, 난 안될 것 같아. 나는 중간고사 공부를 해야 해.

5 좋은 선택을 하는 법에 대한 글이므로 빈칸에는 ③ '할 수 있는 최상의 결정을 내리다'가 가장 적절하다.

[오답]

① 좋은 관계를 유지하다

② 시간 낭비를 피하다

④ 당신의 부정적인 감정을 다루다

⑤ 혼자 시간을 보내고 자신을 찾다

6 • based on: …에 기반하여

• rely on: …에 의존하다

7 '…할수록 더 ~하다'라는 의미를 표현하기 위해 「the+비교급 …, the+비교급 ~」을 써야 한다.

8 [보기]의 that은 동격의 명사절을 이끄는 접속사이며, 이와 같은 용법으로 쓰인 것은 ⑤이다.

[보기] 그녀가 구조되었다는 소식에 나는 눈물이 났다.

⑤ 나는 우리가 일찍 출발해야 한다는 그의 생각에 동의한다.

[오답]

① 너는 그렇게 멀리까지 수영해선 안 된다. (부사)

② 그는 그것이 너무 비싸다고 생각했다. (접속사)

③ 그녀는 내가 먹을 수 있는 무언가를 나에게 주었다. (관계대명사)

④ 저런 집에서 살아봤으면 좋겠다. (대명사)

9 ① invaluable은 '매우 유용한, 귀중한'이라는 뜻이다. '유용하거나 중요하지 않은'이라는 영영 뜻풀이에 맞는 단어는 valueless이다.

[오답]

② (신체의) 부분: 몸의 일부분

③ 진가를 알아보다[인정하다]: 무언가의 가치를 이해하다

④ 악기: 음악을 만드는 데 사용되는 도구

⑤ 확인하다, 확증하다: 무언가가 사실이거나 맞다는 것을 보여주다

10 let go of는 '…을 버리다'라는 의미이다.
② 나는 이 기회를 놓치고 싶지 않다.
오답
① 그 사고 후 내 차는 망가지고 있다.
③ 열대 우림은 아마존 지역의 약 80퍼센트를 구성한다.
④ 이러한 종류의 직업들은 급여에 있어서는 아주 좋다.
⑤ 그것이 당신의 갈증을 없애 줄 것이다.

11 오래 전의 인쇄물인 무구정광대다라니경의 발견에 대한 글이므로 ⑤ '세계에서 가장 오래된 인쇄 문서의 발견'이 가장 적절하다.
오답
① 고문서를 연구하는 위대한 전문가들
② 고대에 문서들이 인쇄된 방식
③ 세계의 유명한 고문서들
④ 고대 사람들이 중요한 문서를 사찰에 보관한 이유

12 ② 서양의 종이는 100년이 지나면 망가지기 시작한다고 했으므로 unusable(사용할 수 없는)이 와야 한다.

13 It을 가주어, to부정사구를 진주어로 하는 문장이며, 의문사 why가 이끄는 명사절이 동사 understand의 목적어 역할을 한다는 점에 유의하여 순서를 배열한다.

14 ⑤ 문장의 주어 역할을 해야 하므로 동명사 형태인 finding이 되어야 한다.

15 문맥상 '원인'을 나타내는 말이 들어가야 하므로, ③ '… 때문에'가 가장 적절하다.
오답 ① …에도 불구하고   ② …에 따르면
④ …에 관해서   ⑤ …을 써서

16 ⑤ 한지로 만든 갑옷이 화살을 막을 수 있다는 내용은 있으나, 한지로 화살을 만들 수 있다고는 하지 않았다.

17 주어진 문장에서 언급된 디자이너들이 사용하는 직물에 대한 설명인 (B), 직물의 또 다른 장점을 언급하는 (A), 직물 외에 한지의 또 다른 쓰임에 대해 언급하는 (C)의 순서로 이어지는 것이 적절하다.

18 ⓐ 「One of+한정사+최상급+복수명사」 구문이므로 최상급 newest가 되어야 한다.
ⓑ plates, panels와 make가 수동의 관계이므로 과거분사 made가 되어야 한다.

19 주어진 문장의 These structures가 different structures를 의미하고, 문맥상 신호를 주고받은 후 그 모든 신호를 감정한

다고 하는 것이 자연스럽기 때문에 ④에 들어가는 것이 가장 적절하다.

20 십 대와 성인의 의사결정 시의 차이점에 대해 설명하고 있는 글이므로, ② '성인들은 보통 해본 적 없는 일을 시작할 때 주저한다.'는 문장은 전체 흐름과 관련이 없다.

21 (A) 조건을 나타내는 부사절이므로 aren't가 적절하다.
(B) 문장의 주어가 the types of activities이므로 are가 적절하다.
(C) 「the+비교급 …, the+비교급 ~」 구문이므로 stronger가 적절하다.

22 앞선 문장의 the connections that are related to those activities를 가리킨다.

23 빈칸 앞의 내용과 상반된 선택을 했을 때의 결과를 빈칸 뒤에서 언급하고 있으므로 ⑤ '반면에'가 들어가는 것이 가장 적절하다.
오답 ① 게다가   ② 예를 들어
③ 그 결과로   ④ 다시 말해서

24 앞에서 청소년기는 새로운 재능들이 나타나도록 돕는 중요한 변화가 뇌 안에서 일어나는 시기라고 했으므로 ⑤ '많은 자질과 능력을 발달시키다'가 들어가는 것이 가장 적절하다.
오답
① 미래의 직업에 대해 생각하다
② 성숙하고 책임감 있게 되다
③ 친구들과 많은 시간을 보내다
④ 그들의 뇌가 어떻게 기능하는지 배우다

25 '무언가가 중요하지 않거나, 생각하거나 이야기할 필요가 없다고 결정하다'를 의미하는 단어는 dismiss(일축하다, 묵살하다)이다.

Memo

지은이

김성곤 서울대학교 영어영문학과

윤진호 동덕여자고등학교

구은영 동덕여자고등학교

전형주 경기상업고등학교

서정환 여의도고등학교

이후고 한성과학고등학교

김윤자 세종과학고등학교

강용구 공주대학교 영어교육과

김성애 부산대학교 영어교육과

최인철 경북대학교 영어교육과

김지연 ㈜NE능률 교과서개발연구소

신유승 ㈜NE능률 교과서개발연구소

High School English 내신평정 평가문제집

펴 낸 이 주민홍

펴 낸 곳 서울특별시 마포구 월드컵북로 396(상암동) 누리꿈스퀘어 비즈니스타워 10층
㈜NE능률 (우편번호 03925)

펴 낸 날 2018년 1월 10일 초판 1쇄 발행
2019년 8월 15일 8쇄

전   화 02 2014 7114

팩   스 02 3142 0356

홈 페 이 지 www.neungyule.com

등 록 번 호 제1-68호

I S B N 979-11-253-1960-3

정   가 10,000원

NE 능률

고객센터

교재 내용 문의 : contact.nebooks.co.kr (별도의 가입 절차 없이 작성 가능)

제품 구매, 교환, 불량, 반품 문의 : 02-2014-7114

☎ 전화문의는 본사 업무시간 중에만 가능합니다.

내신과 수능을 한 번에!
문법과 구문을 동시에!

최신 수능 경향을 반영하여 지문 대폭 교체!
내신 및 서술형 평가 대비를 위해 문제 유형 재정비!

최신 수능 경향 반영
e-mail, 안내문 등 실용문 추가 (기초세우기, 구문독해)
수능 기출 문장 중심으로 구성 된 '구문훈련' (구문독해)
수능 중요도 상승에 따라 빈칸 추론 유닛 확대 (유형독해)
최신 수능 유형과 소재 분석 (종합실전편)

서술형 주관식 문제 재정비로 내신 대비 강화
(기초세우기, 구문독해, 유형독해)

실전 대비 기능 강화
배운 구문과 문법 사항 재정리가 쉬워지는 Review Test (기초세우기)
수능 독해 MINI TEST를 통한 실력 다지기 (구문독해, 유형독해)
MINI TEST에 장문과 고난도 지문 추가, '필수구문'의 문항화 (구문독해)
모의고사 3회분 수록 (종합실전편)

 휴대용 어휘 암기장
(별책부록)

 독해지문
MP3 파일

www.nebooks.co.kr ▼

NE 능률

NE능률 교재 MAP

아래 교재 MAP을 참고하여 본인의 현재 혹은 목표 수준에 따라 교재를 선택하세요.
NE능률 교재들과 함께 영어실력을 쑥쑥~ 올려보세요!
MP3 등 교재 부가 학습 서비스 및 자세한 교재 정보는 www.nebooks.co.kr에서 확인하세요.

중1

중학영어1 자습서 (김성곤_2015 개정)
중학영어1 평가문제집 1학기 (김성곤_2015 개정)
중학영어1 평가문제집 2학기 (김성곤_2015 개정)
중학영어1 자습서 (양현권_2015 개정)
중학영어1 평가문제집 1학기 (양현권_2015 개정)
중학영어1 평가문제집 2학기 (양현권_2015 개정)

중2

중학영어2 자습서 (김성곤_2015개정)
중학영어2 평가문제집 1학기 (김성곤_2015개정)
중학영어2 평가문제집 2학기 (김성곤_2015개정)
중학영어2 자습서 (양현권_2015 개정)
중학영어2 평가문제집 1학기 (양현권_2015 개정)
중학영어2 평가문제집 2학기 (양현권_2015 개정)

중2-3

생활 일본어 자습서 (2015 개정)
생활 중국어 자습서 (2015 개정)

중3

중학영어3 자습서 (김임득_2009 개정)
중학영어3 평가문제집 (김임득_2009 개정)
중학영어3 자습서 (김충배_2009 개정)
중학영어3 평가문제집 (김충배_2009 개정)

고1

영어 자습서 (김성곤_2015 개정)
영어 평가문제집 (김성곤_2015 개정)
내신100신 기출예상문제집_영어1학기
(김성곤_2015)
내신100신 기출예상문제집_영어2학기
(김성곤_2015)
영어 자습서 (양현권_2015 개정)
영어 평가문제집 (양현권_2015 개정)
기초 영어 자습서 (2009 개정)
기초 영어 평가문제집 (2009 개정)
실용 영어 I 자습서 (2009 개정)
실용 영어 I 평가문제집 (2009 개정)
실용 영어 회화 자습서 (2009 개정)
영어 I 자습서 (2009 개정)
영어 I 평가문제집 (2009 개정)

고1-2

영어 I 자습서 (2015 개정)
영어 I 평가문제집 (2015 개정)
내신100신 기출예상문제집_영어 I
(2015 개정)
실용 영어 자습서 (2015 개정)
실용 영어 평가문제집 (2015 개정)
일본어 I 자습서 (2015 개정)
중국어 I 자습서 (2015 개정)
실용 영어 독해와 작문 자습서
(2009 개정)
실용 영어 독해와 작문 평가문제집
(2009 개정)

고2

영어 독해와 작문 자습서 (2015 개정)
영어 독해와 작문 평가문제집 (2015 개정)
영어 회화 자습서 (2015 개정)
실용 영어 II 자습서 (2009 개정)
실용 영어 II 평가문제집 (2009 개정)
영어 회화 자습서 (2009 개정)

고2-3

일본어 II 자습서 (2015 개정)
중국어 II 자습서 (2015 개정)
영어 독해와 작문 자습서 (2009 개정)
영어 독해와 작문 평가문제집 (2009 개정)

고3

영어 II 자습서 (2015 개정)
영어 II 평가문제집 (2015 개정)
영어 II 자습서 (2009 개정)
영어 II 평가문제집 (2009 개정)
심화 영어 자습서 (2009 개정)